THE CONFLICT OF GENERATIONS
IN ANCIENT GREECE AND ROME

THE CONFLICT OF GENERATIONS IN ANCIENT GREECE AND ROME

EDITED BY

STEPHEN BERTMAN

1976

B. R. GRÜNER — AMSTERDAM

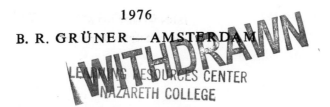

THE CONFLICT OF
GENERATIONS
IN ANCIENT
GREECE AND ROME

EDITED BY

STEPHEN BERTMAN

ISBN 90 6032 033 6

TABLE OF CONTENTS

Contents

ACKNOWLEDGMENT

Special thanks go to the 1970–71 Program Committee of the American Philological Association: John Jay Bateman, John Joseph Keaney, Edward Togo Salmon, William Hailey Willis, and their Chairman, Agnes Kirsopp Lake Michels. Their willingness to sponsor a colloquium on "The Conflict of Generations in Ancient Society" at the 1971 meeting of the American Philological Association helped to generate the discussion and contributions upon which this anthology is based.

οἵη περ φύλλων γενεή, τοίη δὲ καὶ ἀνδρῶν.
φύλλα τὰ μέν τ' ἄνεμος χαμάδις χέει, ἄλλα δέ θ'ὕλη
τηλεθόωσα φύει, ἔαρος δ'ἐπιγίγνεται ὥρη·
ὣς ἀνδρῶν γενεὴ ἡ μὲν φύει ἡ δ' ἀπολήγει.

"Even as are the generations of leaves such are those likewise of
men; the leaves that be the wind scattereth on the earth, and the forest
buddeth and putteth forth more again, when the season of spring is
at hand; so of the generations of men one putteth forth and another
ceaseth."

The Iliad of Homer, Book 6, 146–149
(as translated by Lang, Leaf, and Myers)

Prologue

THE FACE OF JANUS

Janus was the god of passage from old to new.[1]) God of two faces, he looked both forward and back, to future and to past. Though a Roman deity, Janus has presided over modern times too, times torn between old and new, between generations facing away from each other's truth.

With a past that seems more and more remote and a future closing in that he cannot grasp, contemporary man may well feel lost. Denied the perspective of time, he can only cling in isolation to an uncertain present.

Yet if he could, by turning back to the experience of mankind, find some likeness to his own condition, he might well draw strength from the knowledge that men had met and transcended such crises before. Thus, though caught in the winter wind of a Janus-month,[2]) he might yet find reason to hope, and by hoping endure.

To serve this end the present anthology reaches back two thousand years and more to the roots of Western civilization, to the world of Greece and Rome, searching for examples of ancient generational conflict.[3]) The initial essay, by Meyer Reinhold, identifies two periods in the Classical past that witnessed such conflict, the Fifth and First Centuries B. C. Arranged in chronological sequence, the essays that follow explore these times of crisis in greater detail by examining their history and literature, or look closely at other times in the Classical past when such conflict was muted or still.

Stephen Bertman

[1]) Appropriately enough, Janus is also the patron deity of Introductions (see Horace, *Satires*, Book 2, 6: 20–23).

[2]) The month January is named for the god Janus.

[3]) For a close study of 19th and 20th century parallels to the contemporary generation gap see Lewis Feuer's *The Conflict of Generations; The Character and Significance of Student Movements* (New York: Basic Books 1969). An especially valuable chapter is the first, "The Sources and Traits of Student Movements". While Feuer notes the existence of generational conflict as a theme in Greek philosophy (*op. cit.*, pp. 27–30; reprinted below), his focus is essentially modern.

CLASSICAL AUTHORS AND THEIR DATES

Listed below are some of the Classical authors discussed in the anthology. The dates are those given in the *Oxford Classical Dictionary*, ed. by N. G. L. Hammond and H. H. Scullard (2nd ed.; Oxford: The Clarendon Press 1970).

Greek Authors

Homer (8th century B.C.)
Aeschylus (525/4–456 B.C.)
Sophocles (496–406 B.C.)
Euripides (ca. 485–ca. 406 B.C.)
Thucydides (ca. 460/455–ca. 400 B.C.)
Aristophanes (ca. 457/445– ca. 385 B.C.)
Plato (ca. 429–347 B.C.)
Aristotle (384–322 B.C.)
Menander (342/341–293/289 B.C.)

Roman Authors

Plautus (?–184? B.C.)
Catullus (ca. 84–ca. 54 B.C.)
Vergil (70–19 B.C.)
Horace (65–8 B.C.)
Persius (A.D. 34–62)

Introduction

THE GENERATION GAP IN ANTIQUITY*

Meyer Reinhold

University of Missouri — Columbia

How universal is generational conflict? Was the younger generation in all past societies in a state of tension with the older generation because of Oedipal hostility of sons against fathers, or political and socio-economic ambitions of the rising youth against gerontocratic power structures? Dare we say even of the Greeks on historical grounds that "... to the ancients the primacy of generational struggle in history was entirely familiar and obvious. Every form of government seemed to breed its own distinctive form of generational contradiction. Generational conflict seemed to them an everlasting threat to political stability"?[1]) Can we find in antiquity generational consciousness among the youth as a result of competition or disillusionment with the older generation resulting in deep psychological cleavage between fathers and sons and "de-authoritization" of the older generation?

* Reprinted with permission from *Proceedings of the American Philosophical Society* 114 (1970) 347–365.

[1]) L. S. Feuer, *The Conflict of Generations* (New York, 1969), p. 28. On Freud's concept of primordial patricide as the "original sin" of mankind, presupposing a stage of intense generational conflict between fathers and sons based on sexual rivalry, see, e.g., E. Wellisch, *Isaac and Oedipus* (London, 1954), pp. 9–10. Rejecting father-son conflict as a universal human phenomenon stemming from the libido, E. Fromm. "The Oedipus Myth," *Scientific American* 180 (Jan. 1949): pp. 22–27, considers the main theme of the myth of the father-slayer the struggle against paternal authority in patriarchal societies. I do not deem it profitable to elaborate here on the lack of historical evidence for Freud's universalist theory in antiquity.

The following abbreviations will be used: *AJA = American Journal of Archaeology; BCH = Bulletin de Correspondence Hellénique; CAH = Cambridge Ancient History; CR = Classical Review; DS =* Daremberg-Saglio, *Dictionnaire des Antiquités Grecques et Romaines; RE = Paulys Realencyclopädie der Klassischen Altertumswissenschaft; TAPA = Transactions of the American Philological Association.*

The peoples of the ancient Near East could not even have conceived of the possibility of generational tensions or disequilibrium. The conception of a generation gap is irrelevant and unthinkable in societies such as those of the Near East in antiquity whose basic ideological principle of the flux of society is that change in any form is a threat to the well-being and security of all. Given a pragmatically successful pattern of affairs – political, social, religious, technological – society's aim, nay duty, was to maintain this structure in every possible manner. Accordingly, every mode of human and animal behavior, every natural phenomenon, every significant event that was believed to have contributed to the establishment and continuity of the "good society" was cherished. Hence the diligence in isolating the archetypal happenings of the culture, and the validating of the present through constant repetition of the same rituals, periodical retelling of ritual myths, and inculcation of behavior patterns through paradigmatic myths of heroes. Hence also their "terror of history," and the rejection of any concept of the uniqueness of past events. For Near Eastern cultures the past was regarded as a repository of significant precedents for present success; occurrences in the past had value only as criteria by which to test the validity of each new event for the continuity of society. As examples, the Akkad Dynasty in Mesopotamia, notably the reign of Sargon I, served as the paradigm for future rulers and future events; and among the Jews the concept of their selection by Jehovah as the people chosen to act as the vehicle of history colored their evaluation of all events that affected them subsequently.[2]

Against this ideological complex of yearning for the continuity of successful societal orders, the concept of change by human agency was inconceivable. The younger generation, moreover, was in so close a

[2] M. Eliade, *Cosmos and History. The Myth of the Eternal Return* (New York, 1954); R. C. Dentan, *The Idea of History in the Ancient Near East* (New Haven, 1955); J. J. Finkelstein, "Mesopotamian Historiography," *Proc. Amer. Philos. Soc.* 107 (1963): pp. 461–472; S. H. Hooke, *Middle Eastern Mythology* (Baltimore, 1963); E. O. James, "The Nature and Function of Myth," *Folk-Lore* 68 (1957): pp. 474–482; C. Kluckhohn, "Myths and Rituals: a General Theory," *Harv. Theol. Rev.* 35 (1942): pp. 45–79; J. Fontenrose, *The Ritual Theory of Myth* (Berkeley, 1966); P. M. Kaberry, "Myths and Ritual: Some Recent Theories," *Bull. Inst. Class. Stud., Univ. Lond.* 4 (1957): pp. 42–54.

dependency relationship with the family, even where large urban complexes existed, that, as an elementary matter of survival, the principal concern of the youth was to imitate their parents and train themselves for speedy absorption into the life patterns of their elders. Fear of insecurity apart from the family or tribal organization was so basic that the younger generation strove in every way to obtain the approval of the older generation, submitting to often arduous discipline and initiation ceremonies. In short, insecurity and fear of change served to maintain basic generational harmony as being mutually advantageous to both younger and older generations. This generational equilibrium was directed from the top, for the elders controlled not only the mechanisms and mysteries by which order and continuity were assured, but also the apprenticeship systems and career ladders which the younger generation had to master and climb in order to attain the tools of survival and advancement.[3]

Yet the older generation in such patriarchal and gerontocratic societies did not assume that generational balance would automatically ensue because of economic dependency of the youth. It methodically, as a matter of social policy, indoctrinated the youth with obedience to and respect for elders, in regard to both their superior wisdom and ways of doing things. For example, as early as 2450 B.C., in "the earliest formulation of right conduct in any literature," Ptah-hotep, a vizier of the Fifth Dynasty of Egypt, in his popular and famous pamphlet of advice to young aspirants for high status in Egypt, proclaimed the necessity to "hearken," to heed ". . . the thoughts of those who have gone before." "If you are held in high esteem," advises Ptah-hotep, speaking to parents, "and have a household, and beget a son who pleases the god – if he does right, and inclines to your nature, and hearkens to your instructions, "and his designs do good in your house, and he has regard for your substance as it befits, search out for him everything that is good. . . . But if he does wrong and trespasses against your designs, and acts not after your instructions, and his designs are worth-

[3] Margaret Mead, "The Generation Gap," *Science* 164 (Apr. 11, 1969) believes that for the first time in world history there exists today a worldwide generation gap and revolt of young people against the adults who control the societal mechanisms. Dr. Mead's study, *Culture and Commitment. A Study of the Generation Gap* (Garden City, 1970) sheds little light on ancient cultures.

less in your house, and he defies all you say, then drive him away, for he is not your son, and he is not born to you."

Further, "How good is it when a son hearkens to his father, and how happy is he to whom this is said! A son who is good as a master of hearing, namely one who has heard, he is honored of his father." "If a son accept it, when his father says it, not one of his plans miscarries."

"A son who has heard ... prospers after he has heard. When he has grown old and has attained honor, he talks in like manner to his children and renews the instruction of his father. And everyone who is so instructed should talk to his children, and they again to theirs. May the people who shall see them say: 'He is as that one was.' "[4]

Thus it is obvious that as early as the twenty-fifth century B.C., the older generation in authoritarian Egypt had to "work at it" to mold the younger generation in its own image. Ptah-hotep assumes the possibility of rebellious sons; the control is the threat of exclusion from the family hearth. Isolated instances of rebellious children do not, of course, constitute generational disaffection. For generational consciousness to exist, there must occur some traumatic "generational event" that is shared by the youth, leading to disillusionment with and opposition to the older generation.[5] Our first historical record of such generational conflict comes also from Egypt. About 2100 B.C. the aging pharaoh Wahkare-Achthoes II, of the Ninth/Tenth Dynasty, prepared for his son and heir a document of "Instruction for King Meri-ka-re." This dynasty, with its capital at Heracleopolis, came to power in a time of troubles for Egypt, the massive political and social crisis in the transition period between the Old and New Kingdoms. While our sources are extremely fragmentary, it is clear that some sort of generational tension affecting the youth existed. The pharaoh warned against the danger: "The contentious man is a disturbance to citizens; he produces two factions among the younger generation."[5a]

---

[4] Transl. by J. Kaster, *Wings of the Falcon. Life and Thought of Ancient Egypt* (New York, 1968), pp. 166, 169, 172–173; *cp.* Feuer, *op. cit.*, p. 30. Text of the "Maxims of Ptah-hotep" also in J. H. Breasted, *The Dawn of Conscience* (New York, 1939), pp. 129, 130, 134; *Ancient Near Eastern Texts*, ed. by J. B. Pritchard (Princeton, 1950), pp. 412–414; Z. Zaba, *Les Maximes de Ptahhotep* (Prague, 1956).

[5] *Cp.* Feuer, *op. cit.*, p. 25.

[5a] It is possible that a new generation of army recruits, aged twenty, is meant.

The future pharaoh Meri-ka-re was advised to "foster thy younger generation ... and increase thy adherents with recruits ..."; to "increase the younger generation of thy followers. ..." Wahkare was pessimistic: "Generation will oppress generation, as the ancestors prophesied about it." It is perhaps as a result of Meri-ka-re's restoration of generational balance that an era of peace was brought to Egypt for several decades.[6])

Despite the societal conditions fostering generational harmony and the managerial techniques employed to assure dynamic equilibrium between the younger generation and their elders, the theogonic myths current in the Near East in the second millennium B.C. contain significant stories of generational conflict. It is indeed surprising that authoritarian, ideologically static societies that value mythico-historical precedents as paradigms for present behavior should place father-son conflict at the very summit of the divine origins. The Hittite theogony of 1400–1200 B.C., from the royal archives at Hattusas (translated or adapted from Hurrian myths of the fifteenth century B.C., whose roots lie in earlier Babylonian-Sumerian traditions), depicted the divine succession as a struggle for kingship in the sky, involving a three-generational conflict characterized by cruelty of the heavenly fathers against their children and their displacement by rebellious sons. The story of dynastic progression for control of the kingship in the sky, involving mutual violence and cruelty between older and younger generations of gods, is an age-old cosmogonic myth. In the now famous Hittite version, the Kumarbi "Kingship in Heaven" text, Alalu is first dethroned by his son Anu, god of heaven, who in turn oppresses his son Kumarbi, presumably originally a vegetation god. Aroused against his father Anu, representing the forces of the past holding back youth, Kumarbi armed himself with a *harpe* (the common reaping tool of the Near East), castrated his father and seized control of heaven. In turn Kumarbi, fearing his son Teshub (the Hittite-Hurrian weather god), sought to control his son by swallowing him,

[6]) *Ancient Near Eastern Texts*, ed. by J. P. Pritchard (Princeton, 1950), pp. 414–418; A. Scharff, "Der historische Abschnitt der Lehre für König Merikare," *Sitz. Bayer. Akad. Wiss., Philos. Hist. Abt.* 1936, Heft 8: pp. 11, 15–16, 21; A. H. Gardiner, "New Literary Works from Egypt," *Jour. Eg. Arch.* 1 (1914): pp. 20–36; W. C. Hayes, "The Middle Kingdom in Egypt," *CAH²* (1961), 1, chap. XX, p. 5.

2*

but a stone was substituted in place of Teshub. Eventually, Teshub overthrew Kumarbi and finally brought order to the cosmos. A Ugaritic text of *ca.* 1400–1350 B.C. tells of a similar dynastic struggle involving El (who is equated with Kumarbi); and an age-old Phoenician myth deriving from theogonic literature of the second millennium B.C., preserved in the *Phoenician History* of Sanchuniathon, contains a similar tradition of generational struggle among the gods.[7]

Such Near Eastern theogonic concepts, involving divine succession through violence and generational conflicts for power, found their way – the route is not certain – into Greek mythology. Our prime source is the great theogonic poem of Hesiod. The recovery of Near Eastern antecedents of the myth of divine succession in heaven compels us to regard the parallel stories in Hesiod's *Theogony* as an adaptation to Greek mythic and cultural patterns of widely diffused theogonic literature current from the second millennium B.C. The cruelty of the Greek sky god Uranus toward his children by Gaea; the revolt of his son Cronus (a vegetation god); Cronus' castration of Uranus with a *harpe*, and his seizure of control of the kingdom in the sky; his own fear of and cruelty toward his children, whom he swallowed; the substitution of a stone for Zeus; the overthrow of Cronus by his son Zeus, a weather god – all these elements are present in Near Eastern myths. The generational conflict depicted in the Greek myth is an age-old tradition rather than new mythic creations reflecting awareness of intergenerational power struggles in Greek society.[8]

---

[7] On the Hittite-Hurrian, Ugaritic, and Phoenician myths of generational conflict, see A. Lesky, "Hethitische Texte und griechischer Mythos," *Anz. Ost. Akad. Wiss., Philos.-Hist. Kl.* 87 (1950): pp. 137–160; *idem*, "Griechischer mythos und Vorderer Orient," *Saeculum* 6 (1955): pp. 35–52; H. G. Güterbock, "The Hittite Version of the Hurrian Kumarbi Myth," *AJA* 52 (1948): pp. 123–134; B. C. Dietrich, "Some Eastern Traditions in Greek Thought," *Acta Classica* 8 (1965): pp. 11–30; M. L. West, *Hesiod. Theogony* (Oxford, 1966): pp. 18–31.

[8] Hesiod, *Theogony*, pp. 156–182; 453–506. *Cp.* M. L. West, *op. cit.*, pp. 1–31; A. Heubeck, "Mythologische Vorstellungen des alten Orients im archaische Griechentum," *Gymnasium* 62 (1955): pp. 508–525; H. Otten, "Vorderasiatische Mythen als Vorlaufer griechischer Mythenbildung," *Forschungen und Fortschritte* 1949: pp. 145–147; U. Bianchi, "Teogonie Greche e Teogonie Orientali," *Studi Materiali dit Storia delle Religioni* 24–25 (1953–1954): pp. 64–75; P. Walcot, *Hesiod and the Near East* (Cardiff, 1966); see also n. 7, *supra.* E. R. Dodds, *The*

Yet the Greeks did incorporate in this way the concept of generational conflict in their myths. To halt the pattern of divine succession,
Zeus swallowed his consort Metis, because of fear of a rebellious child.
The subsequent birth of Athena out of his own head brought him
instead a dutiful daughter. Even after the final victory of Zeus against
all the forces of chaos (notably Typhon and the Aloades), Zeus' reign
was challenged by a palace plot involving his children Poseidon and
Athena and his wife Hera, who sought unsuccessfully to throw him
into chains. Civil war on Olympus was averted by the intervention of
the Nereid Thetis who brought about the release of Zeus. Conflict
between divine son and divine mother is recorded in the myth of
Hephaestus' hostility to Hera. In exile from Olympus, Hephaestus
sent his mother a magic throne; when she sat in it, she was unable to
move, bound by invisible chains. Efforts to induce Hephaestus by
threats to return to Olympus and release Hera failed. Finally, Dionysus
made him drunk, escorted him back to Olympus, and induced him to
unchain his mother.

Other Greek myths authenticated the reality of conflict between
young and old, between fathers and sons. For example, in the *Iliad*
Phoenix, tutor of Achilles, tells how he left his home "fleeing from
strife against my father Amyntor." In this case the cause of the tension
between father and son was sexual rivalry: at the urging of his jealous
mother, Phoenix seduced his father's concubine. In consequence,
Amyntor invoked a curse upon his son, as the result of which, Phoenix
believed, he remained childless.[9]) It was Phoenix who preached to
Achilles the disasters stemming from youthful pride and passion, citing
also the conflict between the Aetolian hero Meleager and his mother
Althaea. Because of the deaths of her brothers in the war between
Calydon and the Curetes of Pleuron in Aetolia, Althaea cursed her son

Greeks and the Irrational (Berkeley, 1951), p. 61, n. 103, probing the psychology
of the Greeks in adopting the Hittite-Hurrian Kumarbi succession myth finds
in the father-castration theme "... a reflex of unconscious human desires ...,"
reflecting "... the son's attainment of sexual freedom through removal of his
father-rival."

[9]) Homer, *Iliad* IX. 448–477. According to some versions of the myth, Phoenix
was blinded by his father as punishment. Blinding was a frequent penalty for sexual
crimes.

and prayed for his death.[10]) In the opening scenes of the *Iliad*, aged Nestor reminds the younger kings Agamemnon and Achilles that it is proper to be guided by elders."Nay, hearken to me; you are both younger than I am."[11]

Can it be that in the period when Homer wrote, an innovative time when many basic societal changes were in process of emerging, age-old patterns of social cohesion were breaking apart, and that the stories of Phoenix and Meleager reflected contemporary dislocations? At any rate, Hesiod, writing at the end of the eighth/early seventh century B.C., was sensitive to generational imbalance in his time. For in characterizing the last of the five ages of man, the Iron Age, he proclaimed the end of harmony between father and children, and bemoaned a time when "men dishonor their parents," carping at them, and denying them support in their old age.[12])

The Greek mythological tradition preserved more than a few father-son conflicts. It is likely that in their primitive form these myths recorded struggles for power within royal dynasties. But in the later Greek rationalized versions that have survived, they appear as efforts of fathers to avert dread oracular pronouncements that the son would kill the father. The most famous of these myths is, of course, the unwitting slaying by Oedipus of his father Laius, as the result of which he succeeded to the throne of Thebes. A similar myth was told of Minos' son Catreus, king of Cnossus, who was warned by an oracle that he would be killed by one of his children. To avoid accomplishing this fate, his son Althaemens fled to Rhodes. But later Catreus was unwittingly killed by his son Althaemenes, who was so horrified by the deed that he prayed to be swallowed up by the earth, and so atoned for

[10]) *Iliad* IX. 527–573. *Cp.* W. Kraus, "Meleagros in der Ilias," *Wiener Studien* 63 (1948): pp. 8–21; W. Wolfring, "Ilias und Meleagrie," *Wiener Studien* 66 (1953): pp. 24–49.

[11]) *Iliad* I. 259.

[12]) *Works and Days*, pp. 182, 185–189, 331–332. T. A. Sinclair, *Hesiod, Works and Days* (Hildesheim, 1966, reprint) un his commentary on these passages associates Hesiod's pessimism concerning parent-children relationships with the later tradition of apocalyptic literature. *Cp.* Mark 13.12: "Now...children shall rise up against their parents, and shall cause them to be put to death"; Orac. Sibyll. 1.74; A. Rzach, "Sibyllinische Weltalter," *Wiener Studien* 34 (1912): pp. 114–122.

his patricide. So also did Odysseus' son by Circe, Telegonus, unknowingly kill Odysseus. Premeditated patricide in mythical royal families is also recorded: Carcabus killed his tyrannical father King Triopas of the Perrhebeians, in order to deliver the people; Temenos, a Heraclid, king of Argos, was murdered by his sons to ensure that the royal power would pass to them rather than to his favored son-in-law Deiphantes. While such cases are simply by-products of typical palace intrigues, they do, nevertheless, afford precedents for unfilial behavior.

To guard against the dangers of generational cleavage and discontinuity, one of the prime social controls was the age-old injunction, incalculated in the young everywhere, but first elevated into a divine commandment by the Jews, "honor thy father and mother."[13] In the Near East, as well as among the Indo-Europeans, the patriarchal family was the keystone of stability in society. Jewish law proclaimed the solidarity of the family as a cornerstone of the community by placing respect due to parents under the surveillance of Jehovah. Religious fears of divine punishment for disrespect of parents, and by extension of the older generation, were supplemented by legislation making violence or curses against father or mother crimes punishable by death.[14] In the traumatic crisis of the Babylonian Captivity, at a time when separation from the ancestral cult center in Jerusalem and disillusionment with the elders endangered generational continuity, the family was accorded a new importance for the solidarity of the Jewish people in exile; moreover, in the post-exilic period protective laws were sharpened against the disruptive force of conflicts between parents and children.[15] For example, in *Deuteronomy* extraordinary provisions were made for disciplining the incorrigible son: "If a man have a

[13]) Exodus 20.12: "Honor thy father and mother, that thy days may be long.... " *Cp. Proverbs* 1.8; 23.22: "Hearken to thy father who begat thee, and despise not the words of thy mother."

[14]) Exodus 21.15, 17. *Cp.* NT, Mark 7.10; Matth. 15.4.

[15]) *Cp.* S. W. Baron, *A Social and Religious History of the Jews*[2] 1 (New York, 1952): p. 261; J. Gaudamet, *Institutions de l'Antiquité* (Paris 1967), pp. 121–122; Reallexikon für Antike und Christentum, article "Eltern," 4: pp. 1198–1203; S. J. Feigen, "Disrespect toward Parents in the Torah and the Near Eastern Laws" [in Hebrew], *Sefer ha-Shanah li-Yehude America* 10–11: pp. 301–315, was not available to me.

stubborn and rebellious son, that will not obey the voice of his father, or the voice of his mother, and though they chasten him will not hearken unto them," the son is to be hailed before a council of the elders of the city, and if convicted is to be stoned to death by all the men of the city, "so shalt thou put aside the evil from the midst of thee; and all Israel shall hear, and fear."[16]) Against rebellious children was hurled the imprecation, "Cursed be he that setteth light by his father or his mother."[17]) Mockers and scorners of parents were subject to capital punishment, and disrespectful children were also threatened with refusal of proper burial.[18]) As a corollary to the injunction to honor father and mother was the principle of respect due to elders. When Job, for example, complains[19]) that in his fall from wealth and station some of the youth[20]) mocked him, there is almost stunned disbelief: "They abhor me, and keep at a distance from me, and they spare not to spit in my face." Job's friends are compassionate, but it is from the mouth of one of them, Elihu son of Barachiel, the Buzite, that we hear not merely the conventional respect for elders, but for the first time, by way of challenge to the older generation, the demand by the youth to be heard if they possess wisdom and understanding:

"I am young in days, whereas you are aged. Therefore was I in dread and afraid to declare my knowledge to you... It is not the aged that are wise, nor is it the old who understand right; therefore I say, listen to me; I also will declare my knowledge."[21])

But such expressions of generational consciousness on the part of Jewish youth were negligible. The continuity of the family and the people remained overriding forces throughout Jewish history in antiquity, and, indeed, until modern times.

---

[16]) Deuteronomy 21.18–21. Stoning to death for filial disobedience is a unique penalty, and we are properly reminded that, "The present law will hardly, however, have often been carried into practice...," by S. R. Driver, *Critical and Exegetical Commentary on Deuteronomy* (New York, 1895), p. 248.

[17]) Deuteronomy 27.16.

[18]) Leviticus 20.9; Proverbs 30.17.

[19]) Job 30.1, 9, 10.

[20]) The text appears to isolate here the very poor and low class youths (perhaps shepherd boys or brigands).

[21]) Job 32.6, 9; *cp.* 32.20.

No less so did the Greek culture area anchor family solidarity and generational harmony upon the injunction "Honor thy father and mother." Stobaeus has preserved for us a large collection of quotations from earlier Greek writers which ring the changes on the theme.[22] They extend over a period of about 700 years, and include Theognis, Pythagorean doctrine, Sophocles, Euripides, Agathon, the tragic poet Dicaeogenes (a centomporary of Agathon), Plato, the writer of Middle Comedy Antiphanes, Isocrates, Anaximenes of Lampsacus (rhetor and sophist of the second half of the fourth century B.C.), Philemon, Menander, and Diphilus, the three leading writers of New Comedy, Neopythagorean literature, and the late Stoic Hierocles. Besides the general concept of the duty to honor one's parents, we find such specific exegesis as: "It is a duty of children to obey the commands of a father" (Euripides); "it is necessary for children to obey the father, and it is just to think as he does" (Euripides); "it is proper not to say or do evil to one's parents, but to obey them in both little and important matters..., in wellnigh everything, even in madness" (from a Neopythagorean work attributed to Perictyone[23]).

Aside from such moral instruction inculcated in the youth, in the Greek city-states the laws prescribed the precise obligations of children to their aged parents and grandparents: provision of food, lodging, and burial. In Athens the law appears to have originated in the legislation of Solon in the early sixth century B.C. Such filial duty was accorded such weight that in the scrutiny of newly chosen officials they were questioned about their treatment of their parents. Athenians who did not fulfill their filial obligations were subject to indictment under the law concerning mistreatment of parents ($\gamma\varrho\alpha\varphi\grave{\eta}$ $\gamma o\nu\acute{\epsilon}\omega\nu$ $\varkappa\alpha\varkappa\acute{\omega}\sigma\epsilon\omega\varsigma$). Conviction of breaking this law carried with it as punishment partial loss of civic rights. A similar law at Delphi, fragmentarily preserved, reads, in part:

[22] Stobaeus, *Anth.* 4.25 *passim; cp.* Isocrates, *Demonicus* 14, 16. Stobaeus (4.25.5) quotes the tragedian Cleaenetus: "It is beautiful to die for one's parents." On parent-children relationship in Greece, *cp.* Reallexikon für Antike und Christentum, 4: pp. 1191–1194.

[23] Pseudonym of author of work written first century B.C./first century A.D. See K. von Fritz, "Perictyone," *RE* 19: cols., 794–795.

"If anyone does not feed his father and mother, when this is reported to the council, if the council shall find the person guilty, they shall bind him and conduct him to the civic jail.... "[24]

Further weight was given to the honor and duties owed to parents by religious sanctions of various kinds. Parents were often equated with the gods, so that disrespect, violence, or neglect of obligations to them was equated with impiety. Accordingly, Olympian Zeus and the Erinyes of the underworld take the lead in punishing such violations.[25] The insecurity of the older generation must have been considerable in some periods, for sinners against parents were even threatened with punishment in Tartarus in the afterlife.[26] More fearful was the threat to the younger generation that violence to or thwarting of a parent might let loose the dread curse of the father or mother upon the child. Impressive in the mythic tradition were the effective curse of Amyntor on his son Phoenix, of Theseus upon the innocent Hippolytus, Althaea upon Meleager, Oedipus upon his sons Polynices and Eteocles, and Pelops upon his sons Atreus and Thyestes. "Countless other parents," says Plato, "cursed countless other

[24] L. Lerat, "Un Loi de Delphes sur les Devoirs des Enfants envers leurs Parents," *Revue de Philologie* 17 (1943): pp. 68–86; Thalheim, article Κάκωσις in *RE* 10: cols. 1526–1528; G. Glotz, *La Solidarité de la famille...en Grèce* (Paris, 1904), pp. 359–360; R. Flacelière, *Daily Life in Greece at the Time of Pericles* (New York, 1966), p. 80; B. E. Richardson, *Old Age Among the Ancient Greeks* (Baltimore, 1933—The Johns Hopkins Univ. Studies in Archaeology, No. 16), pp. 48–54; W. K. Lacey, *The Family in Classical Greece* (London, 1968), pp. 116–118. *Cp.* Vitruvius VI, Praef. 3: "The laws of all the Greeks provide that parents be fed by children, but among the Athenians not all, only those who have taught them a trade."

[25] An Orphic fragment (Stobaeus, *Anth.* 4.25.28); Euripides, frag. *Alcmaeon* (Stobaeus 4.25.15); Plato, Laws 880E; Euripides, frag. *Heraclidae* (Stobaeus 4.25.2); Antiphanes, frag. 262 (Koch = Stobaeus 4.25.7a); Menander, frag. 805 (Edmonds = Stobaeus 4.25.26); Pempelos of Thurii (*cp.* K. von Fritz, *RE* 19: col. 416), frag. of a pseudopythagorean work "Concerning Parents" (Stobaeus 4.25.52); Hierocles, frag. (Stobaeus 4.25.53).

[26] Plato, *Phaedo* 113E; Perictyone (see n. 23 *supra*): "If anyone despises his parents..., the sin is written down among the gods; both while alive and in death he is hated by men, and under the earth, together with the sinners there, he is for all eternity justly afflicted by the gods below who have been assigned as overseers of these matters."

sons, and regarding such curses of parents upon children it is clearly proved that the gods listen to parents; for a parent's curse upon children is as no other man's curse upon any other, and quite justly so."[27]) Is there any wonder then that we find Greeks confessing to guilt feelings in relations with their parents?[28])

Besides such control mechanisms that must have imposed on most of the youth a self-censorship motivated by guilt and fear, the city of Athens made provisions for generational continuity through an early "coming of age" of youths (18th year), which extinguished the father's paternal authority over his son, and two years of civic and military training among the ephebes.[29]) In Sparta the bridging of the generations was the aim of attaching in close personal relationship each young Spartiate in his mess to an older citizen. It is interesting to find in early Spartan history, before the rigors of the Lycurgan system were imposed, a notorious incident involving a clash of generations. After the long First Messenian War, in the last quarter of the eighth century B.C., the younger generation of Spartans which had grown up during the war was excluded from distribution of the conquered lands on the grounds that they had not participated in the war. When these "war babies" stirred up a confrontation in protest, they were designated *partheniae* ("bastards") or half-breeds, and declared legally ineligible for full Spartan rights. After a threatened *coup d'état* on the part of these youths was thwarted, they

---

[27]) Plato, *Laws* 931C. On curses and their significance in antiquity see Ziebarth, article "Fluch," *RE* 6: cols. 2771–2773; J. Th. Kakridis, '*Aραί* (Athens, 1929); E. Kagarov, *Griechische Fluchtafeln*, in Eos Suppl. 4 (Paris, 1929). *Cp.* E. R. Dodds, *op. cit.*, pp. 46,60, n. 102. Dodds would date the origin of Greek myths concerning curses of fathers to a period when the position of the father was being undermined among the Greeks by allegiance to the *polis*, that is, the post-Homeric period.

[28]) E.g., Menander, frag. (Stobaeus, Flor. 2.25.14 = Edmonds 586): "I am only ashamed before my father, Cleitophon. I shall not be able to face him if I do wrong"; Timocles, writer of Middle Comedy, frag. (Stobaeus 4.25.17): "Whoever fears his father and feels shame before him, that man will be a good citizen"; Antiphanes, Middle Comedy, frag. 261 (Koch = Stobaeus, 4.25.7): "Whoever at such an age still blushes in the presence of his parents is not evil."

[29]) R. Sealey, "On Coming of Age in Athens," *CR* 71 (1956): pp. 195–197; G. Glotz, *op. cit.*, p. 359; P. Girard, *L'Education Athénienne*² (Paris, 1891), pp. 270–327.

were rounded up and shipped overseas, in 705 B.C., to form the nucleus of the only colony ever established by Sparta, Taras (later Tarentum).[30]

One wonders to what extent the numerous other colonies planted in the western Mediterranean and around the shores of the Black Sea were constituted in their origins of the younger generation of the mother cities. We are ill-informed about the incidence of generational tension in the critical period in the Greek city-states that experienced the enormous increase of land hunger as a result of great population increases in the eighth through sixth centuries B.C., and the resort to the safety valve of overseas colonization.[31] While the *patria potestas* of Greek fathers was originally as strong as that among other ancient peoples, it was mitigated much more rapidly than at Rome through the weakening of the authority of the patriarchal families and the clans as the result of the priorities given to the *polis*.[31a] This reordering of societal priorities, together with the unprecedented discontinuities with tradition in all fields, was accompanied by visible gaps in the generational balance of Greek cities, emergent generational conflict, generational anxiety on the part of the older generation, and guilt feelings on the part of the youth.[32]

These incipient dislocations in generational harmony were not likely to wither away as sociological aberrations, given the growing tendencies toward egalitarianism among citizens in Greek cities, and the increasing redirection of allegiances from the patriarchal family to the city-state. Indeed, it was as a result of such an evolution that in Athens in the fifth century B.C. there occurred the first massive challenge to the older generation in the history of mankind. The causes of a decisive cleavage between the generations were complex.

[30] H. Schaefer, article "Partheniae," *RE* 18: cols. 1884–1886; *CAH* 3: pp. 537, 674; G. L. Huxley, *Early Sparta* (Cambridge, Mass., 1962), pp. 37–38.

[31] Fcuer, *op cit.*, p. 29, acknowledges generational balance in some periods of modern times, but characterizes generational friction in antiquity as continuing "with its bitterness unrelieved by any safety valve such as a developing technology or new world."

[31a] L. Beauchet, article "Patria Potestas," *Daremberg-Saglio* 4: pp. 342–343.

[32] *Cp.* E. R. Dodds, *op. cit.*, pp. 45–46; G. Aigrisse, *Psychoanalyse de la Grèce antique* (Paris, 1960), p. 17; W. K. Lacey, *op. cit.*, pp. 16, 20.

First and foremost was the very nature of Athenian democracy under the Periclean dispensation, which elevated all individual Athenian citizens to the highest human dignity the world had ever known. In this time of rapid change, respect for tradition, the age-old concept of honor to parents and elders were in sharp conflict with civic institutions, which placed fathers and sons (from their eighteenth year in Athens) on a level of political equality.

In the fluid, "quick turnover society" of Athens,[33] there came to the surface a polarized two-generational pattern (there is no word for "middle-aged" people in Greek[34]), the νεώτεροι or νέοι and the πρεσβύτεροι, and the tension between them mounted. The age level that separated the generations must have been somewhat fluid, though in one source the cutoff point is thirty, "below which a man is to be accounted young."[35]

In Athens, as in most other Greek cities, a peculiar psychological mechanism, characteristic of slave-owning societies, was operative. Many of the youth, particularly in well-to-do families, were reared by trusted slaves. Such a system is bound to create unclarity as to where authority is centered, because there is a separation between the source of paternal power and the actual exercise of it. Not only does the child not continue to adulthood in respect for his social inferior, but the slave, caught between two masters, as it were, is vacillatory in the exercise of his surrogate paternal power. As a result, in the rearing process, while the child may idealize the father and fear his authority, he learns to circumvent it when exercized by a slave.[36] Add to this conflict the confusion engendered in the Greek value systems by the high estimation placed upon the superior wisdom of the older generation and the idealization of youth in Greek art.[37]

[33] The phrase is A. W. Gouldner's in *Enter Plato. Classical Greece and the Origins of Social Theory* (New York, 1965), p. 74.

[34] Gouldner, *op. cit.*, p. 73; Ehrenberg, *The People of Aristophanes. A Sociology of Old Attic Comedy*[2] (Oxford, 1951), p. 208.

[35] Xenophon, *Memorabilia* 1.2.33–35.

[36] Gouldner, *op. cit.*, pp. 356–358, has a valuable analysis of this social problem in slave societies.

[37] The Greeks did not glorify the elderly in their art. See B. E. Richardson, *op. cit.*, pp. xiii. 16, 31.

But it was above all the growth in respect for reason that increasingly led to the "de-authoritization" of the fathers and the older generation. Aristotle's dictum is applicable to the classical period: "In general all men seek not their forefathers' way, but what is good."[38] In the middle years of the fifth century B.C. the polarization of the generations is explicit. While in the *Persians* Aeschylus put into the mouth of the ghost of Darius the charge of "youthful recklessness" against his son Xerxes as the cause of the disaster at Salamis,[39] in the *Suppliant Women* the chorus implores King Pelasgus, who is "aged in knowledge," to "learn from one of younger birth."[40] It is particularly in the *Eumenides* that we see the traditional dichotomy of the right of authority in the hands of the older generation and the duty of obedience on the part of the younger generation turned on its head, in a dramatic reversal – on the grounds of reason, justice, and the welfare of the city of Athens. The rigid Erinyes, representing an outmoded system of tribal justice and social organization, based upon clan and family, are pitted against younger gods, Zeus, Apollo, Athena, the promoters of civic justice, moderation, reason. Aeschylus is pointedly explicit in stressing the conflict between the older and the younger generation of gods. The Erinyes assail οἱ νεώτεροι for trampling upon the authority of the ancient traditions. It is noteworthy that in this generational conflict on a cosmic level, the younger generation is victorious. "You trample on me, your elder, young as you are," say the Erinyes. The reply of Athena might have become the manifesto of the younger generation of Athens in the Periclean Age:"I will bear with your anger, since you are my elder. And in that respect indeed you are wiser than I am. Yet Zeus hath granted to me, too, no mean understanding."[41]

Sophocles, upholder of traditional piety and patterns, has an illuminating picture in the *Antigone* of intransigent challenge on the part of idealistic youth against the arbitrary authority of the state.

[38] *Politics* 1269A.

[39] *Persians* 744.

[40] *Suppliant Women* 361.

[41] Aeschylus, *Eumenides* 150, 162, 728–729, 731, 778–779, 808–809, 848–850, 883–884. *Cp.* A. J. Podlecki, *The Political Background of Aeschylean Tragedy* (Ann Arbor, 1966), p. 79.

While his rebellious Antigone may represent age-old religious traditions and the solidarity of the family, in his characterization of her and her fiancé Haemon, Sophocles was reflecting a growing consciousness of independence and self-confidence among the younger generation in Athens at the time. The challenge hurled by Haemon against the authority of his father, King Creon, is unmistakable. Sophocles has depicted in this play a double-barreled attack on the authority of the state and on paternal authority. Creon clearly asserts the authority of the father and the obedience due to elders:

"Yes, my son, you should bear this in your heart – in all respects to obey your father's will. It is for this that men pray to have dutiful children grow up in their homes – that they may requite their father's enemies with evils and honor, as their father does, his friend. But he who begets unprofitable children – what shall one say that he hath begotten, but troubles for himself, and much laughter for his enemies."[42]

Spoken like Ptah-hotep two thousand years before! Haemon's formal respect for his father's wisdom and authority[43] is tempered by a demand for the claims of justice and for respect to wisdom in the younger generation. "Nay, forgo your anger," urges the young Haemon to his father, "permit yourself to change. For if I, a young man, have a right to a view, it is best, I say, that man should be endowed by nature with all wisdom; otherwise – and it is not likely to happen so – it is good also to learn from those who speak aright.... If I am young, you should look to my merits, not my years."[44]

Creon can only fall back upon assertion of his authority as ruler and father,[45] and demand respect as an elder. "Men of my age – are we indeed to be taught wisdom by a man of his age?"[46] In the duel between Creon and Haemon we hear for the first time in history (the cautious observations of Elihu to Job along these lines may have been written under the influence of Greek rationalism[47]) the

---

[42]) *Antigone* 639–648.
[43]) *Antigone* 635–636, 701–702.
[44]) *Antigone* 718–723, 728–729, 743, 755.
[45]) *Antigone* 734–735, 742.
[46]) *Antigone* 726–737.
[47]) See *supra*, p. 24.

voice of the younger generation demanding respect for the individuality of its contributions to society, even if at variance with the wisdom of the older generation.

Curiously, Euripides, whose philosophy was iconoclastic, gives us, in the extant plays, no picture of the revolt of the youth. In the *Alcestis*, written in 438 B.C., the quarrel between a father and son takes the bizarre form of King Admetus berating his aged father, Pheres, for his refusal to die in order to save his son's life. Pheres' angry words are based on the traditional relations of the generations: "You are very arrogant," he tells his son, "and, though a youth, you hurl words at me...."[48]) Admetus reverses traditional legal process by formally disowning his father.[49]) Even so, Euripides, like his great contemporaries Aeschylus and Sophocles, all of them perceptive surveyors of the shifting values of contemporary Athens, reflects the changing status and claims of the younger generation.

This generational consciousness and aggressiveness produced under the dramatic circumstances that convulsed the Greek world in the second half of the fifth century B.C. a degree of devaluation of the older generation and of generational disequilibrium unparalleled in the previous history of mankind. The evidence is unmistakable. Increased awareness of an antithesis between the generations took form in Athens.[50]) This cleavage was widened and supplied with a rationale by the Sophists, who elevated the conflict of generations to a vigorous and conscious opposition in Athenian society. Their tendency to analyze phenomena in bipolarized form, their sanctioning of reason and natural rights (*physis*) over legal and traditional institutions (*nomos*), which they held up to critical examination, their advocacy of *arete* in knowledge rather in obedience, of egalitarianism and relativity in morals – all these heightened generational consciousness on the part of the youth. Thus there emerged for the first time the claim of the younger generation to a "natural right"

[48]) *Alcestis* 679.

[49]) *Alcestis* 629–672, 737–738.

[50]) Pherecrates (Old Comedy), frag. 145 (Koch): youth is impulsive, elders deliberate. Euripides, frag. 115.5 (Nauck): "There is an old proverb—the power of youth is in deeds, of the older generation in counsel." See also Jacqueline de Romilly, *Time in Greek Tragedy* (Ithaca, 1968) ch. 6.

to disobey and disregard fathers and elders.[51]) Such vigorous critique and assault on tradition and the customary authority of the fathers and the older generation were accelerated also by the growth of democratic institutions, the weakening of the ties toward the *polis*, and the rise of individualism in Athens.[52]) It is, however, important to recognize that the generation gap in Athens was not motivated by revolutionary political views of the youth, despite realization on the part of many that the older generation had failed as a result of the traumatic experience of the Peloponnesian War. Their unrest and agitation were not directed toward thrusting themselves forward as the "self-anointed bearers of authority"[53]) and the establishment of a juvenocracy in place of their "de-authoritized" elders. The fathers were, indeed, more devoted to the institutions of the *polis* and its democratic constitution than the sons, who had not only experienced disillusionment but, with growing individualism, were likely to repudiate democratic institutions as restrictive, irrational, and contrary to natural law.[54])

The failures of Athens during the Peloponnesian War, the suffering, despair, turmoil, and growing brutalization of warfare and social conflict, unleashed an open critique by the younger generation of the mismanagement of affairs by the older generation. Symptomatic and highly instructive in this connection is a fragment of a political oration "On the Constitution" by the sophist Thrasymachus (well known for his debate on justice with Socrates in the opening pages of Plato's *Republic*): "I could wish, men of Athens, to have belonged to that long-past time when young men were content to remain silent, and when events did not compel them to speak in public, while the older men were correctly supervising the city.")

[51]) E.g., Dodds, *op. cit.*, pp. 47, 61, n. 104; V. Ehrenberg, *op. cit.*, p. 209; E. B. Castle, *Ancient Education and Today* (Baltimore, 1961), pp. 53–54; F. A. G. Beck, *Greek Education, 450–350 B.C.* (New York, 1964), pp. 147–187; 304–305; W. Jaeger, *Paideia* 1² (New York, 1945): pp. 286–331; H. I. Marrou, *Histoire de l'Éducation dans l'Antiquité*⁶ (Paris, 1965), pp. 87–106.
[52]) *Cp.*, e.g., G. Glotz, *op. cit.*, pp. 415, 606–607; Castle, *op. cit.*, p. 49.
[53]) Feuer, *op. cit.*, p. 19.
[54]) *Cp.* S. Luria, "Väter und Söhne in den neuen literarischen Papyri," *Aegyptus* 7 (1926): pp. 244–245.

But now because of grave mistakes, "...it is necessary to speak.[55]) A person either has no feeling or has too much patience who goes on offering himself up to whoever wishes as the object of their mistakes, and is ready to assume the blame for the guile and wickedness of others. ... " As a result, instead of harmony "[we have] reached the point of hostility and conflict with one another."[56]) In another context, the sophist Antiphon (about whom little is known – he was an opponent of Socrates) took a stance on the side of the younger generation. In an essay "On Truth" Antiphon held that blind obedience and piety toward parents were irrational and contrary to natural law; and that there was nothing morally wrong in disregarding legal restraints, so that guilt feelings toward parents, for example, were irrational.[57])

That contacts between the younger and older generation in Athens in the last quarter of the fifth century were abrasive is underlined by the crystallization of a stock motif of Old Comedy, strained relations between fathers and sons.[58]) The growing friction between and changed outlooks of the generations are especially reflected in Aristophanes' *Clouds*.[59]) In the debate between Right Logic and Wrong Logic it is obvious that Aristophanes' sympathies were the older generation and its values. "Boys," proclaims Right Logic, the symbol of traditional ways, "should be seen and not heard," they should be trained in the ways of their fathers, revere their parents, show respect for elders, not talk back to fathers or call them "old Iapetus."[60]) In this connection there was created in Old Comedy the stock figure of the "father-beater," symbolizing the young generation, belligerent, scornful, emancipated from restraints imposed by the fa-

[55]) *Cp.* Eupolis (writer of Old Comedy, fl. 430–410 B.C.), *frag.* 310 (Edmonds): "The young lads stand up and speak before the men."

[56]) H. Diels, *Die Fragmente der Vorsokratiker*,[10] ed. by W. Kranz (Berlin, 1960) 2: pp. 322–324; K. Freeman, *Ancilla to the Pre-Socratic Philosophers* (Oxford, 1948), p. 141. *Cp.* K. Oppenheimer, "Thrasymachus," *RE* Zw. R. 6: cols. 584–592; S. Luria, *op. cit.*, pp. 250–251.

[57]) P. Oxy. XI, 1364, lines 135–139; *cp.* pp. 92–93. *Cp.* S. Luria, *op. cit.*, p. 268; E. Wellmann, *RE* 1: col. 2529.

[58]) V. Ehrenberg, *op. cit.*, p. 208.

[59]) *Cp.* Ehrenberg, *op. cit.*, pp. 210–211.

[60]) *Clouds* 963, 993–994, 998–999. *Cp.* Ehrenberg, *op. cit.*, pp. 210–211.

thers.[61]) In the *Clouds* of Aristophanes, for example, there is a confrontation between the generations in the characters of Strepsiades and Phidippides. Young Phidippides, arguing with his father over his own preferences for modern poetic and musical styles while Strepsiades supports older modes, strikes his father. In the ensuing analysis of this unprecedented act, which the father calls unjust and illegal, Phidippides defends the right of sons to use violence against the fathers on rational and sophistic grounds. When parents act in an immature manner, reasons Phidippides, they must be chastised like children; laws permitting parents to strike children were made by the older generation. The solution is simple: "change the law so that sons may beat fathers."[62]) Similarly in the *Birds* Aristophanes comments on the belligerent attitude of the younger generation by depicting Cloudcuckooland as a place where the young are permitted by law to strike their fathers.[63])

The generational disequilibrium, hostility, and tensions in Athens are also confirmed by the growing importance and application of two intergenerational legal processes: *apokeruxis* – disownment of a son by a father, and *graphe paranoias* – charge of mental incompetence by a son against a father.[64])

In the anxiety of the older generation to restrain the youth there was developed in Athens as a protective device the use of the term "youth" in a derogatory sense in the ideological warfare of the time among members of the older generation. For example, we find a politician in his fifties labeled "the most powerful of the younger scoundrels."[65]) Similarly, middle-aged democratic politicians were called οἱ νεώτεροι as compared with their more conservative predecessors.[66]) In the debate

[61]) A. Bork. *Der Junge Grieche* (Zürich, 1961), pp. 65–67; Dodds, *op. cit.*, p. 61.

[62]) *Clouds* 1321–1436.

[63] *Birds* 755–759, 1347–1352. *Cp.* F. Wehrli, *Motivstudien zur griechischen Komödie* (Zürich, 1936), pp. 56–69.

[64]) S. Luria, *op. cit.*, pp. 243–268; Ehrenberg, *op. cit., pp.* 209–211. *Cp.* P. Oxy. XIII, 1608, a fragment of the dialogue *Alcibiades* of Aeschines Socraticus, one of Socrates' most devoted pupils. In this work (lines 1–6, 34–51) Themistocles' unfilial relations with his parents, leading to disinheritance, are discussed.

[65]) Eupolis, frag. 122b–c (Edmonds) πανούργων... νεωτέρων. The reference is to Diognetus, a brother of Nicias. In 411 B.C. he was between fifty and sixty years of age.

[66]) Aristophanes, *Wasps* 1099–1100.

over the Sicilian expedition between Nicias and Alcibiades which Thucydides incorporates for the year 415 B.C., Nicias downgrades Alcibiades as "still too young to command, ... a rash youth." "It is of youths such as these," says Nicias, "when I see them sitting here in answer to the summons of this same man that I am afraid; and I make a counter-appeal to the older men. ...."[67]) Alcibiades concedes his youthfulness, and warns against Nicias' effort to cause friction (the ominous term *stasis* is used) between the younger and older generations. This, declares Alcibiades, is detrimental to civic harmony and the national imperial goals, for "just as our fathers did, young men should take counsel with older men ... [for] youth and old age without one another are worth nothing."[68]) Thus in this illuminating Thucydidean paradox the older Nicias is depicted as exacerbating generational conflict, while the younger Alcibiades appears as a supporter of generational harmony! It is noteworthy that Alcibiades was at this time thirty-six years of age![69]) A similar instance of the term "youth" as a rhetorical cliché with derogatory implications is to be found in the debate in Syracuse in 415 B.C., in which the popular leader Athenagoras, an older man, attacks the oligarchs, whom he calls *neoteroi*, as overly ambitious for power. Though their leader Hermocrates, the anti-Athenian statesman and general, could hardly have been a young man at the time, Thucydides has simply put into Athenagoras' mouth a typical ideological association of the politician being attacked with irresponsible young men.[70])

[67]) Thucydides, 6.12.2, 13.1. *Cp.* Dover, *Thucydides Book VI* (Oxford, 1961), p. 20.

[68]) Thucydides 6.17,1, 18.6. On Nicias' conflict with Alcibiades and the generational conflict of the time, *cp.* V. Ehrenberg, *op. cit.*, p. 210; J. de Romilly, *Thucydide et l'Impérialisme Athénien* (Paris, 1947), pp. 174–176.

[69]) On the rhetorical cliché "youthful folly" see K. J. Dover, *op. cit.*, p. 20. In Ps-Andocides, *Against Alcibiades* 22 (a forgery of late date), the failure of the Athenians to punish the insolence of the youthful Alcibiades resulted in moral decline. "The young men," taking Alcibiades as their model, "spend their days not in the gymnasium but in the courts. And while the older men are on military campaigns, the younger make speeches."

[70]) Thucydides 6.38.5. *Cp.* Dover, *op. cit.*, p. 50; Lenschau, "Hermokrates," *RE* 8: cols. 883–887.

Because Socrates was on the side of reason, when he thought the sons to be right, despite traditional obligations of obedience and respect, he ranged himself on the side of the sons against the fathers. It is instructive that both factions of the older generation were hostile to him: in 404 B.C. the oligarchs ordered him to cease talking with the youth (that is, those under thirty);[71]) in 399 B.C. under the restored democracy, he was charged with corrupting the youth, found guilty by the democratic courts, and executed. Actually, whatever the effects of his teaching upon individual Athenian youths – and it is clear that on rational grounds his leading pupils turned to conservative political and social philosophies – Socrates had no intention to exacerbate and widen the generational gap in Athens. His views on the generations were a mixture of Pythagorean doctrine requiring veneration of the fathers, and opposition to the despotism of the elders when they thwarted fulfillment of the rational ideals of the youth.[72]) If in his teaching he fostered intellectual revolt of the youth against institutionalized irrationality, he nevertheless inculcated respect for and gratitude to parents as a fundamental duty because they give children the blessings of life. Children owe their parents obligations and respect that are imposed by the laws and public opinion.[73]) This did not deter Socrates' more rabid accusers from charging him with malicious intent in fomenting hostility to and contempt for fathers and tradition, causing sons to become scorners of the gods and morally degenerate.[74]) This he was said to have accomplished by substituting himself as surrogate father, asserting himself to be a wiser guide for the youth in matters of proper conduct than their own fathers.[75]) But, indeed, Socrates in his concern to make respect for reason the overriding obligation, proclaimed that "unreason is unworth" and that, therefore, respect for members of one's family should not be based upon familial ties alone.[76]) Thus in substituting the criterion of reason for the traditional principle of

[71]) Xenophon, *Memorabilia* 1.2.33–35.
[72]) S. Luria, *op. cit.*, p. 268; E. B. Castle, *op. cit.*, p. 51.
[73]) E.g., Stobaeus, *Anth.* 4.25.42: "One must adapt oneself to a senseless father as to a harsh law"; Xenophon, *Memorabilia* 2.2.3, 13.
[74]) Xenophon, *Memorabilia* 1.2.53, 2.55; *Apology* 19.
[75]) Xenophon, *Memorabilia* 1.2.49, 51–52; *Apology* 19–21.
[76]) Xenophon, *Memorabilia* 1.2.55.

unthinking obedience to parents, Socrates in effect contributed to the undermining of the traditional relations between the generations. It came down to this simple proposition: if the older generation acted unwisely, righteousness was on the side of the youths who disobeyed them. "If one does not obey the evil, unjust, or shameful orders of a father or official, or even, by Zeus, a despot, he does not in any way disobey," proclaimed the Stoic philosopher Musonius Rufus, one of the intellectual heirs of Socrates.[77]

With the defeat of Athens in 404 B.C., the generational tensions of the end of the fifth century B.C. took a new turn. The increasing disillusionment with the cultural and political forms of the older generation and the rapidly increasing individualism fostered by social instability did not result in confrontations or programs for reform mounted by the youths. In the first half of the fourth century B C. their scorn for their elders took the form of rejecting integration into the traditional political and social institutions of their elders: instead the energies of the educated and affluent youth were channeled into degenerate practices – dissipation of all sorts, debauchery, drinking, squandering of wealth, general idleness. Isocrates warned that such dissolute living was especially true of "the most promising young men."[78]

The reaction of the older generation in Athens was a form of backlash which was directed mainly against democratic institutions; they

[77]) Musonius (*ca.* 30–102 A.D.) was the teacher of Epictetus. In the fragment of his teaching preserved in Stobaeus, *Flor.* 4.26.51, Musonius reasons that while obedience to parents is a general principle, even on the assumption that parents are basically well-intentioned to their children, if a father acts willfully in ignorance, or orders his son to steal or betray a trust, or commit a shameful act for pay, then a son is wise if he disobeys his father. In the pseudo-Platonic *Theages* (123B), probably of the second century B.C., Socrates is made to say to Theages who has quarreled with his father who does not want him to continue an intellectual education, "What wisdom do you lack, when you blame your father for being unwilling to place you with people who would enable you to become wise?"

[78]) *Antidosis* 285–287 (the date is 354/353 B.C.). On the degeneracy and dissipation of the Athenian youth in the fourth century B.C., see also Athenaeus 12.532D; *cp.* Bork, *op. cit.*, pp. 54–55. Athenaeus (4.165–166) records the story that Ctesippos, son of the Athenian general Chabrias in the middle of the fourth century B.C., in order to indulge his prodigality actually sold one by one the stones of a monument to his father erected with public funds. Unfortunately, we do not know the ages of

urged a return to more authoritarian controls. In 335 B.C. Isocrates, in the *Aeropagiticus*, an "address on the public safety," attributed the intensity of class struggle in Athens to what he called the "extreme democracy." Isocrates singled out as one of the significant elements of social disharmony in Athens the disaffection of the younger generation against their parents and elders. "Let no one suppose," he assures his fellow Athenians, "that I am out of temper with the younger generation." Those who were to blame for the time-wasting and the excesses of the younger generation were the politicians who introduced into Athens an excess of freedom by destroying the power of the Areopagus.[79] He therefore recommended a return to the constitutional and social order of the sixth century B.C., to a time he idealized as the "old democracy" of Solon and Cleisthenes. This he asserted, was the golden age of Athenian democracy when the youth were obedient and modest, when the elders exercised vigilance over the youth (who require firm restraints), when the quality of citizenship was sounder.[80] Earlier, in 374-372 B.C., Isocrates had expressed his concern for the youth in the maxims he set forth for Demonicus: he reaffirmed the traditional injunction, "honor thy parents," recommended to youth their special virtues of modesty and self-control, and, in one of the earliest expressions of the golden rule, urged them to "Conduct yourself toward your parents as you would have your children conduct themselves toward you."[81] It is in line with such thinking that Xenophon turned to less free contemporary cultures as models for harmonious relations of the generations. For example, he admired the Persian prince Cyrus, under whom he served as a mercenary soldier, as a paragon of modesty and

the four Athenians, Cinesias (dithyrambic poet *ca.* 450-390 B.C.), Apollophanes, Mystalides, and Lysitheos, who called themselves κακοδαιμονίσται ("Devil's Club") and feasted together on religiously forbidden days (Lysias, frag. 53.2 [Thalheim] from *Oration against Cinesias*).

[79] *Areopagiticus* 49-51.

[80] *Areopagiticus* 25, 43, 48-49. *Cp.* S. Cecchi, *Isocrate, Antologia daile Orazioni* (Milan, 1960), pp. 127-128; R. C. Jebb, *Attic Orators* (New York, 1962) 2: pp. 202-213; Bork, *op. cit.*, pp. 53-54; W. Jaeger, *op. cit.* 3: pp. 48-49, 119-123; Münschner, *RE* 9: cols. 2206-2208; G. Norlin, *Isocrates* (LCL) 2: p. 100, warns that we must be on guard against exaggerations in Isocrates and the philosophers of the fourth century in their depiction of the degeneracy of Athens.

[81] *Demonicus* 14-16.

obedience to elders.[82]) Xenophon also urged a return to the ways of the ancestors, and asserted that what was especially needed was "Lacedaemonian reverence for older people, seeing that they [Athenian youth] despise all their elders, beginning with their own fathers."[83]) It is perhaps as a result of the moral decay of the Athenian youth that there was created a new group of ten officials, one for each tribe, whose duty it was to superintend the training of the ephebes. They were called *Sophronistae* – Restrainers.[84])

The backlash was given more elegant philosophical underpinnings by Plato, who advocated return to more authoritarian controls, "... the ancient and world-wide traditions."[85]) The youth should learn honor and respect for parents, grandparents, and elders, and show no scorn for or commit acts of violence against them (except in cases of insanity).[86]) Positively, to parents are due the traditional obligations, particularly in old age, and throughout one's life reverence of speech and compliance even when parents act in anger toward their children.[87]) "Everyone shall reverence his elder both by deed and by word."[88]) Yet Socrates had bequeathed to Plato the paradox of respect both for elders and for reason. And so in the *Euthyphro* Plato presents the dilemma of the righteous youth who is torn by the twin duties of honoring his father and prosecuting him for murder because his father had caused the death by exposure of a hired workingman who had committed a murder. Some have thrown up to Euthyphro the charge of impiety for persecuting his father for murder; but Euthyphro believes that it is impious not to prosecute a wrong-doer, even if father or mother, citing as support Zeus' violence

[82]) *Anabasis* 1.9.5.

[83]) *Memorabilia* 3.5.14–15.

[84]) G. Busolt, *Die Griechische Staats- und Rechtsaltertümer* (Munich, 1892), pp. 306–307; J. Oehler, *RE*, Zw. Reihe, 3: cols. 1104–1106.

[85]) *Laws* 881A.

[86]) Plato, Stobaeus, *Flor.* 4.25.43; *Laws* 879B, 880E, 881B–C, 930A, 931E, 932A; *Seventh Letter* 331C. On the authenticity of Plato's *Seventh Letter* see e.g., L. Edelstein, *Plato's Seventh Letter* (Leiden, 1966), pp. 167–169; F. Solmsen, *Gnomon* 41 (1969): pp. 29–34.

[87]) *Laws* 717–718A.

[88]) *Laws* 879C.

against his father Cronus, and that of Cronus against his father Uranus.[89])

But Plato gives greater weight to the traditional deterrents against generational arrogance: inculcation of fear of punishment by the gods, both in this life and in the afterlife, of children who inflict violence upon parents and elders.[90]) True, there may arise differences between fathers and sons that cannot be harmonized, in which extreme cases there may be applied legal procedures for disownment by fathers, and, on the other side, for charging mental incompetence against parents by sons.[91]) But in well-ordered states, according to Plato, elders should be revered, and treated as if they were parents; "an outrage (that is, violence) perpetrated by a younger person against an older person is a shameful thing."[92]) Persons convicted of assault upon parents should be treated as a defiling thing and banished from the city and all sacred places.[93]) Those who neglect their parents shall be reported to magistrates charged with administering the laws. The penalties Plato would impose for neglect include whipping and imprisonment of men under thirty and women under forty. Any person who hears of such mistreatment of parents shall be obligated, under penalty of the law, to report this to the magistrates.[94])

Reflecting upon the unstable conditions of his own times, in particular the generational contradictions in Athens, Plato isolated generational disequilibrium as a significant mechanism in political change. But Lewis Feuer has concluded, erroneously, that Plato and Aristotle set forth generational struggle as a universal theme in history.[95]) Extrapolating a few passages from Plato and Aristotle, Feuer would have us believe that "both ... recognized its [generational strife] primacy as an independent factor in political change ... virtually the basic mechanism in political change. ... Generational conflict seemed

---

[89]) *Cp. Euthyphro.* 4D–E, 5D, 6A. See *supra*, p. 349.
[90]) *Laws* 718A, 879B–C, 880E, 881A–B, 931C.
[91]) *Laws* 928D–E.
[92]) *Laws* 879B–C.
[93]) *Laws* 881D.
[94]) *Laws* 932A–C.
[95]) Feuer, *op. cit.*, pp. 27–30 (reprinted below).

to them an everlasting threat to political stability."[96]) It is true that Plato, in his concern over the loss of respect for their elders by the younger generation of his day, did seek to analyze the relations between the generations prevailing under different types of government. Under certain forms of government, he declares, there tends to develop loss of respect for the fathers. For example, in an aristocracy affluent fathers who are excluded from political power are "de-authoritized" in their sons' eyes in various ways. The mothers, out of status jealousy, complain to their sons that their fathers do not hold official positions because of personal weakness. Even house slaves talk to the sons in the same way. Such loss of respect for the fathers leads to generational disequilibrium and consequent political instability, resulting in the degeneracy of aristocracy into timocracy, which opens up office holding and political power to the men of wealth.[97]) Particularly in a democracy excessive freedom, according to Plato, results in loss of respect for the older generation; attendant egalitarian concepts and leveling downward produce a general adaptation on the part of the older generation to the manners and values of the younger generation. In a democracy the fathers therefore do not discipline their sons, who turn to dissipation and abandon modesty and self-control, becoming rebellious, insolent, and profligate, interested only in the satisfaction of material desires.[98]) Thus does equality of all destroy the authority of the older generation.

"The parent falls into the habit of becoming like a child, and the son like the father. The father is afraid of his sons, and they show no reverence or respect for their parents, in order to assert their freedom. Citizens, resident aliens, and strangers from abroad are all on an equal footing. ... The schoolmaster is afraid of and flatters his pupils, and the pupils make light of their masters as well as their attendants. Generally speaking, the young copy their elders, and compete with them in words and deeds, while the elders, anxious not to be thought disagreeable tyrants, imitate the young, accommodating themselves to the young and filling themselves full of wit and bon mots."[99])

[96]) *Ibid.*, pp. 27–28.
[97]) *Republic* 549C–550B.
[98]) *Republic* 560B–E, 561A–E. *Cp.* Bork, *op. cit.*, pp. 52–53.
[99]) *Republic* 562D–563A.

This condition of affairs Plato calls "anarchy"; the consequence is dictatorship. Thus Plato, in his horror of political instability, non-conformity, and pluralism, and in his efforts to validate an oligarchic and paternal social structure, advocates a return to a vigorously policed hierarchical organization of society which would assure firm restraints of elders over the youth.

One of the by-products of the generational tensions of the fourth century B.C. was the study of the psychological makeup of each generation and the formulation of the characteristic ethos of each in bi-polarized form.[100] The lead in this formal analysis was taken by the conservatives, who tended to characterize the youth as unstable in views, mercurial, and insolent in behavior. It was Aristotle who laid down the classic formulation of the antithesis between the natures, values, and conduct of the order and younger generations.[101]

"The young are changeable in their desires and quickly sated; they have violent desires which are soon appeased. .... Owing to ambition, they cannot bear to be slighted, and they become indignant if they think they are being wronged. .... They are ambitious for honor but more so for victory. .... These two they desire more than money because they have not yet experienced want. .... They are not prone to evil, but rather to goodness, because as yet they have not seen much vice. .... For the most part they live by hope; for hope belongs to the future, as memory to the past, and for young men the future is long and the past short. .... They are rather courageous, for they are full of passion and hope, and passion keeps men from being fearful, while hope makes them confident. .... They are shy, for as yet they have no independent standards of propriety, but have been trained by convention alone. They are high-minded, for they have not yet been humbled by life, they are inexperienced in its necessities. .... They prefer honorable before expedient actions, for they live by their disposition rather than by calculation. .... They are fond of their friends and their companions rather than of persons of other ages. .... All their mistakes are due to excess and vehemence. ..... They think they know everything and are positive; this, indeed, is the cause of their excess in all things."[102]

---

[100] E.g., Plato, *Seventh Letter* 328B; *Laws* 716A.
[101] *Rhetoric* 2.12.3–16.16.
[102] *Rhetoric* 2.12.3–14.

By contrast, the older generation is materialistic and ungenerous, guided by expediency rather than principle; and so it appears temperate. "Their life is guided by calculation rather than by what is noble."[103])

All these tendencies, suggestions for controls, and theoretical formulations affirm that in the highly unstable conditions of the fourth century B.C. friction between the generations was a historical fact of life. But revolutionary programs or violent gestures on the part of the young did not develop.[104]) The older generation was largely "deauthoritized," but there were safety valves, such as employment in the ever growing mercenary armies of the time, escape into dissolute living, and, above all, in the last third of the fourth century into the massive Macedonian-Greek imperialistic scheme to invade the Persian Empire, the success of which was to siphon off vast numbers of Greek youth into the great reaches of Asia.

In the new cultural patterns created by the conquests and policies of Alexander the Great the conditions that had produced generational consciousness in the fifth and fourth centuries B.C. on the part of the youth in Athens and the tensions between the older and the younger generations were largely eliminated. In the Hellenistic world democracy quickly withered away, the autonomy of the Greek city-states came to an end, and, despite ever-increasing individualism, political despotism and authoritarian societal patterns prevailed. In this atmosphere generational disequilibrium, such as Isocrates, Plato, and Aristotle had sought to combat, ceased to be a major concern.

Symptomatic of the altered relations between the generations in Athens is the social outlook of the New Comedy. In the plays of

---

[103]) *Rhetoric* 2.13.6, 9, 13–14. *Cp.* Aristotle, *Rhetoric* 1.5.6 on self-restraint and courage as the *aretai* of the youth.

[104]) *Cp.* Feuer, *op. cit.*, p. 30. I fail to see as evidence for "...the immense political significance of generational struggle in the Greek towns..." the political struggles for office in the oligarchic cities of Massilia, Ister, Heraclea, and Cnidos, cited by Aristotle, *Politics* 5.5. Rather than involving generational confrontations, the passage deals with provision made to prevent members of the same families—older and younger brothers, fathers and sons—from holding magistracies at the same time. In *Nic. Ethics* 7.6.2, Aristotle tells of a man who when indicted for beating his father defended himself by testifying that it ran in the family: his father beat his father, and he fully expects his own son to beat him. Dinarchus' *Against Aristogeiton* (338 B.C.) involves a case in Athens of a man accused of mistreating his father.

Menander the stock type of the younger generation is now the "Good Young Man," who is the worthy son of the "Good Old Man." Between father and son there exists a harmonious relationship of love, trust, and affection. True, Menander, his contemporaries Diphilus and Philemon, and their Roman imitator Terence, reflected principally the lives of the rich strata of the period. Their older men – extremely wealthy, industrious, wise – are intent on preserving the conventional moral standards of the family as the nucleus of their neat, respectable little worlds. Their conventional young men, mostly of the leisure class, sure to succeed to their father's estates, feel nothing but the highest respect for their fathers; they may occasionally deviate from the rules in their amorous adventures, and the fathers may generously indulge their sons' pecadilloes. But the aims of both the older and the younger generation are identical: adherence to respectability and maintenance of familial harmony.[105] "How sweet is harmony of parents and children!" wrote Menander,[106] epitomizing the ideals and practices of the Hellenistic Age.

It is, nevertheless, curious that it was in the Hellenistic Age that the first efforts in world history took place to organize the youth into associations. Beginning at the end of the fourth century B.C. associations of *neoi* appeared and gradually spread all over the Greek world, especially in the Near East, enduring as an institution for seven centuries. Recognized by the Hellenistic rulers and the Roman emperors – even sponsored by them – these corporate associations of *neoi* (*neoteroi* or *neaniskoi*) accepted as members Greek youths who had

[105] P. S. Dunkin, *Post-Aristophanic Comedy. Studies in the Social Outlook of Middle and New Comedy* (Urbana, Illinois, 1946, Studies in Language and Literature, No. 21 [3–4]), pp. 24–30, 52–54, 106–137. F. Wehrli, *op. cit.*, pp. 56–69. *Cp.*, e.g., Diphilus, frag. 93 (Edmonds; Koch = Stobaeus, *Anth.* 4.25.16): "If I appear to speak better than my father, I wrong myself and am no longer reverent to the gods, for I harm my sire and do not love him."

[106] D. L. Page, *Greek Literary Papyri* (LCL), No. 56 (4). *Cp.* Menander, frag. 663 (Edmonds; Koch): "He who gladly makes himself a proper and true guardian for his son will not have someone around waiting for him to die"; Ariston (Peripatetic philosopher of the third century B.C. [*RE* 2: cols. 952–957], frag. (Stobaeus, *Anth.* 4.25.44): "Those who have recently studied philosophy, and question all, beginning with their parents, are like new born puppies. Not only do they bark against outsiders, but also those inside."

passed the ephebic age, that is young men from nineteen or twenty up. Though their membership and titles indicate generational conscious-ness, these youth associations existed largely as sports clubs for foster-ing gymnastic and athletic competitions.[107]) Though generationally motivated, these youth clubs, except in rare instances, did not engage in political activities. Such exception is to be found in the intense polit-ical struggles on the island of Crete in the early Hellenistic period, when organized youth groups obtained official recognition and some influence. For example, in the revolutionary situation in the city of Gortyn, which involved generational conflicts between young and old in the third century B.C., a council of youths (νεότας) was invested with official authority and judged cases concerning illegal currency.[108]) Polybius tells us, tantalizingly, that in the Lyttian War of 221–219 B.C. Gortyn was in a state of civil war, in which "the older generation was in a state of conflict with the younger generation, the elders siding with Cnossus, the youths with Lyttus."[109]) The generational cleavage and civic disunity in Crete about this time – end of third century/early second century B.C. – led the elders to impose legal sanctions to strengthen their hold on the youth and keep the younger generation in line. At Drerus the youth as a separate group, were required to swear an oath, hedged around with powerful religious sanctions, that they would not aid the Lyttians in any way, that they would maintain loyalty to the city of Drerus and allied Cnossus, would not foment revolution, would oppose all who did so, and would denounce any who so con-spired.[110]) But this was a special localized phenomenon, affecting a limited area of Crete under still unclear circumstances.

In general, indeed, our knowledge of the Hellenistic Age does not reveal generational friction, and we may assume that, whatever were

---

[107]) C. A. Forbes, *Neoi* (Middletown, 1933 = Amer. Philol. Assn., Monographs, No. II): F. Poland, *Neoi, RE* 16: cols. 2401–2409; P. F. Girard, *Neoi*, DS 4: p. 59. R. F. Willetts, *Aristocratic Society in Ancient Crete* (London, 1955), pp. 188–190.

[108]) Insc. Cret. 4.162, 163, 164; H. Schaefer, "Neotas," *RE* 16: col. 2477; F. W. Willetts, *op. cit.*, pp. 187–190.

[109]) Polybius 4.53.7–9.

[110]) Insc. Cret., 1: pp. 84–88, lines 10–14; Willetts, *op. cit.*, pp. 119–120, 182–183; H. van Effenterre, "A propos du serment des Drériens," *BCH* 61 (1937): pp. 327–332. Scholars are in dispute whether the oath of the Drerian youth was a new oath for the occasion or recopied at the time from a much older archetype.

nistic world experienced – frequent
tagnation, growing diminution of the
dual – generational dissension was not

, in a region that was socially, econom-
d as compared with the Greek world,
third century B.C. great upheavals tore
ating instability and confusion in values.
B.C.) succeeded to the royal power, he be-
came a great conqueror and unifier. Grandson of Chandragupta, the
founder of the Mauryan Dynasty, Asoka Maurya united India with
brutal violence (the Kalinga War) and tyranny. But suddenly he was
converted to Buddhism, and eschewing force, he sought to unify his
vast empire of many classes, castes, sects, and religions by proclaiming
the reign of moral law and advocating the spread of Righteousness
(*Dharma*). It was a period in Indian history when the subcontinent
was undergoing great social dislocation and instability attendant upon
the transition from pastoral to agrarian village economy, and when
the family as an institution was developing out of the kinship-based
tribal castes. Because previous human relations had disintegrated
Asoka sought to cement them on a new level through centralization
and authoritarian restrictions on individual liberty.[111]) Accordingly,
he presented himself as a "father figure," and stressed the importance
of the harmonious family as the ideal nucleus for spreading *Dharma*
and thus achieving harmony throughout the empire. Hence in the
edicts inscribed along the borders of his empire, through which he
published his code of piety and morality in the form of advocacy of
specific approved forms of human and social relations, Asoka pro-
pounds as one of the basic bonds of social unity the duty of obedience
to father, mother, and elders. We may assume that the unrest of his
times had involved generational frictions, for he tells us (in the Greek
text of a recently discovered bilingual inscription set up at Kandahar
[in Afghanistan] in the Indian province previously part of the Persian
and Seleucid Empires) that ten years after his conversion and the
promulgation of his code, "Whosoever were lacking in self-control,

---

[111]) R. Thapar, *Asoka and the Decline of the Mauryas* (Oxford, 1961), p. 213.

have ceased from such lack of control, each according to his ability, and they have become obedient to their fathers and mothers and eld- ers, contrary to what had been the case previously. And in the future, by so acting, they will live better and more advantageously in every respect."[112]) In other edicts addressed to all the people, written in Prakrit, Asoka constantly reiterated the obligations and advantages of obedience and respect to superiors, elders, and parents.[113]) Though Asoka tells us that, after "he made men more pious..., he caused all to flourish throughout the entire country," we do not know how his program of social harmony in the rapidly changing society of India worked out in actual practice. Suffice it to say that after his death his experiment with *Dharma* disappeared. Asoka's experiment is, how- ever, instructive as another example of the possibilities of generational dislocations in antiquity in times of great crisis and of the efforts, usually successful, to control the younger generation through main- taining the unity of the family.

Turning our eyes westward to Italy, we find in the Roman expe- rience an idiosyncratic pattern of self-renewing social and legal tradi- tions and of stern controls that methodically channeled each new generation into the ways of the fathers. For over a thousand years of their history, the Romans—except for a brief period at the end of the Republic—succeeded in preventing generational deviation. The ex- traordinary authority of the *mos maiorum*, the cult of the ancestors, whose worship held up to each new generation behavioral paradigms authenticated in the past, the systematic inculcation of such Roman virtues as *disciplina* and *pietas*—all these served to mold each genera- tion in the image of the elders and forefathers. Above all loomed the

---

[112]) D. Schlumberger and L. Robert, "Une Bilingue Greco-Araméenne d'Asoka" *Journal Asiatique* 246 (1958): pp. 2–3. The Aramaic text of the same edict (p. 22) is slightly different: in place of "contrary to what had been the case previously," it reads "in conformity with the obligations which fate has imposed upon each."

[113]) Rock Edicts II, III, IV, XI, XIII; Pillar Edict VII. On the texts and signif- icance of Asoka's edicts see *The Edicts of Asoka*, ed. and transl. by N. A. Nikam and R. McKeon (Chicago, 1959); J. Bloch, *Les Inscriptions d'Asoka* (Paris, 1950); V. A. Smith, *Asoka, The Buddhist Emperor of India* (Oxford, 1920), pp. 149–230; R. Thapar, *Asoka and the Decline of the Mauryas* (Oxford, 1961), pp. 147, 164, 180, 213–217, 250–266 (texts in English); B. G. Gokhale, *Asoka Maurya* (New York, 1966); G. Woodcock, *The Greeks in India* (London, 1966), pp. 47–61.

his household beginning with the second century B.C., the Roman government was disinclined to interfere with the *patria potestas*, and the total power it embodied remained as a legal right until the end of Roman civilization, indeed into the Christian period. "The legal authority of the power which we have over children," wrote the jurist Gaius, "is peculiar to Roman citizens; there are no other men who have such power as we have over our sons."[115])

Reverence and obedience to fathers were second nature to Roman youths; it was also "the duty of a young man to respect elders."[116]) For Cicero the virtues peculiar to the younger generation—particularly modesty and self-control—were better cultivated if the younger generation did not segregate itself from the older generation even in its pleasures.[117]) Extraordinary sanction was given to filial duties of the youth by associating the Roman concept of *pietas* with both parents and gods, thus giving identical religious content to correct relations with both authorities.[118]) And just as among the Greeks, the Romans hedged around filial duty with the threat of the father's curse. An early Roman law read: "If a boy strike

---

[114]) See *supra*, p. 352.

[115]) Gaius 1.55. On *patria potestas* see, e.g., R. Paribeni, *La Famiglia Romana* (Rome, 1948), pp. 11, 31–33, 45–46; M. Borda, *Lares. La Vita Familiare Romana* (Rome, 1947), pp. 2–3; M. Pellison, *Roman Life in Pliny's Time* (New York, 1897), pp. 19–20; L. Beauchet, "Patria Potestas," *Daremberg-Saglio* 4: pp. 344–347; M. Johnston, *Roman Life* (Chicago, 1957), pp. 106–109; M. Kaser, "Der Inhalt der Patria Potestas," *Zeitschrift der Savigny-Stiftung für Rechtsgeschichte, Rom. Abt.* 58 (1938): pp. 62–87; Reallexikon für Antike und Christentum, 4: pp. 1194–1198.

[116]) Cicero, *De Off.* I. 122.

[117]) *Ibid*.

[118]) C. Koch, "Pietas," *RE* 20: cols. 1221–1232; R. Heinze, "Zum Römische Moral," in *Vom Geist des Römertums* (Stuttgart, 1960), pp. 82–86.

his father, and the father complains, let the boy be accursed."[119])

In consequence of the Roman high estimation of the fathers and devaluation of the legal and social personality of children, the term "youth" was associated with shallowness, foolishness, and ineptitude. In the second century B.C., when the Roman as an individual was emerging out of the rigid Roman family controls and the absolute subordination to the state, "youth" appears as a derogatory appellation. For example, Plautus, in reworking the Greek New Comedy for Roman ears, made the stock "Good Old Man" of Menander into a tedious moralizer, and the "Good Young Man" into a spineless, shallow, trivial, often roguish figure.[120]) At about the same time, the Roman poet Naevius expressed his view as to how a powerful state might be destroyed in a line which Cicero admired: "New orators came forth, foolish young men."[121])

Motivated by the needs and traditions of Roman society, early Roman educational procedures and aims were directed not at intellectual achievements but principally at the inculcation into the young of discipline, duty, and filial submission. This was achieved mainly by the constant companionship of the son with the father, "the living representative of Roman authority," whom he imitated and served, as it were, as apprentice and understudy.[122]) In this connection Cato the Elder undertook personally to instruct his son even in the elements of learning, rather than allow a surrogate father in the form of a slave or freedman teacher to intervene.[123])

Any sense of generational consciousness or disaffection with the older generation was rendered negligible not only by Roman traditions and education, but also by the frequent wars and the safety valve of colonies sent out by the Roman government first in Italy and later in the provinces. Harmony with the older generation was especially cultivated by the Roman upper class youth which was eager to

---

[119]) Festus, p. 230, Müller; p. 260, Lindsay.

[120]) Dunkin, *op. cit.*, pp. 64–102; F. Wehrli, *op. cit.*, pp. 56–69.

[121]) Quoted by Cicero, *De Senect.* 6.60.

[122]) See, e.g., A. Gwynn, *Roman Education from Cicero to Quintilian* (Oxford, 1926), pp. 12–21.

[123]) Plutarch, *Cato Maior* 20.3–8.

assume its place on the ladder of the administrative and military organs of the world power.

But the world crisis during the hundred years from the Gracchi to Augustus eventually had the impact of a generational event that aroused massive disaffection from the Roman government and the ways of the fathers. Yet this "de-authoritization" of the Senatorial Order, and the disillusionment with the older generation in Rome did not lead to either strong generational consciousness among the youth or generational conflict. It is characteristic of the Romans that many alienated youth, such as Vergil and Horace, remained strongly devoted to their fathers while seeking peace of mind from the insecurities, anxieties, and turmoil of the times in the doctrines and living style of Epicureanism. Others expressed their rejection of society through unrestrained dissipation of all sorts.[124] In the troubled and chaotic times of the last decades of the Roman Republic, Cicero reiterated the merits of inculcating the Roman virtues and of maintaining the traditional father-son relationship, reaffirming the efficacy of self-restraint, filial duty to parents, devotion to kin, the practice of attaching a young man as understudy to a wise elder experienced in public affairs.[125] Cicero was, nevertheless, fully aware of the disaffection and alienation of the youth of the ruling classes. Indeed, in 44 B.C. he expressed the conservative view that the history of other societies showed that great states were undermined by the younger generation and restored by the elders.[126]

[124] The collapse of traditional Roman moral standards in the first century B.C. is too well known to require documentation here. A good example is Cicero's son Marcus. Cp. J. Carcopino, Cicero, The Secrets of his Correspondence (London, 1951) 1: pp. 151–177; F. F. Abbott, "The Career of a Roman Student," in Society and Politics in Ancient Rome (New York, 1963, reprint), pp. 200–213. On the nonconformism and retreat from national commitment on the part of many of the Roman youth in the first century B.C. in both politics and literature see the suggestive comments of J. Granarolo, "La jeunesse au siècle de César d'après Catulle et Cicéron," Assoc. G. Budé, Congrés de Lyon, Actes (Paris, 1960), pp. 483–519.

[125] Cicero, De off. 2.13.46: "And if they associate constantly with such men they inspire in the public the expectation that they will be like them, seeing that they have themselves selected them for imitation."

[126] De Senec. 6.20.

4*

Cicero's pessimistic valuation and fears of the dissolute Roman youth were shared by many. But in the debates of the time more forward-looking political theorists like Sallust, while equally aware of the collapse among the Roman youth of a sense of social direction, sought basic reforms to overcome the moral crisis. The corruption of the youth, asserted Sallust, was brought about by the riches that poured into Rome from the second century B.C. "As the result of riches, luxury and greed united with insolence took possession of our youth."[127] Those affected were not only the upper-class youths, but also those among the common people in the country, who flocked to the city of Rome preferring dissolute idleness on the dole there to poorly paid manual labor in the fields.[128] All the youth, asserted Sallust, "were utterly thoughtless and reckless," indulging in all sorts of depravity—gluttony, sexual dissipation, self-indulgence, illicit gain, and extravagances.[129]

Some of the youth—Sallust occasionally uses the term *homines adulescentuli* in a derogatory sense—sought to achieve influence through political adventurism. Sallust was critical of several young men, "whose age and disposition made them aggressive," who obtained the tribuneship after 70 B.C. and used their political authority to inflame the plebs against the Senate by doles and promises.[130] It was especially the young men of the upper classes—greedy for gain, reckless, impressionable—who were attracted to the revolutionary program of Catiline in 64–63 B.C., and whom he particularly courted.[131] When Caesar held supreme power in the early 40's, Sallust advised him that a basic reform in the spirit of the youth was indispensable. "If our youth continue to have the same desires and habits as at present, beyond doubt that eminent renown of yours will come to a speedy end, along with the city of Rome."[132] Above all, advised Sallust, what was needed to curb the license and lack of restraint of the Roman youth was a turning away from materialism and a return

---

[127] *Catiline* 12.1.
[128] *Catiline* 37.7.
[129] *Catiline* 3.3–5, 12.1–2, 13.4–5; *Epist. I ad Caes.* 5.5–6.
[130] *Catiline* 38.1; cp. 52.26.
[131] *Catiline* 14.1–4.
[132] *Epist. I ad Caes.* 6.1.

to respect for and practice of the old Roman values of discipline, industry, and integrity.[133] The analysis and recommendation of Sallust, while motivated in part by partisan politics, are a valuable commentary on the retreat of the Roman youth into pleasure-seeking and on their susceptibility to participation on violence.[134]

The advent of the principate of Augustus did not succeed in effectively controlling either materialism in the Roman world or the disposition to and opportunities of many of the youth for pleasure-seeking as a way of life. In this connection one of Augustus' mouthpieces, the poet Horace, commented in 28 B.C. on the degeneracy of both the young men and young women of Rome. "The age of our parents was worse than that of our grandparents; it made us even more worthless, and soon we shall produce a more corrupt generation."[135] But the imperial power did put brakes on the recourse to violence as a tool of change endemic in the last century of the Republic. It is characteristic of the Roman mind that Augustus (and the emperors after him) assumed the role of father image for many Romans and the provincials, and that *pietas* was redirected for the Romans to a new level of submission and duty to the emperor. Henceforth we do not hear of generational disaffection in the Roman Empire. Both the authority of the emperor and that of the *paterfamilias* in each household imposed on the younger generation submission and obedience as the normal way of life.

Augustus' concern for the youth, particularly of the two upper classes (Senatorial and Equestrian Orders) led to the institution and spread of associations of youths in the Roman world, comparable to the *neoi* of the Greek East. *Collegia iuvenum*, each one approved by the Roman government, common at first in the cities of Italy and then in the western provinces, are known during the first three centuries of the Empire. These youth associations had high status in their communities and played a substantial role in their civic life as municipal youth clubs. But their functions were limited to participation in

[133] *Epist. I ad Caes.* 5.6, 6.4, 7.2.

[134] On Sallust's views see, e.g., K. Vretska, *C. Sallustius Crispus: Invektiven und Episteln* (Heidelberg, 1961) 1: p. 70; 2: pp. 224, 239. The genuineness of Sallust's letters to Caesar seem well established in contemporary scholarship.

[135] *Odes* III.6.21–32, 45–48.

sports, athletic contests, and religious ceremonies, as were the Greek associations of *neoi*.[136]

Thus, after the turmoil and dislocations of the first century B.C. which produced the only generational friction in Roman history, we find generational balance and harmony restored under the imperial regime. This remained one of the foundations of social life in the Roman Empire to the end of the urban civilization of antiquity, when the rigidities of feudal society descended.

---

[136]) See, e.g., Zeibarth, "Iuvenes," *RE* 10: cols. 1357–1358; C. Jullian, "Iuvenes," *Daremberg-Saglio* 3: pp. 782–785; "Iuvenes," *Dizionario Epigrafico di Antichità Romane* 4: pp. 317–320; S. L. Mohler, "The Iuvenes in Roman Education" *TAPA* 68 (1937): pp. 442–479; M. Rostovtzeff, *Römische Bleitesserae, Klio,* Beiheft 3 (1905); *idem, The Social and Economic History of the Roman Empire,*[2] rev. by P. M. Fraser (Oxford, 1962), pp. 103, 107, 127–128. Rostovtzeff considered the *collegia iuvenum* as "seminaries of future soldiers" which provided military preparation for future officers, soldiers, and local militia. By contrast, Mohler regarded these associations as clubs of schoolboys for the promotion of sports and social activities for school youth.

Chapter 1

CONFLICTS BETWEEN YOUNG AND OLD IN HOMER'S *ILIAD*

Carlyn A. Querbach

University of Windsor

The earliest evidence of generational conflict in the Greek and Roman world appears in Homer's *Iliad*. In that work the conflicts we find generally occur between the young and old of the same social class, particularly that of the princes ($\beta\alpha\sigma\iota\lambda\tilde{\eta}\varepsilon\varsigma$)[1]. Two types of such conflict exist, one which emanates from the view of the elders that they were at one time superior to their younger counterparts in strength and warlike spirit and one that involves the idea that the elders are superior in wisdom by virtue of their advanced age. The conflicts are fairly subtle and subdued by the constraints of a rigid society in which the young warriors for the most part desire to emulate the conduct and values of the preceding generations.

The first type of conflict arises from the fact that the older Achaian men are not involved in the activity of battle to the same extent as the young warriors are. To compensate for the emotional consequences of their reduced usefulness in battle and to assure the younger men as well as themselves that they were once valorous, these elders love not only to recount their former deeds of glory, but also to assert that these deeds required a strength and courage which far surpassed that demonstrated by their younger counterparts. Nestor, who represents the oldest generation of Greek chieftains at Troy, makes such assertions frequently throughout the *Iliad*. In Book Two he severely rebukes the Argives for fighting with words rather than deeds, the implication being that this is not what he would do, were he a young man (II, 337–368). In Book Seven he makes an even stronger and clearer statement about the inferior valor of the younger warriors (VII, 124–160). Agamemnon has just discouraged Menelaus from engaging in

---

[1] This social class consisted of the rulers of the various states of Greece and their immediate families. At Troy these men were, as a general rule, the military commanders of the contingents of fighting men from their native areas.

single combat with Hektor, and no one else has volunteered to take Menelaus' place. Nestor speaks of the occasion when, during a battle between the men of Pylos and the Arcadians, none of the Pylians was willing to fight in single combat against Ereuthalion, the champion of the Arcadians. Only Nestor, who was the very youngest of the Pylians, volunteered to combat him. Furthermore he indicates that he would combat Hektor in the present situation, were he young again:

> But you, now, who are the bravest of the Achaians,
> are not minded with a good will to go against Hektor
>   (VII, 159–160).[2])

In Book Four Nestor, advising his own contingent from Pylos as to battle strategy, concludes by recalling the precedent for warlike spirit which was established by the preceding generations:

> So the men before your time sacked tower and city,
> keeping a spirit like this in their hearts, and like
>   this their purpose (IV, 308–309).

This very mention of such a precedent implies that he has reservations about the degree to which this quality exists in the younger generation.

The younger warriors engage in hard and strenuous combat, and the elder men do not dispute this. Nestor does involve himself in the fighting, and he is a strong man; nevertheless he is too old to be one of the foremost warriors (IV, 317–325; cf. XI, 635 f.). He can primarily serve the function of instilling enthusiasm into his troops and advising them on the basis of his previous experience (IV, 295–310). In a society which values physical prowess and the demonstration thereof as a major criterion by which to determine worth, it is understandable that the older warriors, who have lost much of their physical strength, might suffer from a somewhat weakened self-image. In order to compensate for this lack of self-esteem, the old men find it necessary to assert that in their youth not only were they stronger and braver than their young counterparts but also engaged in combat with more formidable foes. In Book One Nestor asserts that he fought in company

---

[2]) All quotations from the *Iliad* are taken from *The Iliad of Homer*, translated with an introduction by Richmond Lattimore, copyright 1951 by the University of Chicago.

with the strongest generation of men against the strongest foes, the mountain-beast men. He further claims to have fought singlehandedly against these monsters whom no man of the younger generation would have the strength to combat (I, 254–274).

It is not sufficient, however, for the elders to rely on the superiority of their past accomplishments. They also need to feel superior in some respect or other in the present time. When the old hero Nestor is told by Agamemnon in Book Four that his fighting spirit still surpasses that of the younger men (IV, 311–316), Nestor agrees with this and finds in this assurance the kind of compensatory superiority which he needs. He cannot after all compete with the younger warriors in actual display of physical ability. At least, however, even in his old age he can feel superior to the younger men in valorous spirit if not in actual achievement. He can furthermore assure himself that in his youth he was decidely superior in both respects.

There are those among the young warriors, however, who are not entirely willing to concede all of these claims to the old. In Book Four Agamemnon rebukes Diomedes for failing to match his father, Tydeus, in battle, and by such criticism tries to evoke a better perform-ance from him (IV, 370–400). But Agamemnon receives a return rebuke from Sthenelos, Diomedes' companion, who well illustrates the resentment of the young toward this assertion:

> Son of Atreus, do not lie when you know the plain truth.
> We two claim we are better men by far than our fathers.
> We did storm the seven-gated foundation of Thebe
> though we had fewer people beneath a wall that was stronger.
> We obeyed the signs of the gods and the help Zeus gave us,
> while those others died of their own headlong stupidity.
> Therefore, never liken our fathers to us in honour.
>
> (IV, 404–410).

Sthenelos uses Nestor's technique of referring to a past event, but instead of presenting the men of the past as superior, he clearly regards them as having acted in a reckless and foolish manner. He indicates that he and his companions stormed a stronger wall with fewer men and far surpassed the performance of their fathers in so doing. He also claims that he and his companions exercised greater caution and presence of mind. Diomedes rebukes Sthenelos for speaking rudely to the king, but he in no way disagrees with what Sthenelos has asserted.

This particular generational conflict in the *Iliad* is, however, verbalized almost exclusively by the old, particularly by Nestor. Agamemnon, who is of the middle generation of princes at Troy (he is younger than Nestor and older than Achilles and Diomedes) uses this idea as an expedient form of rebuke to the younger warriors. The young warriors, however, although they sometimes praise the ability of their fathers to demonstrate the quality of their own lineage, do not speak of them as stronger and braver than they themselves are. Neither do they openly assert the superiority of the young over the old. Sthenelos, after all, spoke with provocation in response to a direct rebuke against Diomedes. The young in the *Iliad* do not need to make compensatory claims of superiority because they are still useful in terms of their society's criteria. They feel no need to justify their worth because it is not doubted either by themselves or by their older peers.

The second area of conflict arises from the idea that the older men are wiser in counsel by virtue of their advanced age and broader experience. This view furthermore assumes that the young are more inclined toward reckless behavior (III, 105–110; cf. XX, 407–412; XXIII, 603 f.). Indeed the elders foster this view of themselves. It is their only claim to distinction inasmuch as the princes both young and old are about equal in social status. That the old should be regarded as the wisest counsellors may be a form of compensation, which is granted to them because they have lost the ability to make a more active contribution. In Book Four, for example, Nestor states that although he is too old to fight, he will serve the warriors in an advisory capacity, He further claims that this is the special prerogative of old men (τὸ γὰρ γέρας ἐστὶ γερόντων). The choice of the word γέρας, which commonly means "prize," seems to imply that this advisory prerogative is a form of compensation which remains when all other distinctions have been lost (IV, 318–325).[3]) The giving of counsel is

---

[3]) Compare the formula, τὸ γὰρ γέρας ἐστὶ θανόντων (XVI, 457, 675), which similarly seems to imply that there remains for the dead some reward, albeit empty,

the only area in which the old men can still do something of value.

The younger men perhaps accept this theoretically, but in actual practice they listen politely and then proceed to follow their own best judgement. They do sometimes adhere to the advice of the old, but only when that advice is uncontroversial and the young have no objection to it (II, 337–368; IX, 52–78; X, 191–193). No one, for example, is opposed to building a wall to protect the Greek ships. Therefore all agree to Nestor's advice (VII, 327–344). Often in the *Iliad* advice which is uncontroversial is also quite obvious and trivial and as such is unobjectionable to the younger men. In Book Ten Nestor advises Agamemnon to awaken certain other chieftains to accompany them on an inspectional tour of the sentinels. The advice is so obvious that Agamemnon and Menelaus have already thought of it (X, 120–127).[4]) In Book Nine Nestor tells the Greeks not to quarrel among themselves and to prepare a feast (IX, 52–78). It is not surprising that this advice, hardly brilliant or significant, evokes no objections.

Frequently in the *Iliad* the more significant counsel proves also to be the more controversial. When the younger men do not agree with the advice of the elders, they do not adhere to it, irrespective of how sound it may be. Nestor's analysis of the conflict between Agamemnon and Achilles is insightful, and his advice for alleviating it is sensible; but neither man pays him any heed. Indeed Nestor himself seems to know that it will be difficult to persuade them and finds it necessary to impress them with his qualifications as a counsellor (I, 254–274).[5]) In Book Nine Nestor advises Agamemnon to make some kind of

despite the loss of almost everything that men value. The same notion appears in connection with the funeral games for Patroclos (XXIII, 618–623), where Nestor is given an honorary prize (ἄεθλον) to compensate for his inability to participate in the contests.

[4]) Finding no real disparity in the treatment of this subject between Book Ten and the rest of the *Iliad*, I am quoting examples from the Book, despite the considerable uncertainty as to its authorship.

[5]) It must be noted that the quarrel between Achilles and Agamemnon is essential to the plot construction of the poem and that perhaps the poet had no choice but to prevent a reconciliation between the two princes. Nevertheless, with this reservation kept in mind the passage should be mentioned as an example of the failure of Nestor to deter the younger men from their respective positions.

amends to Achilles. Agamemnon agrees to this because he is disturbed at the reversal of his army's fortunes and is therefore inclined to reach an understanding with Achilles. This is in his own self-interest and certainly in the best interests of the Greek army, but the younger Agamemnon makes only those amends which his weakened self-image will permit. He does less than Nestor intended and much less than the situation requires. He offers Achilles many gifts, and that is all, although Nestor had at least hinted at some form of a mild apology.[6] Thus, Agamemnon agrees to part of Nestor's suggestions but rejects that other part which he is not emotionally prepared to accept.

Another example of advice not taken from an elder is found in the passage where Nestor through Patroclos suggests that Achilles should re-enter the battle. It is noteworthy that Nestor's own doubts about the potency of his advice lead him to propose also a milder alternative, that of sending Patroclos to fight in Achilles' stead (XI, 785–802). Achilles rejects this advice because he is not emotionally capable of renouncing his wrath. He accepts that part of the advice which does not require any change in his position or loss of face among his peers (XVI, 46–100).[7] Neither does he follow the advice of Phoenix to

[6] Nestor's words are:

$$\text{``}\dot{\alpha}\lambda\lambda' \ \ddot{\varepsilon}\tau\iota \ \varkappa\alpha\grave{\iota} \ \nu\tilde{\upsilon}\nu$$
$$\varphi\varrho\alpha\zeta\dot{\omega}\mu\varepsilon\sigma\theta' \ \ddot{\omega}\varsigma \ \varkappa\dot{\varepsilon}\nu \ \mu\iota\nu \ \dot{\alpha}\varrho\varepsilon\sigma\sigma\dot{\alpha}\mu\varepsilon\nu\sigma\iota \ \pi\varepsilon\pi\dot{\iota}\theta\omega\mu\varepsilon\nu$$
$$\delta\dot{\omega}\varrho\sigma\iota\sigma\dot{\iota}\nu \ \tau' \ \dot{\alpha}\gamma\alpha\nu\sigma\tilde{\iota}\sigma\iota\nu \ \ddot{\varepsilon}\pi\varepsilon\sigma\sigma\dot{\iota} \ \tau\varepsilon \ \mu\varepsilon\iota\lambda\iota\chi\dot{\iota}\sigma\iota\sigma\iota.\text{''}$$

"But let us even now think how we can make this
good and persuade him
With words of supplication and with gifts of
friendship."
(IX, 111–113)

Agamemnon agrees to make amends with a contribution of many gifts, but he does not specifically agree to the kindly and conciliatory words, which Nestor also suggests.

$$\text{``}\ddot{\alpha}\psi \ \dot{\varepsilon}\theta\dot{\varepsilon}\lambda\omega \ \dot{\alpha}\varrho\dot{\varepsilon}\sigma\alpha\iota \ \delta\dot{\sigma}\mu\varepsilon\nu\alpha\dot{\iota} \ \tau' \ \dot{\alpha}\pi\varepsilon\varrho\varepsilon\dot{\iota}\sigma\iota' \ \ddot{\alpha}\pi\sigma\iota\nu\alpha.\text{''}$$

"I am willing to make all good, and
give back gifts in abundance."

(IX, 120).

[7] This passage again may be essential to the plot construction, but with that kept in mind, I think that it is reasonable to mention it as an example of advice not taken by the younger man.

accept Agamemnon's gifts and re-enter the battle (IX, 607–619).[8])
We also get a subtle hint from the poet that Achilles did not follow
aged Peleus' advice to avoid quarrels at Troy (IX, 252–261). It would
seem, therefore, that there is abundant evidence that Achilles often
rejects the notion that he must follow the advice of his elders. If it is
not to his liking, he rejects it. In fact, rarely if ever in the *Iliad* does
an older man actually convince a younger man to desist from something which he is determined to do.

One of the most interesting and subtle generational conflicts in the
Iliad, that between the aged Nestor and the youthful Diomedes, involves the open objection of a young man to the opinions of an old
man. Diomedes is not, as Achilles is, rebellious against the traditional
values of the heroic society. Apart from their difference in age, he and
Nestor are very much alike; they share the same status and the same
ideals and can boast of similar achievements in battle. Nevertheless
Diomedes is often at odds with Nestor and, for all his external deference, is particularly disturbed by the notion that age in itself gives
Nestor an advantage in the councils of the princes.

[8]) An interesting relationship exists between Achilles and Patroclos and between
Achilles and Phoenix. Patroclos and Phoenix are both of a lower social status than
is Achilles. Both presume to advise him by virtue of being his elders. Consider the
following words of Nestor in Book XI:

> "My child by right of blood Achilleus is higher
> > than you are,
> but you are the elder. Yet in strength he is far
> > the greater.
> You must speak solid words to him, and give him
> > good counsel,
> And point his way. If he listens to you it will be
> > for his own good."

Nestor indicates that it is appropriate for Patroclos to advise Achilles because he is
older, even though Achilles definitely possesses higher social standing (γενεῇ ...
ὑπέρτερός) (IX, 785–788).

Phoenix is not only older than Achilles but his pedagogue as well. This lends a kind
of superiority to his position. It is apparent that men of a lower social standing can
appropriately give advice to a younger man of higher birth. It may also be implied
that the people of the inferior social position must have a positive relationship to
the younger man for other reasons. To be aged is not enough if one is inferior in
lineage.

The first example of this conflict occurs when Nestor commends the gifts which Agamemnon will send to Achilles. Nestor agrees that such gifts would be scorned by no one. They will in fact be scorned by Achilles, and it seems significant to me that it is Diomedes who points this out to Agamemnon (IX, 697–709). He is in conflict with Agamemnon to be sure, but he is far more subtly in conflict with Nestor, who has after all commended the idea of offering Achilles a virtual bribe. Diomedes, for all the supposed inexperience of his youth, has understood Achilles better than did either Agamemnon or Nestor. In this instance Nestor has not given Agamemnon completely sound advice. The gifts were quite inappropriate because Achilles did not want to be bought. He is only further insulted by the offer of gifts without an apology. While Diomedes is still far more an adherent of Nestor's value system and does not condone Achilles' withdrawal, he yet understands Achilles in a way in which Nestor cannot. The younger man's counsel, even though after the fact, of leaving Achilles alone and letting him decide when he will fight again, is far more preceptive of the realities of the situation. The Achaian princes finally acclaim the words of young Diomedes, who has subtly revealed the inherent weaknesses in the old man's advice.

When Nestor suggests that a spy be sent among the Trojans to gain information about their battle strategy, Diomedes offers his services. He also supplements Nestor's advice by suggesting that it would be better to send two men (X, 220–226). He speaks with great deference to Nestor, but gently reveals the weaknesses in Nestor's advice. The young man has thought out his reasons for sending two scouts and expresses them convincingly.

Another example of this conflict occurs when Diomedes saves Nestor's life. The old man tries to urge him to leave the battle. Diomedes hesitates and requires signs from Zeus before he will retreat. The old man's counsel, although sound, is not readily accepted by the young man until he himself is convinced. In this particular relationship we find that the young man questions the older man's advice by means of subtle criticism and outright objections. Later, in Book Fourteen, Nestor suggests that the wounded kings should not return to the battle. Diomedes directly contradicts him and asserts that they should return. The young man's advice is followed. Diomedes demonstrates that the impetuosity which he sometimes displays and an ability to analyze a situation and make sound suggestions for improving it are not mutually exclusive traits. The old would assert that they are.

Diomedes has also demonstrated that a young man sometimes gives sounder counsel than does an old man, a view which the old could not accept. An interesting illustration of this generational conflict is seen in Nestor's reply to a rebuke made by Diomedes to Agamemnon before the assembly. Nestor applauds the valor and the words of the young man, but states that an old man can present a more complete account of a matter to the assembly. He in effect asks Diomedes to yield place to him in addressing the assembly because he is older (IX, 53–78). The actual feelings of the younger man about this discrimination are revealed in Book Fourteen. In response to Agamemnon's quest for advice, Diomedes asserts (as noted above) that the wounded kings should return to battle. His opening lines reveal the discomfort with which he, the young man, addresses his elders:

> If you are willing to listen to me,
> and not be each astonished in anger against me
> because by birth I am the youngest among you (XIV, 110–112).

He is defensive and insists that his status and lineage should entitle him to counsel his elders despite his youth. The old man Nestor, on the other hand, feels completely secure in addressing the assembly of princes. He does not have to justify the appropriateness of this act. The old men take such a prerogative for granted. The young men cannot. Nestor even says quite confidently that Agamemnon himself cannot dishonor the things he says (IX, 61–62). With this prerogative the old man maintains his status, but the young man resents that his counsel is thought to be of less value simply because he is young.

Interestingly enough the advice of the old men is very rarely solicited in the *Iliad*.[9]) Nestor, for instance, simply stands up and speaks.

---

[9]) The only incident in the *Iliad* which would seem to contradict this statement is found in Book Ten, lines 17–20, where Agamemnon decides to awaken Nestor and ask him to devise a plan which might reverse the setbacks which the Greeks have been suffering. Actually all that he finally asks Nestor to do is to accompany him on an inspection of the sentinels to warn them not to fall asleep.

This illustrates to some degree how much the younger men in the *Iliad* value the opinions of the old. The old adhere to the integral association of age and wisdom because it is in this area alone that they can claim with any credibility to be superior to the young. While the old man views his length of service as the most important criterion, the young man argues that the quality of his lineage and deeds should offset his inferiority in age. Herein lie the foundations of generational conflct. Ironically, Nestor himself as a young man showed a degree of impetuosity and assumed that he could handle with maturity and good sense a situation wherein his father doubted his ability (XI, 716–720). The old men underestimate the good judgement of the young, and the young both resent this and refuse to act in accordance with it.

Yet despite the generational tensions that exist in the *Iliad*, there does not seem to be any fundamental discrepancy between the basic value systems of the young and old. There is, for example, no evidence of a radical youth culture; instead most of the young are striving to emulate the values of heroic society. While there is one actual conflict of values in the *Iliad*, it involves Achilles versus the others both young and old.[10] He literally withdraws from the society because he cannot accept its criteria for determining a man's worth. In the *Iliad* he is the only serious critic of his society's rules, but nonetheless it is significant that he is a young man.

---

[10] The conflict in values between Achilles and the others is admirably treated by Cedric Whitman in *Homer and the Heroic Tradition*, (Norton Library, 1965), chapters VIII and IX.

Chapter 2

THE GENERATION GAP IN THE *AGAMEMNON**

Jay M. Freyman

University of Maryland – Baltimore County

The *Agamemnon* contains much about the relation between old and new, age and youth. Very frequently in the play, this takes the form of an expression of the parent-child relationship and the responsibilities of one generation to the next. Such expression appears both explicitly and implicitly. The present study will trace the interplay of old and new, especially as it is embodied in the conflicts of parents with children, generation with generation, through the play. This is not to ignore the role of the *Agamemnon* in the *Oresteia* as a trilogy so composed, but rather to demonstrate how the theme under consideration, which is much more explicit in the *Choephoroe* and the *Eumenides*, plays an important part in the first drama of the three and thereby prepares for its more overt expression in the next two plays.

Yet, because it seems that the expression of this theme is in many instances implicit, the burden of gleaning its full import in the play as a whole would appear to rest heavily upon the audience and upon the mind-set with which the audience entered the theater. For instance, the audience would know the outcome of the familiar story of the trilogy even as the events in the *Agamemnon* were being unfolded before them.

The underlying importance of the theme in the *Agamemnon* requires recognition in view of such passages as 40–54 where there is the description of birds which realize that their young, the result of their toil, have been destroyed, or 104–21[1] where we hear of the Greek youth sent to die at Troy, or 228–57 where the picture of Iphigenia being sacrificed is given. The simile in the first of these three passages (all of

---

* Presented at the April 1971 Meeting of the Classical Association of the Atlantic States.

[1]) Cf. in particular ἥβας in *Agamemnon* 109.

66

which are contained within the first long choral ode and which are rather evenly spaced – beginning, middle, end – throughout the passage to maintain the impression) is moving and sets the scene for the second and third passages noted. The birds are humanized by the implication that they *feel* as humans do on realizing their young are dead. (But, by a similar token, in being put in the same situation as these unreasoning creatures, men are dehumanized somewhat and made more instinctual.)

In the *Agamemnon*, there is the fact of age's learning from or by youth as it is expressed, for example, in 584. By the end of the *Agamemnon*, the audience is reminded of the universal truths by which one ought to direct his life while keeping in mind that their application within the family has broad implications for the whole community. Rightly applied, they prepare a livable world for generations to come. Wrongly applied, they leave the next generation nothing but a world in which it must suffer, and learn, if it can.[2])

Perhaps, the most succinct expression of this, an expression which the *Agamemnon* has been building up to and foreshadowing, in the *Oresteia* as a whole occurs approximately in the middle of the trilogy, at *Choephoroe* 418–9, in the words of Electra:

> But what could we say and hit the mark? What, indeed, other than that the distresses we suffer are at the hands of the very ones who brought us into the world?

In this passage, the "poetic" plural $\tau\varepsilon\varkappa\omega\mu\acute{\varepsilon}\nu\omega\nu$ is used. It is employed for non-specific reference to an individual and in this case would refer to Clytemnestra. Denotationally, Electra would consciously be referring to Clytemnestra, which would be supported by the use of $\mu\alpha\tau\varrho\acute{o}\varsigma$ in 422, as well as by the diction of 132–4 and 190–1. Connotationally, though, the reference may be to both parents and all her elders.[3])

The responsibility for the expedition to Troy, and therefore, for its outcome, rests at the same time on both sons of Atreus ($\zeta\varepsilon\tilde{v}\gamma o\varsigma$

[2]) *Agamemnon* 174–8.
[3]) H. W. Smyth (*Aeschylus*, Loeb Classical Library, vol. II, Cambridge, Mass., 1963, Harvard University Press) takes $\tau\varepsilon\varkappa\omega\mu\acute{\varepsilon}\nu\omega\nu$ in the former sense; R. Lattimore (*Greek Tragedies*, vol. 2, Chicago, 1960, University of Chicago Press) in the latter.

’Ατρειδᾶν, 44) and on each separately. The reason for deciding to sacrifice Iphigenia was to save the "flower of the Argives," ἄνθος ’Αργείων, as they will be called at 197 in the last section of the ode. The irony lies in the more universal implication of the decision. Immediately, it is true, the Argive youth are saved from a wasting death at Aulis, but how and to what end? One of their own generation must die; and most of them, indeed, are to die at Troy. Agamemnon's generation has become a threat to the next one just as Atreus' generation had through his killing his brother's children and serving their flesh as food for their father and through Thyestes' subsequent curse on his brother's house.

Immediately on setting forth their tale of the expedition to Troy, the chorus are concerned with parents and children, elder and younger (109–20):

> How a fearsome bird-omen sent the double-throned force of the Achaeans, Hellas' youth's allied authority, against the Teucrian land with avenging spear and hand, for there were for the kings of the ships one black king of birds and one white in its tail feathers, and they appeared hard by the palace on the side of the spear-wielding hand in a very conspicuous place, feeding upon the offspring of a hare, still full with the burden of the womb, arrested from its last running-away.

The continuity which should exist from one generation to another is made clear as the hare and its offspring, the latter yet unborn, are destroyed at the same time. Aeschylus' ambiguity in γένναν (119), as in many cases in the *Agamemnon*, is poignant; the need to question whether it means here "that which is born" or "bearer"[4] is significant. The answer is that it is both. The hare is at one and the same time itself an offspring and a mother pregnant with offspring. The implication is that the young of the hare which fall victim to the eagle-kings symbolize Greeks and Greek youth as much as they do Trojan; and

---

[4]) Cf. the note of J. D. Denniston and D. Page (*Aeschylus: Agamemnon*, Oxford, 1968, Oxford University Press) on *Agamemnon* 118 f.

we must look in the past, i.e., Thyestes' children, the present, i.e., Iphigenia,[5]) and the future (λοισθίων, 120)[6]) for the consequences of the injustice done by one generation to the next. We are to learn, then, from the story of the eagles and the hare that the very fact of conceiving young exposes them to destruction. How much greater the danger is when the young are allowed to be born Thyestes and Agamemnon and Clytemnestra could testify.[7])

The Achaeans have sent the ἥβη, youth, to Troy. They go as πράκτωρ, avenger. The one generation has created the situation; the toil and suffering remain for the next. Here, there is a vicious circle in force. The parents are responsible for a given situation in which the children must work as avengers. A responsibility, artificial and created by the society of their parents, devolves upon innocent children. In discharging it, though, through a process of retribution, they lose their innocence and only necessitate the same for their children.

The emphasis on youth continues through the choral ode. Calchas has much to say of the young of animals, according to the chorus. But, he is then concerned with events on the human level. His whole prayer (146-55) builds to a final, climactic word which (along with its possible ambiguity[8]) as to whether the first part stands in a subjective or objective relationship to the second part [for there will in the course of the trilogy be vengeance both for and by a child of the house of Atreus]) is the distillate of the action of the whole trilogy and of its mythic background — τεκνόποινος, child-avenging.

In the retelling of the events at Aulis, Iphigenia is not mentioned

[5]) Edwards, W. M., "The Eagles and the Hare," *Classical Quarterly*, XXXIII (1939), 204-7. If we accept the identification of κτήνη in *Agamemnon* 129 with the δῆμος of the city, the collectivity and impersonality give us all the more reason to view the young of the hare as symbolizing youth in general, youth which has not been given the chance to realize its potential, Greek and Trojan alike.

[6]) Dawson, H. S., "On *Agamemnon* 108-120," *Classical Review*, XLI(1927), 213-4.

[7]) Cf. Lucretius V. 222-34 on exposing a child to danger merely by bringing him into the world.

[8]) Cf. Stanford, W. B., "Γυναικὸς ἀνδρόβουλον ἐλπίζον κέαρ (*Agam.* 11)," *Classical Quarterly*, XXXI(1937), 92-3.

once by name.[9]) Without its being spoken, the violent emotions created by the chorus' story are, in a way, psychologically confined. Mention of her name might be *expected* here. Yet, Aeschylus no more desires to release the tension of this confinement in this manner than he does by allowing the knife in the hand of her father actually to fall (in the words of the chorus). The audience are waiting for this; Clytemnestra may even be beginning to turn around from the altar to face them. But, the matter is dropped with the ironical words, "well-fated song for the third libation," ($\tau\rho\iota\tau\acute{o}\sigma\pi\sigma\nu\delta\sigma\nu$ $\epsilon\check{v}\pi\sigma\tau\mu\sigma\nu$ $\pi\alpha\iota\tilde{\omega}\nu\alpha$, 246–7); yet, the audience know that all three elements will be controverted. The third libation, that for $ZEY\Sigma$ $\Sigma\Omega THP$, Zeus Savior,[10]) is to be of no avail. Both the song and the girl will come to anything but a good end. The healing, connoted in $\pi\alpha\iota\tilde{\omega}\nu\alpha$,[11]) is not to come for a long while.

The chorus allow feelings to remain tense:[12])

What happened after that I neither saw nor say; the skills of Calchas are not vain. Justice allots it to those who suffer to learn.

How, at such a time, can the chorus suddenly lapse into a gnomic statement, just when feelings are running amidst the irrational and the last thing that the audience and Clytemnestra would expect, or want, to hear is a rational precept? Yet, it is to the purpose. It leads one to think again of 177 where the same sentiment is voiced in the play of *pathos* and *mathos*. Suffering is supposed to bring learning. What happens next at Aulis is for the audience to imagine, and they will imagine suffering. What happens next at Argos will be suffering. But, learning will come. Hence, the purpose (and it seems to be achieved) of the chorus' words is to raise the situation of Iphigenia to the realm of the universal.

[9]) In fact, her name appears only twice in the whole trilogy (*Agamemnon* 1526 and 1555) though her death is much in the forefront and is the immediate cause of the plot's action. Iphigenia's silent but, perhaps, intentional curse is hinted in $\grave{\alpha}\rho\alpha\tilde{\iota}\sigma\nu$ of *Agamemnon* 237.

[10]) Cf. Pindar *Isthmian* VI. 7–8.

[11]) This recalls $\Pi\alpha\iota\tilde{\alpha}\nu\alpha$ in *Agamemnon* 146.

[12]) *Agamemnon* 248–51.

Within Agamemnon's mind, this rift between generations takes the form of a conflict between a man's positions as king and, at the same time, as father. Agamemnon was given a choice at Aulis—not really whether to sacrifice his daughter, but whether to proceed with the expedition against Troy. Deciding the latter question automatically decides the former. Agamemnon might well have been shamed before his people; but he would have affirmed the bond of parent and child and would have broken the curse and the circle of *pathos*, if he had decided not to proceed.

The chorus in 717–81 immediately precedes the arrival of Agamemnon. In the story of the young lion raised in its master's house as a pet but in the end the cause of suffering to that house, the chorus again refer to the animal world in explicating the theme of the responsibility of parents to and for children. After all, the young lion is unnaturally removed from the care of its own mother. The breaking of the parent-child bond is clear. While the example here is meant to show Helen as removed from her own people, "nourished," as it were, in the house of Priam only to bring ruin upon that house, it also applies to another figure in the myth, Paris (and to Aegisthus, who later in 1217–25 is referred to as a lion). He was nurtured contrary to an omen and thus brought ruin to Priam's house. His estrangment from his parents and people came first in his exposure as an infant which failed and then in his carrying off Helen.[13] In any event, the older generation has consented to the cultivation of this ruin. In the case of Paris at Troy and, eventually in the trilogy, in the case of Argos, the youth reverse the direction of inherited suffering and, themselves beset by destruction, cause the destruction of members of the former generation. The upbringing by the parent returns to the parent through the child's later acts and their ramifications. The ἄλγος (733), suffering, or even sickness, for the citizens was caused by the acts of one generation of Atreus' house (both in the case of Atreus himself and in that of Agamemnon). These acts were committed against the next generation. In a reversal of direction, Helen and Paris brought suffering upon both Troy and Argos.

That the ill workings of parents continue the circle of *pathos* for

---

[13] Throughout the *Iliad*, the hostility of the Trojans toward Paris is evident.

their children, that is, that suffering begets only suffering, is aptly stated by the chorus in 757-71:

> But apart from others I am single-minded. For the deed of sacrilege brings forth more after, more which is like its own kind. For the fate of straight and just houses is always to have beautiful children. It is customary for Insolence of old to bring forth among evil men a new Insolence at one time or another; when the appointed time and the light of birth come, it brings forth a kindred spirit, unconquerable, invincible, unholy Boldness, black ruin for a house, taking the appearance of its parents.

It will remain for youth symbolically in the person of Orestes to find that one can, if he will, learn from suffering, that the words of 177 are not an empy platitude. In so doing, he will bring to an end in Atreus' house the curse and evil which brings forth its own kind.

There is bitterness in Clytemnestra's words that Iphigenia will greet her father in the lower world (1551-9). The younger generation will always be present in some form to confront the older with the latter's wrongs. Almost pitifully, Clytemnestra would have *this* point mark the end of the curse (1567-77); but this may not be. Aegisthus expresses the reason for the suffering of his generation (1582-6) and further on, through the story of his father, Thyestes, implies, to an extent, the reason that an escape from it may not come for them. The older generation may have been able to learn something from youth (584), but it is too far astray to attain the necessary, full *mathos* (1621-4).

Clytemnestra closes the play in a passage framed by the verbs παθεῖν and μαθεῖν (1657-61). Again, the maxim of 177 is brought sharply to mind. Some suffering, linear, not cyclical, is necessary for learning. Suffering in the circle of *pathos* in which it just leads to more suffering is useless, futile. Suffering, linear, future-oriented, with *mathos* as the goal, no longer produces more of its own kind as its only result; it, therefore, is useful.

Youth are for their elders a promise of a better world to come, but of a world in which the elders themselves can never take part. Assurance that youth can achieve, at least in part, this better world is given in the *Oresteia*, as Orestes, the representative of the younger generation, is absolved of a crime grounded in past generations and as the formerly Dark Goddesses, representative of suffering for the past, reverse their nature and exit in a procession of light. This way of viewing the relationship between generations is evident elsewhere in the fifth century in the words of Pericles about the importance of children as related by Thucydides and even in the father-son relationship portrayed in Aristophanes' *Clouds*. The feeling seems to have lasted into the fourth century and is contained in Diotima's words about parents and children to Socrates in Plato's *Symposium*. Also, that philosopher's stress on education of children in the *Republic* stems from a similar origin.

To an extent, the older generation has done right by the younger. The former has indeed nourished and reared the latter. On the other hand, the older has failed miserably and has left a legacy of perpetuated suffering for the younger. Orestes has the actions of both his parents to blame, both for his suffering and for what he does.[14]

Orestes' absolution seems to be a particular example of vindication of a universal principle which youth seems to espouse, i.e., that everything must be done for the sake of the future. The past, it is true, holds valuable experience gained from suffering; but, unless this suffering teaches one that he need not fear innovation, the future, but must pursue it, the suffering only breeds more of its own kind and learning is never achieved. The propensity of youth to innovate must be encouraged and guided by elders; otherwise, it is stifled, progress is impossible and a vicious circle results.

Aeschylus is saying that this principle is always there and will always be; it has, in fact, always been there. But, he is also realist enough to perceive that much of the time men do not see it clearly. His warning is that safety lies in continually striving to understand and interpret it, in *keeping it in mind*. This is the meaning of φρονεῖν in *Agamemnon* 176. Because the older generation seem to discourage change, the younger generation must suffer to learn the value of innovation. Even so, retributive justice, wild and savage, is changed in the *Oresteia* by the doings of youth into an ordered system of statutory justice. The validity of the principle of innovation and future-orienta-

---

[14] So, indeed, does Electra, as she intimates in *Choephoroe* 421–2.

tion is eternal, despite the danger of losing sight of it. It is permanent as the now Light Goddesses' place is in Athens. The past, then, is to be used, not worshiped. When parents perpetuate the vicious circle and do not encourage and guide their children in the direction of new thoughts for the future they are failing in their responsibility to and for their children.

Implicit in this future-orientation and attainment of knowledge is a principle of action arising from the maxim expressed in *Agamemnon* 177–8 and 250–1. Fear of acting has no place in true knowledge. *Pathos* is suffering, passion, passivity. The person is acted upon by the world. But, when the vicious circle of suffering is broken and *mathos* is attained, one is not completely under the control of the past. One controls his future and is active, not passive. In the *Oresteia*, youth learn not to fear to act, to innovate. They are no longer helplessly and passively caught up in suffering begetting suffering.

If there is a moral in the parent-child theme of the *Oresteia* for the Athenians at the height of their state's power, indeed for any people at any time, it is that the deeds of a generation should be performed with their effects on the succeeding, not merely with their origins and causes in the preceding, generations in mind.

More particularly, the *Agamemnon* gives a concrete example of the destruction worked for one generation by members of the preceding generation. "As surely as Atreus had failed him as a father, Agamemnon has failed Iphigenia." In addition, the killing of the Greek youth at Troy was no less brutal than that of Iphigenia and Thyestes' children. Both Clytemnestra and Aegisthus are motivated by the same kind of crime, the older generation's killing the younger, a crime which runs its course in the house of Atreus because of a curse. Aeschylus seems to have this in mind at the outset in his ambiguous use of the word οἶκος, house or family, in line 37 of the watchman's speech.

Chapter 3

THE CONFLICT OF CODES IN EURIPIDES' *HIPPOLYTUS*

Fred Mench

Stockton State College

The conflict of two not totally isolated but nevertheless distinguishable codes or cultures is a basic motif of the *Hippolytus*. In his play Euripides continually stresses the antithesis between appearance and reality, between the reputation-based morality of the older generation and the conscience-based morality of the younger generation. It is a distinction reflected in both the actions and words of the characters in the tragedy.

The older generation represents what Dodds[1]) terms a "shame-culture", basically that of the Homeric epics[2]), which judges not by the intent of the doer but by the event itself, especially its success or failure. The emphasis is on reputation (δόξα or εὔκλεια) and appearing (δοκεῖν); its principal term of moral censure is αἰσχρόν, "shameful" or "ugly." To this culture belong the older characters, Aphrodite, Theseus, and Artemis. One could also add the old servant, but the nurse is a special case, pragmatism being her guide. Phaedra is frequently governed by this code even though she is younger than its other adherents and even though she is aware of and tries at times to follow the newer code.

The younger generation represents what Dodds[3]) calls a "guilt-culture" and embodies a newer morality, which rejects appearances and concentrates on being (εἶναι) rather than seeming. Its term of moral censure, not αἰσχρόν "shameful", but κακόν, "bad", reflects an

---

[1]) E. R. Dodds, *The Greeks and the Irrational*, U. of Cal. Press, 1951, p. 17.

[2]) See the analysis of these terms and the cultures to which they belong in A. W. H. Adkins' *Merit and Responsibility*, Oxford, 1960, pp. 154–187. Adkins discusses the moral currents of Euripides' day. Of course, a certain degree of conflict between older and younger generations or different cultural codes is temporally and spatially universal, but Euripides is describing and utilizing the conflict of his own day, fifth-century Athens, not that of the play's mythological setting. Hippolytus is to some degree a counterpart of Socrates or one of the Sophists, but less personable and more immature.

[3]) *Loc. cit.*, n. 1 above.

absolute standard dependent not on the evaluation of others but on the deed's rightness and the individual's conscience. This code manifests itself most clearly in Hippolytus, the youngest of the principals, the representative of a new generation.[4])

In this paper I concentrate on the statements of the two most crucial characters, Phaedra and Hippolytus, as illustrative of their motives and the nature of the cultural conflict, very briefly showing how the other principals belong to the older code.[5])

Phaedra starts by referring to her mad desire as $κακόν$, "bad" not $αἰσχρόν$, "shameful", (248), and considers it a sin that her hands are clean but her heart defiled (317: $χεῖρες μὲν ἁγναί, φρὴν δ'ἔχει μίασμά τι$). These two statements suggest that Phaedra is aware of guilt, not just shame, but her awareness of a different code of conduct and her occasional attempts to conform to it do not suffice to make it the principal determinant of her action. She herself says, "Many know the

---

[4]) It is interesting to note the similarities—and the differences—found in the scheme constructed by David Riesman in *The Lonely Crowd* (Yale Press, 1950). Riesman posits three societies: "tradition-directed", "inner directed", and "other-directed". These are, in Riesman's analysis, three phases through which society passes and are produced by the rise and fall of birth and death rates. Riesman's description of "tradition-directed" culture fits, in many superficial respects, that of the older generation in the *Hippolytus*, but in the source of the motivation to action his "other-directed" society is also remarkably similar to that older generation. At page 22 he says, "What is common to all other-directeds is that their contemporaries are the source of direction for the individual...The goals towards which the other-directed person strives shift with that guidance; it is only the process of striving itself and the process of paying close attention to the signals from others that remains unaltered throughout life." In describing the "inner-directed" society Riesman states that "the source of direction for the individual is 'inner' in the sense that it is implanted early in life by the elders and directed toward generalized but nonetheless inescapable destined goals." This is clearly a society that has a greater rigidity (or capability for implantation) than exists in Hippolytus' case and code, but the source of the motivation is basically the same.

[5]) In this paper I am, of course, concentrating on one individual thread of a complex fabric at the conscious expense of such important themes as the conflict of the rational and irrational, Artemis and Aphrodite as life forces, Hippolytus' basically negative *sophrosyne* which lacks understanding and measure, or the examination of the metaphorical language. Such treatments are crucial to reaching an understanding of the play, but I am aiming simply at one part of Euripides' structure and meaning which has a particular applicability to our own society.

right; we know good but cannot effect it." (379–81).[6]) Just five lines after stating that a defiled heart is a sin, Phaedra betrays her upbringing: "May I not be seen (ὀφθείην) doing evil to Theseus" (321). The choice of verb is significant; her concern is directed not toward avoiding evil but toward escaping its social consequences. Is it basically a concern for reputation, not for absolute right or wrong, that motivates Phaedra? This single instance does not, alone, support such a contention. Does Phaedra, originally ashamed of her guilty passion as well as afraid for her honor, fall prey to the nurse's "too fair-seeming arguments" (433–481)? Phaedra's language before the nurse's arguments suggests not; time and again she talks in terms of "not being seen" or "not being caught" in any wrong action. Phaedra says that if the reason for her noble abstinence were known it would bring her honor (329: τιμή).[7]) When Phaedra, however, says that she is making something fine out of something bad (331) she chooses as her term of censure αἰσχρόν (unpleasant to look at). And immediately after she tells how she tried to stifle her love, she says that she wants her good deeds known but few witnesses to her shameful behavior (430–4). In her resolution to die rather than face public disapproval, Phaedra shows that it is less the deed itself which she abhors (she calls it ill-famed, δυσκλεές, 405) than the possibility of public scandal.[8])

[6]) Cf. Herman Melville's characterization of Claggart in *Billy Budd* as "apprehending the good but powerless to be it."

[7]) If Phaedra had died in silence no one would have known how virtuous she had been. She talks in such a way as to be compelled to surrender her secret and thus gain the praise of the chorus (431–2). As Bernard Knox says ("The *Hippolytus* of Euripides," *YCS* 13, 1952, p. 9), "She can act nobly, die rather than yield to her passion, and yet not pass unnoticed... Phaedra can have her cake and eat it too." Hazel Barnes (*Hippolytus in Drama and Myth*, U. of Nebraska Press, 1960, p. 86) goes one step farther, pointing out that a secret, once told, inevitably spreads, but it is Hippolytus, not Theseus, who will hear it. "Phaedra's rational will is resolved on dying rather than giving in to the passion she condemns. But her emotional nature whispers the hope that perhaps if Hippolytus knew...." If Miss Barnes is right, Phaedra has misjudged, even if sub-consciously, her man and his moral code, attributing to him her own shame-culture code, within which an accomodation might have been possible.

[8]) Like Willie Loman in Arthur Miller's *Death of a Salesman*, Phaedra is so dependent on the opinion people have of her that, once that opinion (in Loman's case reflected in his sales record) is destroyed, she can think of no alternative to suicide.

In lines 413–430 Phaedra begins condemning adultery but soon
wonders why adulterers are not afraid of being caught: "May I never
be caught shaming Theseus" (420: ἁλῶ); "May I never been seen
among the evil" (430: ὀφθείην; cf. 321 cited above). To the nurse's
arguments that the example of the gods justifies adultery Phaedra
replies that she wants not pleasing words (an interesting self-revela-
tion in itself) but something that will lead to good repute (488–9).
Can we suppose that the nurse's specious reasoning could convert a
mind resolutely opposed on principle to adultery? Artemis claims that
Phaedra was trying to overcome her passion by will when she was
destroyed unwillingly by the nurse's revelations to Hippolytus
(1304–6). But Artemis knows only the external events, failing to fathom
the psychology of the mortal characters, especially of Phaedra, who
does not know her own motives. Phaedra rebukes the nurse for her
suggestions but admits that, if the nurse continues to talk prettily
(καλῶς) of shameful things (αἰσχρά), she will succumb. In her three
speeches following the nurse's arguments the lady protests too much.
The exchange sounds like that between Anna and Dido in *Aeneid* 4:
nurse (Anna) says what she knows Phaedra (Dido) wants to hear,
whatever disclaimers the latter may utter. After the nurse's ambiguous
promise of philtres (509) Phaedra simply asks whether the charm will
be a salve or a potion (516), not what it is intended to accomplish.
If Phaedra had not been considering the feasibility of adultery the
nurse would have needed more than the barest minimum of sophistry
about its rightness to cloak her assurances of success in the affair.
Phaedra's language allows us to glimpse her sub-conscious values and
motives.

Crucial to the interpretation of Phaedra's character is what she
thought the nurse meant by a "cure" for Phaedra's love (570ff). Since
Phaedra does not question her closely, she could have thought the
nurse was seeking some antidote for love. Yet, though explicitly fearing the nurse will tell Hippolytus, she makes no effort to stop her.
Phaedra should not have allowed the nurse to leave so easily on so
doubtful an errand. In fact, she probably has deduced[9]) that the nurse
will try to win Hippolytus with a love-philtre or with words. Thus

---

[9]) Cf. Hazel Barnes, *op. cit.*, n. 7 above, p. 88.

Phaedra appears willing to commit adultery provided it can be managed discreetly. Unfortunately, for Phaedra, the attempt fails as she and the nurse could have foreseen if they had really understood Hippolytus. Phaedra tried to resist her love, but the goddess was too strong, her own sense of guilt too weak.

Once the secret is out and her reputation stained, Phaedra says that her only recourse is to die as quickly as possible (599). After Hippolytus' tirade against women, Phaedra reproaches the nurse and complains that she will no longer die well-esteemed (687-8: εὐκλεής) and must think of some way of restoring her reputation. She decides, maliciously, on the tablets. The principal determinant of the action which causes the death of Hippolytus is Phaedra's concern that she leave an uncontaminated name to her children. Something more than mere reputation may, however be at work here; Phaedra fears Hippolytus will denounce her to Theseus, who might then transfer the succession from her children to Hippolytus. Thus to protect her children's position Phaedra must discredit Hippolytus in advance. She can therefore justify to herself the destruction of her enemy as an act of maternal protection, not merely as simple vengeance for a love which has turned to hate. Nevertheless, it is this destruction of Hippolytus, rather than any failure to contain her passion, that causes Phaedra to forfeit our sympathy.

The nature of Hippolytus' code is made clear by Euripides as early as lines 19-96 in the scene between Hippolytus and the old servant. The servant, by Socratic questioning, tries to get Hippolytus to admit that certain actions are pleasing and certain displeasing to other people (which Hippolytus admits), and that some make a man liked by others and some make him hated (which Hippolytus admits), and that some contribute to a good reputation and others to a bad. But the servant never gets far enough to make Hippolytus admit that a man's actions should be determined by consideration for reputation. Hippolytus senses that his servant is trying to lead him to a worship of Aphrodite and refuses, regardless of what people may say. Hippolytus says, "I greet her from afar because I am holy" (102). The episode, however, is not intended by Euripides merely to demonstrate Hippolytus' attitude to Aphrodite but to reveal something more basic about Hippolytus. Hippolytus is an absolutist (some would even say a prig),

his actions uninfluenced by concern for society's approval. Just as
Phaedra is aware of moral values found in the new morality but is not
in the final analysis motivated by them, so Hippolytus is not oblivious
to appearance and its social consequences; he simply does not allow
them to dictate his conduct. He gives Aphrodite the long farewell not
because he wants to be called holy but because he is – or thinks himself
– holy. The same absolutist bent is seen in his diatribe against women
when he displays his concern for the thing *per se* (see esp. lines 630–2),
not its mere appearance.[10]) He needs, he says, to purge himself of even
hearing such a wicked proposition: "How could I be evil ($\varkappa\alpha\varkappa\acute{o}\varsigma$) when
simply hearing the proposition makes me feel unholy?" (653–5).

Hippolytus' statements about reputation are instructive. In his
first long speech of defense before Theseus he points to his spotless
reputation and asserts that he deserves every bit of it. He did not touch
Phaedra – not because he felt he could not succeed but because he did
not want to. "If ever," he says, "I have been wicked ($\varepsilon\dot{i}$ $\varkappa\alpha\varkappa\grave{o}\varsigma$ $\pi\acute{e}\varphi\upsilon\varkappa'$-
$\dot{a}\nu\acute{\eta}\varrho$) may I be destroyed, unreputed, unnamed, uncitied, unhoused,
etc." (1028–9. Contrast this with Phaedra above at line 403–4).
Hippolytus is concerned with truth, not reputation, with being ($\varepsilon\tilde{i}\nu\alpha\iota$)
not seeming ($\delta o\varkappa\varepsilon\tilde{i}\nu$), good. If he is good, he wants people to know it;
if bad, he will not hide it to escape its deserved punishment. Ideally,
the new generation wants reputation to be a true reflection of the
character of its bearer, not a counterfeit ($\varkappa\acute{\iota}\beta\delta\eta\lambda o\nu$) as Hippolytus
asserts is the case with women (616).[11]) The opinion of other people is
to be a *result* of one's actions, not their cause.

A few of Hippolytus' statements seem to run counter to this supposed contempt for reputation. At 1016–7 he declares, "I would be
first in the Hellenic games but second in the state." One could argue
that the games are a means of serving Artemis or that Hippolytus is
simply using a barrister's argument to prove to Theseus that he does
not want to be first in the state, i.e., that he had no political motive
for his supposed action. But the answer is simpler: Hippolytus is a

---

[10]) The wickedness of women that Hippolytus sees may be largely in his own
mind, just like the phoniness that J. D. Salinger's Holden Caulfield *(Catcher in
the Rye)* is constantly seeing. Remember that Holden is mentally unbalanced.

[11]) Cf. Harry C. Avery, "My Tongue Swore, But My Mind is Unsworn," *TAPA*
99 (1968), p. 26.

young athlete who wants to compete in the games – and, of course, to win; he is perfectly willing to accept valid acclaim and feels no compulsion to hide his excellence, physical or moral. In fact, he *is* excellent, and that is why many readers dislike him as smug and complacent.[12]) Secure in his own goodness (cf. 1100–1), he does not care what society thinks.[13]) Not only do others call him noble (ἐσθλός, 1254, spoken by the messenger) and just (δίκαιος, 1298 and 1308, spoken by Artemis)[14]), but he himself reiterates (three times in exactly the same words, 1301, 1075, and 1191) "If I have been a bad man" (εἰ κακὸς πέφυκ' ἀνήρ) may some disaster strike. Hippolytus, heedless of reputation, allows himself to be wrongly abused without taking the one chance left that might save his name, i. e., breaking his oath (1060–63). True, Hippolytus says he will not speak because he will not convince Theseus anyhow and would then have broken his oath in vain. But would he have spoken even if he could thereby have saved himself? Doubtless he had ratified his oath by swearing to the gods (perhaps to Artemis, as in 1451?) and might fear divine wrath if he broke it. More convincing, however, is the fact that he had given his

[12]) Theseus claims that Hippolytus has had plenty of practice in self-worship (1080).

[13]) Why do we dislike Hippolytus? He is, after all, correct when he speaks of his maiden soul (993–1006) or of affliction coming upon one who was responsible for no wickedness (1364–5). True, he is rather insistent about it. Even taking into account that Theseus is enraged at the time, lines 948–57 ("You are the one who was supposed to be so holy?") suggest that Hippolytus made no secret of his purity and his companionship with Artemis. Perhaps we dislike him because he rejects so ostentatiously what apparently does not tempt him at all. Lytton Strachey's biography, *Queen Victoria* (pp. 316–7), tells of the biographies Victoria commissioned of her late dear Albert. She wanted her subjects to see him as she had, flawless in every way, but failed to "understand that the picture of an embodied perfection is distasteful to the majority of mankind. The cause of this is not so much envy of the perfect being as a suspicion that he must be inhuman." Euripides, of course, does not present Hippolytus as unflawed; the great absolutist, like so many idealists, lacks moderation, despite Hippolytus' own statement that he was not only reverent and devout but also excelled all in temperance (σωφροσύνη 1364–6). And Charles Segal's recent "Euripides, *Hippolytus*, Tragic Irony and Tragic Justice" (*Hermes* 97, 1969, pp. 297–305) suggests that Euripides wanted us to see other flaws of some consequence in Hippolytus.

[14]) Cf. also lines 1390, 1402, 1419, and 1454.

word, even though tricked into doing it, and would stick by it. He
allows himself to be judged by appearances, since the only way he can
explain his actual purity is by breaking the oath and speaking.[15])

According to the messenger (1192–3) Hippolytus prayed, as he was
about to leave the country as Theseus had ordered: "May my father
know how he has dishonored me either while I am still alive or after
I am dead." Is this inconsistent with his supposed unconcern for
repute? The prayer seems to turn on the word "father" ($\pi\alpha\tau\acute{\eta}\varrho$).
Hippolytus had said (1071) that what brought him to tears was that he
should appear so evil and that Theseus should think him so, that his
father should think him capable of such wickedness. In 1084–90
Hippolytus warned Theseus' servants that they would touch him at
their peril. But when Theseus said that he would drag him away
himself if Hippolytus did not leave, the son meekly bowed his head
and walked off, unwilling to raise his hand against his father. The
messenger reports that subsequently Hippolytus, after delaying to leave
the country awhile, finally acquiesced with, "a *father's* words must be
obeyed" (1182). Hippolytus wanted his father, someone he loved, to
know how he had misjudged him. Hippolytus was somewhat hyper-
sensitive about his father's feelings toward him because of the contin-
ual consciousness of his bastardy and the apparent estrangement
that had developed between Theseus and the son he could not
understand. But the desire on Hippolytus' part for his father's love
and respect bears little resemblance to a general desire for society's
approval.

Hippolytus' lonely adherence to this inner-directed code can be seen
in the actions and the words of the other characters. Aphrodite's first
words (1–2) set the tone of the play: she is great among men and not
without name. Even the gods, she says, delight in being honored by
men (7–8). Aphrodite makes it clear that it is not because she is a deity
in whom there rests some part of an ineffable and beneficent godhead
that she should be so honored but because she is a powerful person;
anyone who crosses her she will strike down. Aphrodite does not object
to Hippolytus' consorting with Artemis but to his calling her the vilest
($\varkappa\alpha\varkappa\acute{\iota}\sigma\tau\eta\nu$) of goddesses (13). For this affront to her reputation (and

---

[15]) Cf. Avery, *op. cit.*, n. 11 above, p. 25.

doubt of her power) she will destroy him; that Phaedra and Theseus will be destroyed in the process is of no concern to her.

Aphrodite's opening speech resembles that of Dionysos in the *Bacchae* (1–63): Dionysos states there that the play will spring from his desire to prove himself a god and Semele the mother of a god against the slanders of her sisters and the studied neglect of Pentheus, who omits Bacchus' name from sacrifices (46). Bacchus represents the same type of force as Aphrodite – passion and abandon. Compare the remark of Cadmus (*Bacchae* 1348) to Bacchus, that gods should not be moved by mortal passions, with that to Aphrodite by the old servant (*Hippolytus* 120), that gods should be wiser than mortals.[16])

Aphrodite's insistence on honor is balanced by Hippolytus' own failure to see the importance of at least simulating respect for the goddess. Hippolytus refuses to act hypocritically; he does not know how to temporize.

Artemis, when she exclaims, "Had I not been afraid of Zeus, I would never have fallen into such shame (ἐς τόδ' αἰσχύνης) as to let Hippolytus be destroyed by Aphrodite" (1331–34), reveals that the blow to her reputation grieves her at least as much as Hippolytus' undeserved death. She announces she will destroy one of Aphrodite's favorites and compensate Hippolytus for his suffering with honors (1416–30). The death of Aphrodite's favorite will not, however, add any honor to Hippolytus but simply prove that Artemis is no less powerful than Aphrodite, thus restoring the luster to Artemis' reputation. Artemis is more concerned throughout her speech with Hippolytus' reputation (partially as a reflection of her own) than is he. In her first speech to Theseus she says, "I've come to show the just heart of your son, so he can die with good repute" (1298–9). She correctly states (1402) that Aphrodite acted out of slighted honor, but fails to understand Hippolytus' psychology in thinking the honors she prophecies for him (1423–30) will comfort or even concern him. She correctly interprets Phaedra's writing of the letter as basically an attempt to prevent falling into disgrace (1310: εἰς ἔλεγχον μὴ πέσῃ

---

[16]) See A. R. Bellinger's "The *Bacchae* and *Hippolytus*", *Yale Classical Studies* 6 (1939), p. 26, for the comparisons Dionysus/Aphrodite, Pentheus/Hippolytus, Agave/Theseus, and Teiresias/old servant.

φοβουμένη) but does not see that Phaedra might act out of vengeance or for the protection of her children. That Euripides meant his audience to question somewhat the validity of what Artemis says is suggested by the juxtaposition of her fine-sounding statement that the gods destroy the wicked (1340-1) and the entrance of the mangled Hippolytus in the very next line as the example of the absurdity of the statement. Artemis' one action suggestive of a higher motive is her reconciling Theseus to Hippolytus; here she seems moved by pity and rightly understands that the restoration of Hippolytus to his father's love was a concern of his. Pity also seems to motivate her injunction to Hippolytus to forgive his father[17]) (1435). Yet, when Hippolytus had lamented his father's misfortunes as well as his own (1405), he seemed moving of his own accord toward forgiveness.

No reference to reputation need explain Theseus' punishment of the supposed rapist responsible for his wife's death. Yet Theseus says, "Isthmian Sinis will never witness that I killed him if I let you get away, but will say that I boast in vain; the Scironian rocks will say that I am soft on the wicked" (976-80). The phrasing is significant; Theseus cannot let Hippolytus off because people might think he had acted out of fear and that his reputation as a hero was thus a fake. To protect this reputation, Theseus precipitously curses Hippolytus and decrees his banishment, thus, as Artemis points out (1290-95), inadvertently destroying his reputation.[18])

Ironically, in so doing Theseus expresses the wish that men had two voices so that false and true could be distinguished – essentially what Hippolytus sought in his tirade against the false appearance of women (616ff). Unfortunately, Theseus fails to recognize that the voice he is hearing from his son is true, as it has been all along. He concludes that

---

[17]) Bernard Knox, *op. cit.*, n. 7 above, remarks: "Artemis does indeed tell Hippolytus not to hate his father (1435). But... she does not , on her own plane, forgive Aphrodite, rather she announces a repetition of the terrible events we have just witnessed" (p. 29). "To err is human, as Artemis says to Theseus, but to forgive is not divine." Only man can do this; Hippolytus does and calls to witness "Artemis of the conquering arrow" (1451), an unconscious reminder of Artemis' vow of vengeance (p. 30). "Hippolytus' forgiveness of his father is an affirmation of purely human values in an inhuman universe" (p. 31).

[18]) Similarly Phaedra had lost her reputation because of the lying letter she left, the letter that she had hoped would be the means of preserving her reputation.

Hippolytus' piety has been a sham, a reaction suggesting that Theseus had never been particularly sympathetic to Hippolytus' often-trumpeted purity. In judging Hippolytus a hypocrite, Theseus judges by his own moral code – that someone base within would carefully cultivate a false appearance for the sake of reputation.

One other exchange between Hippolytus and Theseus may be indicative of Theseus' code. As Hippolytus is dying Theseus says, "Are you leaving me with my hand still unholy?" (1448). Hippolytus replies, "No; I free you from murder." Theseus, scarcely believing this, asks (1450), "What? You mean you are freeing me from blood-guilt?" Hippolytus swears, with unconscious irony, by Artemis (1451) and Theseus exclaims (1453), "My dearest son, how noble you have proved to your father." The point is that Theseus can talk about his *hand*[19]) being unholy and about a blood-guilt that can be expiated, in this case by the forgiveness of the victim. Even in the midst of his grief, Theseus thinks in terms of some external stain that must, and more importantly can, be washed off.[20])

By age and temperament the nurse belongs to the older generation. However, she differs from them in that she is not acting in her own interest. The nurse, more pragmatist than moralist, adapts her attitudes, or at least her words, to Phaedra's needs. Nevertheless, she is well aware of the importance of reputation in the mind of Phaedra and argues accordingly. The nurse urges Phaedra to go on with her love, pointing out that Aphrodite is a powerful god (439–50) and that Zeus and Eos had affairs and did not on that account lose any reputation in heaven (451–8) – both arguments for the fact that it must not be wrong to yield to love. Then, tipping her hand, she clinches the argument with "besides, you can get away with it" (462–6). People won't talk, she insists, because the whole thing will be hushed up, for wise men overlook things that are not nice ($\mu\grave{\eta}$ $\varkappa\alpha\lambda\acute{\alpha}$) – 465–6. But the nurse puts aside questions of morality and reputation as she loses patience and tells Phaedra that it is better to have Hippolytus if it will save her life than to maintain a mere reputation ($\tau\grave{o}$ $\check{o}\nu o\mu a$) – 501–2. In the final

---

[19]) Reading $\chi\acute{e}\varrho a$, "hand" and not the less suitable $\varphi\varrho\acute{e}\nu a$, "heart."

[20]) Cf. Apollonius, *Argonautica* 4, 698–717, where Circe washes off the blood-guilt of Jason and Medea.

analysis, the nurse denies the right to consider reputation as the determining guide for action. In this she agrees with Hippolytus, but her reason is different: she argues that anything is right if expedient while
Hippolytus maintains that nothing is right unless holy.

The values of the two cultures are basically incompatible; reputation
dominates the older culture, conscience the newer. Unluckily for
Hippolytus, the principal actions of the play spring largely from reputation: Aphrodite's machinations start because she feels slighted;
Phaedra leaves the letter to discredit anything that Hippolytus might
say against her;[21]) Theseus rushes into his curse because he does not
want to seem weak or hesitant. Because Phaedra and Theseus are what
they are (and Hippolytus what he is) the tragedy set in motion by
Aphrodite takes its inevitable course.

Euripides realized that not all cultural conflict is a simple function
of age. Phaedra and Hippolytus are separated by a gulf created in part
by difference of social position[22]) (Phaedra, the palace; Hippolytus,
the hunt) and ancestry (Pasiphae, the sex-crazed taurophile; Hippolyta,
the chaste Amazon).[23]) Phaedra's stress on repute follows logically
enough from her mother's bad name while Hippolytus' bastardy drives
him to stress purity.[24]) Phaedra is caught to some degree between two
generations, between two cultures. This internal conflict is a principal
element in the pathos of her plight. She feels the pull of the morality
that Hippolytus embraces; when she speaks of doing ill (380) she
speaks of doing it unwillingly. Phaedra is not the shameless slut that
Euripides probably portrayed in his earlier *Hippolytus*[25]), rather a

[21]) If Knox is correct in footnote 7 above, reputation, the need for her nobility
to be known, was also the reason for Phaedra's not going off quietly to a swift
suicide right at the start.

[22]) Cf. R. P. Winnington-Ingram's "Hippolytus: A Study in Causation,"
Fondation Hardt pour l'Étude de l'Antiquité, 6, (1958), pp. 169–198.

[23]) Cf. *ibid.* and Hazel Barnes, *op. cit.*, n. 7 above, p. 93. Note Phaedra's evoca-
tion of her mother and sister at 337–41.

[24]) Is Hippolytus' consciousness of his bastardy (an important motif) partly
responsible for the vehemence of his diatribe against Phaedra (note the ambiguous
κιβδήλον "counterfeit/illegitimate," 616) because of the specific nature of the
proposal? Or is its violence due to a more general fear of women on the part of
Hippolytus?

[25]) See W. S. Barrett's *Euripides: Hippolytus*, Oxford, 1964, pp. 10–15.

woman trying to be virtuous but failing. But her words show her innermost feelings, ones that she may not be entirely aware of herself. She is influenced by the new morality, but it is not sufficiently in her fiber to keep her from defecting to the code in which she had been raised.

But for the conflict of the codes Phaedra and Hippolytus might have worked out Phaedra's problem.[26]) If Hippolytus had been content with merely seeming good, he could, if he had chosen, have satisfied Phaedra with no one the wiser. If, on the other hand, Phaedra had really been good, she might have succeeded in fighting her passion or, failing that, at least have left no incriminating letter when she committed suicide.

Whereas Phaedra is to a degree the example of a person caught between two moralities, Hippolytus is the example *par excellence* of the new generation breaking sharply with the old. He refuses Phaedra because his deterrent is not fear of discovery and consequent scandal but moral abhorrence of the deed itself. It is ironic that Hippolytus patterns his life on what he imagines Artemis to be while in fact the peevish goddess is no better than anyone else in the older generation. Hippolytus, however, manages in one sense to transcend his model because he himself is noble and capable of imagining a deity holier than exists. He creates god in his own image, imputing to that god his own purity.

Part of the trouble that Hippolytus encounters, however, is not simply that he is pure but that he makes such a loud noise about it. This is what convinces Phaedra that he will tell Theseus anyhow and may also be partly responsible for his lack of closeness with his father. It is certainly what got him into trouble with Aphrodite in the first place; had he stayed quietly celibate, she probably would not have cared, even if he had quietly ignored her altars. Those imbued with moral certitude (especially, though not exclusively, the young) tend to adopt a tone of brusque self-righteousness. Since they believe what they are saying is true, they feel no need to couch it in terms of politeness.

---

[26]) In fact, had Hippolytus belonged to the older code, the tragedy would never have arisen because he would have sacrificed *pro forma* to Aphrodite, either recognizing her real power—even though disliking her—or being forced by social pressure (as the old servant urges). Thus Aphrodite would have had no reason for revenge.

Hippolytus irritates by his polemical manner as much as by what he says, just like the notable Saint Peter Mavimenus who, when certain Arabs came to see him at Damascus when he was sick, said, "Every man who does not embrace the Catholic Christian faith is damned as Mohammed, your false prophet, was."[27] Mavimenus was forthwith slain by the Arabs, quite possibly less for his faith than for his bad manners. Youth traditionally tends to arrogate to itself the morality of substance, insisting, rightly or wrongly, that the older generation hypocritically concerns itself only with form and appearance. Such a dichotomy creates a destructive communication gap.

The gap between Phaedra and Hippolytus, in this case more cultural than generational, is neither bridgeable nor discussable; it crushes the two of them.[28] The most Artemis can do to set things right at the end of the play is to restore Hippolytus' reputation, something that he considered of negligible importance – itself a fact illustrating the gulf between Hippolytus and his patron goddess. The break between Theseus and Hippolytus is a generation gap in its most classic form, causing a fatal interruption of understanding and communication between father and son. This gap, nevertheless, turns out to be the only one that is bridged in the play. Theseus and Hippolytus are reconciled, but to effect it there is needed a divine revelation of the true state of affairs; and the price is the death of Hippolytus. In these final moments of the play Hippolytus and Theseus become simply two mortals alone in a world governed by capricious forces over which they have only the most limited control; this realization and their shared grief (Hippolytus for his father; Theseus for his son) suffice to span the chasm – though this is a high price for a momentary rapport.

---

[27] See *The Roman Martyrology*, edited by Canon J. B. O'Connell, Newman Press, Westminster, Md., 1962, p. 37 (February 21).

[28] One tends to sympathize somewhat with the exclamation of the chorus (114–119) that they would prefer to have a character neither too unbending (= Hippolytus) nor counterfeit (= Phaedra?)—δόξα δὲ μήτ' ἀτρεκὴς μήτ' αὖ παράσημος This is the voice of common sense speaking; the chorus, like the Vicar of Bray, wants to veer with the wind.

Chapter 4

FATHER-BEATING IN ARISTOPHANES' *CLOUDS*

Kenneth J. Reckford

University of North Carolina — Chapel Hill

Were today not my birthday, I might have begun with the problem. Say that late fifth-century Athenians suffered like us from generational conflict, and from related anxieties about the alienation of youth from its traditional ties to family and society, the polis and its gods: I might have discussed the focusing of these anxieties in the charge against Socrates, of 'corrupting the youth',[1]) or asked how far the waning of traditional loyalties was caused by political, social, and economic factors (notably, the special democratic experiment of Athens, emphasizing individual freedom and responsibility at the expense of family solidarity), and how far by the educational revolution itself, the acquisition of intellectual techniques for analyzing, and arguing for or against, all accepted customs, ideas and institutions. Evidently problems of family, including generational conflict, reflected, even as they intensified, all the rest, from the strains of democracy in the war-torn polis to doubts about the gods themselves and the validity of traditional norms of conduct. But evidently too, the Athenians themselves could scarcely grasp what was going on. They were not scholars. Their anxiety, like ours, took many irrational forms, of which hostility to Socrates and Euripides – university and theatre – were, though striking, yet fairly typical.

And yet, despite its intrinsic fascination and enormous relevance today, the intellectual history of the late fifth century not only fails to 'give relief' (as *relevance* should): it is quite the wrong starting-place

---

[1]) There were two charges against Socrates, *asebeia* (impiety) and *diaphtherein tous neous*. The latter is usually translated "corrupting the youth"; our word, 'alienating', better conveys the verb's emotional connotations as well as its manifold applications to family, society, the gods, and the older education and way of thinking. On the fifth-century ferment generally and the generation gap, see Meyer Reinhold's excellent remarks in this volume.

if we want to enjoy and understand Aristophanes. Thoughts of my birthday give the required pitch, diverting us from scholarship's "concentration camp". It is a red-letter day for us, Saint Philip Neri's feast and mine. In the morning I open presents and my children spank me with saturnalian decorum. In the late afternoon we shall attend Mass. In the evening there will be roast beef, good red wine, and laughter with friends, strawberry short cake and champagne, crystal and candle-light, coffee, chocolates and liqueurs. The world is transformed momentarily. To-morrow will be a time to pay bills, save on groceries, discipline children, see about new valve cover gaskets, read a doctoral dissertation, write my Congressman about the war, and struggle on with an overdue essay for a book on Conflict of Generations ... but *today* I celebrate. Which is precisely what Aristophanes was anticipating when he wrote, and his audience doing when they watched, the *Clouds* of 423 B.C.[2])

The returning holiday of the Greater Dionysia brings renewal. It releases us, not only from ordinary work-habits, but from anxiety, "problems", toil of mind and spirit. Its patron is Dionysus, the violent one, "looser" of bonds. Consider the Exekias cup: the prisoner suddenly freed, the ship over-run with ivy, the mast spouting grape-clusters, the pirates transformed into dolphins, to sport gaily in the wine-red sea. And comedy – Aristophanic comedy, the comedy we are now watching – is one of Dionysus' best gifts. It requires us to leave problems and anxieties at the door. It conducts us into a world different from the ordinary, a world of transforming fantasy, where anything is possible and the Iron Laws of 'realife'[3]) are waived for once; and if, in

---

[2]) That play won third prize; Aristophanes apparently revised it in some measure, and we have the revision. The much-debated question of how much was changed scarcely affects the father-beating scene or its interpretation; but I shall assume (and hope to justify the assumption elsewhere) that neither the First Agon, between the Just and Unjust Argument, nor the play's last scene were as drastically changed as many critics believe.

[3]) 'Realife' is used as opposed to play or fantasy, not as co-extensive with reality. It denotes a serious, everyday world, in which we work, struggle, and obey the laws of gravity: what my wife refers to when things go badly and she says, "Life is like that." For the term, and for the concept of game used later in this essay, I am much indebted to my friend and student, Fontaine Belford, and her emerging dissertation on theory of comedy.

this magical green world, our problems and anxieties once more turn up, they do so like the familiar old intruders at the feast, to be dealt with, played out, expelled. This applies to conflict of generations as to everything else – politics, inflation, degeneration of the theatre, the never-ending war. Aristophanes does indeed provide escape. He is, like Dionysus, one of the great escape artists of all time. Yet the escape he offers is not just negative, just *from* problems, but *into* a celebratory perspective of body, mind, and spirit, which at once transforms the old familiar problems and provides a new and joyful perspective in which they may be seen.

No one, not even Euripides or Thucydides or Socrates, saw more deeply into issues of the 420's than did Aristophanes. In the *Clouds* he turns significantly from more obvious spheres of anxiety (politics, inflation, degenerate theatre, the never-ending war) to more fundamental changes in culture and education. No one, too, was more sensitive to the anxieties of ordinary people, their short-sighted reactions to what *they* perceived as the problems of the day, their hopes, fears, stupidities – and often real good sense. Yet if one side of Aristophanes' genius is his inclusive casting of the comic net, to catch such deep-set and extensive ideas and problems, the other matters still more: the comic power that consistently subjects "real" problems and anxieties to the transforming alchemy of comic feeling and comic fantasy, much as those wicked pirates were changed into carefree plunging dolphins.

I shall therefore presuppose three contexts of thought and feeling when I discuss the father-beating scene in Aristophanes' *Clouds*. The first and main one, as said, is festive. Like Aristophanes' other comedies, the *Clouds* reflects back the meanings of religious celebration, holiday leisure, communal solidarity of rite and play, saturnalian gaity in an ordered setting, honoring Dionysus, guaranteed by a still great, still bountiful polis. The second context is historic, Athenian, problematic. Throughout the scene, Aristophanes alludes to a bewildering number of contemporary problems. I shall dwell on these various and significant allusions at more than comic length, as though replaying scenes of comic wit and action in slow motion; but I shall try also to indicate the comic control with which they are constantly handled, so that clarification, in Barber's formula, comes through release. The third context is literary and theatrical: of the play itself, its plot, characters, ideas. These I shall indicate, as briefly as possible, in connection with the immediate scene, from the moment Strepsiades rushes onstage with a bloody coxcomb, shrieking out, "Iou, Iou!"

The Proagon

The exclamation rings a bell. When we first met Strepsiades, he was complaining ("Iou, Iou!") about painful money worries, how to pay the horse- and chariot-bills his son's "galloping consumption"[4]) had incurred. And now, after conceiving the Brilliant Idea of sending Pheidippides to Socrates' Phrontisterion, or "concentration camp", to learn the Unjust Argument that pays no debts; after bravely going himself, when Pheidippides refuses; after being flunked out ignominiously by Socrates, yet recovering himself, and sending Pheidippides after all; and after Pheidippides re-emerges, a pale but all-competent Master of Sophistry, to Strepsiades' enormous exultation – "Bow, bow, ye tradesmen and ye masses!" – and, victory in his hands, he leads his son indoors for a triumphal feast: after all this, what happens? Pheidippides beats his father; we are back ("Iou, Iou!") where we started. Or rather, things are worse than ever.

The *Clouds* is, in fact, a play of reversals. In accordance with Strepsiades' name, Mr. Twister, and with the replacement of Olympian Zeus by Dinos, "Revolution", as king of the universe, the would-be successful wrestler, who would 'twist' out of debts like a comic Odysseus, becomes rather fate's victim, a bouncing ball or spinning top impelled by the lash of "revolution". No wonder his fortunes come full circle. It is the old story, familiar in proverb and fable, of the person who goes from the frying pan into the fire; in addition it exhibits the comic, or poetic, or rough justice of the scoundrel hoist with his own petard. Earlier, when he drags Pheidippides off to the

---

[4]) I owe this pun to a former student, Ward Briggs, who also suggested "bronchopneumonia" for the disease. Unless otherwise noted, translations in this essay are mine; but I strongly recommend to the non-specialist William Arrowsmith's fine translation in the University of Michigan series (Ann Arbor, 1962).

Phrontisterion ("Just do a bit of wrong, now, listen to Papa,") he is warned: "You'll be sorry for all this later!" So too, the teasing Clouds[5]) tell us just before the catastrophe that Strepsiades will pay for his misdeeds; and afterwards, both Pheidippides and the Clouds rub it in. It's his own silly fault, he shouldn't have taken the boy away from his horses, shouldn't have tried to cheat everybody! Reversal and Recognition come close to tragedy; more specifically, to the contemporary Euripidean model. Why then are we laughing so very hard?

Turning to the immediate words and actions of the Proagon (I would give the full Arrowsmith translation here, only it costs too much), we are struck away by the cheerful shamelessness of Pheidippides. This leit-motif is thematic: it recalls the attitude of "Anything Goes!" which the Unjust Argument demonstrated victoriously in the First Agon, and it suggests simultaneously how well Pheidippides has learned his lesson – just as Strepsiades intended! Freed from every normal restraint and inhibition, his shamelessness unfolds with splendid comic timing and escalation. To paraphrase:

    (a) Strepsiades rushes in, screams to the neighborhood for help, and accuses Pheidippides (the audience will bear witness) of Assault and Battery on his Own Father;

    (b) which Pheidippides calmly admits; and

    (c) cheerfully accepts all insults offered, like Villain, Parricide, Burglar, and Gaping Asshole; and

    (d) offers moreover to demonstrate the justice of father-beating by

    (e) beating Strepsiades in argument, even

[5]) Nobody agrees about the clouds' essence or what they are doing; perhaps that is part of their charm. For some recent discussions of this question, and criticism of the play generally, see C. H. Whitman, *Aristophanes and the Comic Hero* (Cambridge, Mass., 1964; Chapter IV, on *Clouds* and *Wasps*, is entitled "The War Between the Generations"); K. J. Reckford, "Aristophanes' Ever-Flowing Clouds," *Emory University Quarterly* 22 (1967) 222–35; C. P. Segal, "Aristophanes' Cloud-Chorus," *Arethusa* 2 (1969), 143–61; and now K. J. Dover, *Aristophanic Comedy* (Berkeley and Los Angeles, 1972) 101–20. For closer study of problems in *Clouds*, Dover's excellent commentary on that play (Oxford, 1968), with lengthy introduction is indispensable; the older commentary by W. J. M. Starkie (London, 1911) still remains very useful.

> (f) to the point that Strepsiades himself will admit that the
> action was right and fitting!

The exchange indicates clearly enough how Pheidippides has been transformed (or corrupted); it also, through various playful echoes, shows the logical escalation of events, the comic justice rebounding on Strepsiades' head. More immediately, though, we participate vicariously in a marvellous removal of inhibitions. In Freudian terms, a long, civilizing process has taught us to restrain ourselves in word and action, to repress our normal instincts, inhibit our feelings, and even censor the thought and language that might give them away: and suddenly, all that huge inhibitive effort is not needed, all that psychic energy is free, to be discharged in laughter. Or in mythic terms, quite appropriate to Aristophanic comedy generally and the *Clouds* in particular: the stern rule of father Zeus is suspended. We may thus re-enter the world of Golden Age innocence, governed by a beneficent Kronos (or Dinos). What is paradoxical is that the apple of knowledge – of sophistic instruction and analysis – has this time *sent us back* to an older, more innocent and liberated world, where shame and fig-leaves are no longer obligatory.

Yet humanity requires order together with liberty, and we must be reassured, while eluding inhibitions, that we are not falling into utter chaos. In this respect we resemble the child whose father pretends to be a bear, hiding under a rug, crawling on four feet, and growling: to a point, she is delighted; but then, if he pretends too far – if he does not show his face now and then, and smile – the game becomes reality, she is terrified and bursts into tears. Daddy must reassure her that he is not really a bear, he is just pretending. Similarly, I think, Aristophanes safeguards our enjoyment of his anarchic game by reminding us constantly, by structure and language, that it is just that, only a game. Superimposed on the Dionysian experience was, first, the ordered ceremonial of ritual worship, to which tragedy and comedy belong; second, the civic ordering of festival, in which laws, magistrates, policemen, and judicial punishment, all ensure a necessary constraint; and third, the shaping artistic order of the theatre and of comedy, where Apollo and the Muses are joined harmoniously, as so often, with Dionysus for his benefit, theirs, and ours. Comedy is not, therefore, just an excuse for free self-expression. Its multiple contexts shape liberated energy, make laughter meaningful. I have stressed this point because Aristophanes' father-beating scene skates over dangerous waters, deep human anxieties about sex, family, and life; and if (to pursue my metaphor) we may skate joyfully, confident that the ice will hold, it is because of the comic machinery itself which Aristophanes inherited and takes pains, as usual, to make visible to us. We are in the theatre, watching a comic fiction. The wild meanings of the Second Agon, as of the First, are controlled by the elaborate and special structure of this form of play; to wit:

A the Proagon, or Pre-contest;

B_1 the ode: a little playful song, egging on the first contestant;

C_1 the epirrheme: first side up; here, Strepsiades' account of how and why he was beaten;

B_2 the antode: egging the second contestant on;

C_2 the antepirrheme: second side up; here, Pheidippides' defense; which is closed by

D a rapid comic finale.

This very formal structure, of the 'epirrhematic syzygy',[6] licenses Aristophanes' comic flirtation with dangerous feelings and ideas. The balanced arrangement of the Contest, the choice of weapons ("Take an Argument, either Argument," says Pheidippides), the egging-on by the mischievous Chorus, the singing, dancing, flute-playing, and dramatic positioning, all make the Contest into a sport, like a duel or tennis-game, which we would expect to watch with a certain detachment. The comparison is thematically apt because (as Strepsiades himself is finally realizing) Pheidippides was torn away from his expensive chariot-racing only to master the far more ruinous sport, sophistic argumentation. One thing we learn from Aristophanic comedy is that human nature abhors a vacuum. Another is that the mind is a good playground, that the play of ideas, intellectual slapstick, can find as

[6] Thomas Gelzer, *Der Epirrhematische Agon bei Aristophanes* (Munich, 1960) 17–19, limits the "epirrhematic agon" proper to lines 1345–1451. I have extended it impressionistically. Also, to be accurate, the little *ode* and *antode* (B_1 and B_2) should be designated *katakeleusmos* and *antikatakeleusmos*, and each of the two epirrhemes ends with a *pnigos* or "choker" (D_1 and D_2).

good a place in the comic repertoire as the old knockabout farce – indeed, that the two make a magnificent combination.

The third reason why we laugh, not cry, at the father-beating scene is most important of all. Strepsiades is a clown, in failure as in success. (Comedy of frustration is as common in Aristophanes and, I would argue, as significant as comedy of vicarious wish-fulfillment.) Earlier, we saw Strepsiades rejected by Pheidippides, peppered with initiatory flour by Socrates, stripped of coat, trousers, and shoes, swaddled in dirty blankets (the better to "cogitate") on a bedbug-infested old cot, and ignominiously kicked out of school as a "terribly stupid, forgetful – most old man"; just as we *also* saw him maniacally displaying his New Learning to Pheidippides, shoving him off to school, shouting a triumph-song at his graduation, abusing creditors, and adding injury to insult – the last one he just now chased offstage with a pointed horse-goad (or erect phallus) to the rear! And now, amid slapstick beating and screaming, we know perfectly well that a good clown (think of Laurel and Hardy) is never really hurt. More important, he can't be kept down for very long. Strepsiades' theme-note emerged in the first scene: "I may have fallen, but I won't just lie here." He always bounces back, like a large rubber ball or Bobo. Knock him down, and he will rise again; murder him, and his death, like Falstaff's, will prove only another "counterfeit". The point is that finally, like the epic wrestler Odysseus, he does manage to survive; and that in itself is a considerable triumph. We may enjoy the victory of Pheidippides, the uninhibited playboy, in the wonderful new game Aristophanes has procured for us; but still more, I think, we enjoy (and are reassured by) the clowning of Strepsiades, the comic hero, who cannot declaim in tragic fashion,

> "In the fell clutch of circumstance
> I have not winced nor cried aloud.
> Under the bludgeonings of chance
> My head is bloody but unbowed."

yet whose power to survive – bloody and bowed, nonetheless survive – merits celebration.

The outward and visible sign of Strepsiades' triumph will be the "last twist", the burning down of Socrates' Phrontisterion. But that comes later. Let us return to the scene of utter (but of course, not final) disaster.

Strepsiades' Story

It happens all the time.[7]) The son comes home from college; the proud father kills a fatted calf, all is good cheer; but eventually, from some trivial point, a heated discussion arises, tempers flare, a frightful hostility is bared.

Recognition of such happenings, what we might call the ordinary disasters of life, represented and magnified on stage has always brought laughter: partly because we enjoy contemplating frustrations, our own or others', at a certain protective distance; partly because they can be shared in the theatre: there is strength in numbers. Add to this the way Strepsiades tells the story on himself, with comic pathos and exaggeration, and also with a certain shamelessness, which doubles the laughter; and notice also the spring mechanism employed by Aristophanes in building up the story to its conclusion. This comic device, based on constraint and sudden release or explosion, may be illustrated by the famous and very funny story of Hippocleides in Herodotus vi, 126-31. To paraphrase:

> Cleisthenes, tyrant of Sicyon, tested suitors for his daughter Agariste's hand by inviting them to his court for a year and observing their behavior. Finally he chose the Athenian, Hippocleides, for his good character and family connections. A day was set for their betrothal, a feast given. Hippocleides drank generously, called for a piper, and began to dance: Cleisthenes disapproved but said nothing. Next Hippocleides leapt upon a table, danced Laconian, then Attic dances, and then, bracing his head on the table, gestured with his feet. Now Cleisthenes had

---

[7]) The reported scene of Pheidippides' intransigence at dinner probably recycles a number of comic motifs earlier worked out on stage in Aristophanes' *Banqueters* of 427; in that play, a prodigal son apparently ridiculed the traditional culture to which his goody-goody brother adhered. Aristophanes says in the parabasis of *Clouds* that the earlier play's success encouraged him to take up the general topic (of education) again.

been angered earlier, but he held back, not wishing to grieve a
family connection; but at last, seeing the upside-down gesticu-
lation, he burst out, "Son of Tisander, you've danced away
your wedding!" And Hippocleides answered (hence the familiar
proverb): "Hippocleides doesn't care!"

Ou phrontis Hippocleidei. It may be, Aristophanes had this story in
mind when he portrayed Pheidippides, another careless playboy with
'horse' prominent in his aristocratic name, who is, curiously, sent to
the *Phrontisterion*, a place of thought and care, yet emerges more carefree and uninhibited than ever.[8]) (Earlier, he at least showed a sense
of shame, asking what the Knights would say if he lost his color in
Socrates' school.) In any event, Strepsiades' story proceeds with the
same mathematical precision, the same inexorable movement toward
a delayed explosion:

(a) Father and son are feasting; Strepsiades asks Pheidippides
to sing something nice from Simonides. But the boy refuses.
Singing at table is "old fashioned and silly", Simonides "a bad
poet". Two slaps in the face. We begin to realize how much
Pheidippides has been alienated from the traditional culture.
But Strepsiades does not take up the challenge; typically, he
humors his headstrong son; all may yet be well. And so:

(b) He suggests a compromise. Let Pheidippides take up the
(customary, ceremonial) myrtle bough and recite (not sing)
something from Aeschylus. Having made this concession,
Strepsiades is rebuffed straightway: Aeschylus is nothing but an
"archaic blustering old windbag".

---

[8]) Compounded of *pheido*, "spare," and *hippos*, "horse," Pheidippides is a
mixed-up kid, reflecting the tension between his easy-going, rustic father and his
snobbish, luxurious, citified mother. The play shows what comes of "sparing the
horses": i. e., diverting a strongminded youth from his normal athletic pursuits in
order to cheat your way out of the debts which he incurred. Curiously Aristophanes'
own father and one of his two sons were called *Philippos*, "lover of horses"; further
psychological-literary speculation is inviting!

I am very pleased with my translation, "concentration camp," for *phrontisterion*.
The verb *phrontizoin* means both "to cogitate" and "to worry," and Aristophanes,
like many people today, equates the two.

(c) Hurt, angry, rejected, Strepsiades still restrains himself, attempts another compromise: "Something, then, from one of your newer people?" And Pheidippides, with that sure instinct with which children drive for the jugular vein, recites a passage from Euripides, a real shocker, "in which a brother, so help me God, screws his own sister!" This is too much for even Strepsiades. At last he breaks out, with violent reproaches; insults are hurled back and forth; and then... Pheidippides beats his father! Somehow, we feel, it had to be.

In this fast-paced account, Aristophanes touches on deep-set Athenian worries, preoccupations "left at the door" earlier. Not that rudeness of children is anything new. Hesiod makes it, around 700 B.C., a mark of the Iron Age that has befallen mankind; and we may wonder whether, in the Golden Age itself, parents did not look backward nostalgically to some earlier time when children showed more respect and consideration for their elders. The generations have always fought, one way or another; they always will. But what made generational conflict particularly scary for parents (and children?) in the later fifth century was the disparity of life styles, value systems, even modes of thinking. Pheidippides has moved into a new world and can't go home again. His rejection of ordinary etiquette – amusingly for us, of singing at table – reflects the basic educational change portrayed in the First Agon, away from "music", with its familiar harmonies and reliable subject-matter, towards a new, open-ended, dialectical learning. Naturally, Strepsiades likes Simonides and Aeschylus because he grew up with them; but they were also upright, patriotic, and morally responsible writers, accepted and acceptable educators of Greece. Again, Strepsiades reacts to Euripides with typical philistine prejudice. He is appalled by the subject matter: here, incest in the *Aeolus*; of course he has no idea of the complexity of the issues Euripides was concerned with or the complex and far more than sophistic stance which the poet (not to be identified with any character or sentiment in his plays) takes toward these issues. Are human beings capable of responsible self-control? Do any values hold, does intelligence avail, in an irrational universe? Now Aristophanes' own comedy of ideas is very much concerned with these same issues. Far from sharing the philistine view of Euripides and Socrates as teachers of immorality, he sees them both quite fairly as spearheads of the educational and cultural revolution of his time; beneath the comic slander (which runs parallel to the philistine prejudice, but must not be taken seriously) both exemplify a *loss of simplicity* in the Greek world, an eating of the apple of knowledge. Moreover, both Socrates and Euripides extended the cultural revolution, brought it home to ordinary people through the media of teaching and theatre (we would say, college and television), and profoundly, in their different ways, disrupted the old mental and cultural bond between child and parent. The real, historical issues are there, in Strepsiades' account of the Quarrel, and they were – indeed, still are – very disturbing.

On all these genuine anxieties – about child-rearing, education, sexual mores, generation gap – Aristophanes operates with healing laughter. And the comic controls mentioned earlier still co-operate: the release of inhibition, not only in Pheidippides' reported liberation, but in Strepsiades' own telling of the tale; the constant awareness of a game being played out; the clowning of the hero, not least when he is down and out. Were this play-frame removed, we would find ourselves in the realm of tragedy, where father-son quarrels generally end in real disaster. Thus Haemon, in Sophocles' *Antigone*, incurs his father's irrational anger and reacts with the ambivalent wish and threat, to kill either Creon (as he later attempts) or himself (as he succeeds in doing); and in Euripides' *Hippolytus*, Theseus' furious curse brings about his son's death.[9] Euripides' plays were especially shocking because he presented, albeit in mythic form, very modern conflicts of fathers and sons, or husbands and wives, as though bringing myth back full circle to the psychological realities from which it largely sprang. In a short while, Aristophanes will allude to a memorable quarrel in Euripides' *Alcestis* of 438. In that scene, Admetus, partially crazed with grief and guilt, denounces his old father Pheres and breaks off relations with him: "I am dead to you" ... "No longer do I account myself your

---

[9] Euripides stresses Theseus' blindness in so quickly cursing Hippolytus, then failing to listen to his rational self-defense; but there is, I think, a further suggestion that the tension between a father and son who live and think altogether differently from each other—Theseus sees Hippolytus as both hippie and hypocrite—might itself tend towards murder. (Ironically, the two share an inner violence.)

son." And Pheres, the cool old scoundrel, swallows all insults and points out Admetus' own selfish cowardice in letting Alcestis die for him. The violent scene must have shocked the Athenian audience and lingered in their minds, like a great father-son fight by O'Neill or Arthur Miller or Tennessee Williams. *Alcestis*, it happens, ends joyfully; it has been called a tragicomedy (and many other things); but it shows well enough how a father-son quarrel in Euripides could uncover an unbridgeable gulf between the generations.[10]) In many other plays, such quarrels issued in death: most often, the death of the innocent, aspiring, or different-minded son.

But comedy counterfeits, it substitutes humiliation for murder. Strepsiades' shameless account of Pheidippides' shameless attack on him moves through recitative,

"He flayed me, spayed me, grounded me, and pounded me to pieces," to a lyrical climax, marking the nadir of Strepsiades' up-and-down career, as the son whose baby wants ("Nana, Wa-wa, Doo-doo") he once looked after so considerately now fails him in his moment of need:

> ... and bawling out, I HAD TO GO
> you wouldn't carry me out, you wretch, but
>   choking, helpless,
>   then and there
> you made me do my Doo-doo!

If we who have attained the higher ranks of the academic profession are not too inhibited to enjoy this sort of thing, but can say, as Oliver Wendell Holmes once said of burlesque, "Thank God I am a man of low tastes," then we can see the dramatic and psychological rightness of this happening. The comic hero seeks rejuvenation. Strepsiades has

---

[10]) As I see it, the utter breakdown of the father-son bond in *Alcestis* makes way for Euripides' romantic vision, quite revolutionary in fifth-century Athens and akin rather to Homer (in the *Odyssey*) or Menander, of an intimate bond of love between husband and wife. The Pheres scene establishes an extreme of selfishness and separatism from which we happily re-emerge along with Admetus into the bright, joyful world of friendship, generosity, and love. Of course, the comic parodist, like the philistines in the audience, isolates the particular shocking scene from its larger context in the drama as a whole.

found it – too much of it! A psychologist might say that he has accomplished what many of us unconsciously seek, a return to the "infantile omnipotence" where perfect power is joined with perfect helplessness. The *Clouds* is full of inversions, as well as reversals; this is one of the most dramatic. At the same time, Strepsiades' "thunder-crap" was, earlier in the play, his comic-heroic response at once to terrifying thunder from heaven and Socratic teaching about the same; and if, as the Clouds' behavior suggests, Zeus' avenging thunderbolt takes the form of the present murderous storm fallen on Strepsiades' head, then what in tragedy would be divine vengeance and parricide is here diverted to an absurd and humiliating but by no means serious end. (The Saturnalian flavor of the scene, with its almost ritual substitution of trivial for tragic, would be more apparent today if Pheidippides "spanked" his father.) But the actual scene – reported, we must remember, by Strepsiades in his usual unabashed way – must have been very enjoyable. The more pain, anxiety, and frustration of both young and old the scene presupposes, the more relief is afforded by the sudden discharge of so much pent-up feeling in wild and glorious laughter.

Pheidippides' Defense

However much we admire the sheer intellectual brilliance with which Pheidippides defends father-beating – the same kind of brilliance, enhanced by paradox, that we find in Gorgias' praise of Helen and in so many "unjust arguments" in Euripides' tragedies – we must first follow Aristophanes' own lead and remind ourselves of the comic setting. Once again, the teasing chorus sharpen our anticipation but remind us that we are watching the usual Contest in the usual playground:

> O, the younger generation must be
>   full of pride,
>
> for if he can show this sort of thing
>   is justified,
>
> then – we wouldn't give a penny for
>   an old man's hide.

In the real world, the question is extremely serious. What value has an old man's life? Other plays, the *Wasps* especially, show an extraordinary sensitivity on Aristophanes' part to old men's concern with their honor and importance; their very anger, or "sting", constitutes an almost sexual potency.[11]) In the play world, such painful matters can be handled through laughter. Sport is substituted for war.

Pheidippides' own prefatory remarks, which I must paraphrase here, recall two other aspects of the game. First, it was Daddy, nobody else, who diverted him from the old ignorant days of horse-racing to the new glories of sophistic argumentation. "I wish to Hell you'd stuck to horses!" says his poor old father. What happens, then, is comic justice. If Pheidippides has turned from a clean-cut athlete into a long-haired radical, it was Strepsiades' own silly fault for sending him to the University to make more money eventually for the family. So viewed, the comic reversal suggests a reassuring order in things, which helps control the anarchic tendency of the following arguments and make them more fully enjoyable. But second: Pheidippides' transformation hints that sophistic argument is, no less than horse-racing, a most delightful sport. He has acquired some fine new tricks, he will try them out (we need only watch) on his father. As ever, Strepsiades will be fairly helpless in the intellectual realm, a clown on ice skates. We will enjoy his comic bafflement. Nor, for all the poignancy (and this is important) of the Athenian issues alluded to, must we take Pheidippides' arguments with final seriousness: for he, in his own way, is charmingly naive; and he has indicated, rather like a magician, that he will be using tricks, trying to fool us ("Now, watch carefully!"). The result is comedy of ideas at its finest.

[11]) This splendid play seems almost a sequel to *Clouds;* see Whitman (above, note 5) and Douglass Parker's fine translation with introduction and notes (Ann Arbor, 1962). The old scoundrel Philocleon is first imprisoned, then (symbolically) killed, then imprisoned again in a sort of domestic welfare state by his reformist son; it is a great joy when he bursts loose from every constraint, gets wonderfully drunk, insults everybody, carries off a flute girl, knocks his son down, and dances wildly around the stage. The *Wasps* is a glorious tribute to human incorrigibility and democratic freedom. Differently, our special motif returns in the *Birds* of 414 in the person of a "father-beater" who seeks his own limited definition of the natural life and is simply expelled, along with other nuisances, from the truly free and happy community of Cloudcuckooland.

Cumulatively, the arguments are overwhelming, a mass of blows beating Strepsiades to the ground. (Studying them in slow motion, we must never forget the timing and total effect.) The first argument (a) sets the over-all tone of silliness, of intellectual slapstick. "Did you beat me, when I was a child?" asks Pheidippides. "Yes, for your own good." "Well, it's right to return favors." (All justifications, it turns out, are two-edged; what is especially amusing is the seal of rectitude, fairness, propriety, which Pheidippides puts on father-beating.)

The second argument (b) also chops logic. "Free citizens aren't beaten; I was born free as you; *ergo*, why should your person be immune, and not mine?" But this time the underlying problem goes deep. Progressive democracy brings one revolution after another; discover the Rights of Man, and some day Women's Rights will be advanced, and Children's, and Slaves', and so on; yet each liberation, however right and desirable, disrupts the stability, order, and equilibrium which states, and individuals too, equally require. Thus Pericles, champion of liberal democracy, assumed the traditional family order in his Funeral Oration and spent a lone sentence on women: their excellence is to be noted as little as possible for good or bad! The same year, Euripides' *Medea* gave a devastating analysis of the unfair treatment of women within the democracy, a speech still relevant and moving today. About the same time, Antiphon the radical sophist, and probably Socrates and others, were asking dangerous questions about 'bad parents' and the moral responsibility and human rights of their children. It may be that such discussions were limited mainly to the leisured upper class who had time to listen to sophists; but everyone went to the theatre, and critics of democracy made the 'licence' given to women, children, and slaves a commonplace of their pleas for "law and order" and return to a more conservative polity.[12] It is interesting that humor generally supports the conservative side in these discussions. Even the animals, says Plato, bump into you in the demo-

[12] See the devastating analysis of Athenian democracy by the "Old Oligarch," (more likely a young, sophist-trained oligarch), who wrote in the 440's or possibly 420's; and Plato's criticism in Book VIII of his *Republic*, written in the 380's but strongly reflecting disillusionment with the late fifth century experience. "Disorder" and "licence" became commonplaces of attacks on the progressive or extreme (Periclean or post-Periclean) democracy.

cratic streets! Similarly, Aristophanes is playing, in our passage, with comic escalation and paradox, much as Samuel Butler moves past the Rights of Animals (familiar enough already in enlightened circles) to the Rights of Vegetables. Yet such humor not only plays on contemporary anxieties about change (two years ago, the *New Yorker* published a large number of cartoons about kindergarten children making demands); it helps us, by clearing the air of emotional tension, face the real and very difficult problems of reconciling liberty and order, change and stability, in the democratic state.

The following verse (c), "If children cry, shouldn't a father also?" is a clever parody from the scandalous father-son quarrel in *Alcestis*, mentioned earlier. The allusion is significant as well as funny. When Pheres, the old egoist, said, *"You* enjoy living, shouldn't your father also?"*, he was expressing an "every man for himself" attitude altogether contrary to the traditional Greek sense of the solidarity, interdependence, and continuity of family (as a man lives on in his descendants). Aristophanes is alluding here at once to the troubling question of individuation and to Euripides as its principal catalyst. Yet the allusion, which goes so deep, flies past; it is a throw-away line. The audience barely has time to laugh at how Pheidippides is quoting from (of course) his favorite poet: you can find anything bad in Euripides!

Two blows follow (d, e) in rapid succession. Pheidippides anticipates an appeal to *nomos*, "custom and law": "You might argue, 'But that's *what one does* with children.' " The answer? "Old men are in second childhood;" moreover, "they have less excuse for wrongdoing, *ergo* they are more deserving of punishment." Once more, of course, the joke lies in the anarchist's appeal to traditional, even proverbial wisdom. The devil can quote scripture. We also catch a fleeting glimpse of those two comic themes, so very appropriate to Strepsiades' case: the "return to childhood" (again, excessive rejuvenation!) and "getting one's just deserts".

Now at last (f) Strepsiades gets a word in, and he indeed falls back on *nomos*. "But you *don't* treat your father like that, nowhere, nohow!" But this ground has become untenable. Pheidippides is child to Democracy and Enlightenment;[13]) he points out that *nomos*, being made by men, can be changed by men. And it's high time! Again, the serious implications are legion. Aristophanes touches here on the instability of law, especially in a democracy; the problem of its underlying sanctions, if it is made by men, not given by the gods; and the possibility that persuasion, that keynote of democratic debate and settlement, is really a means of manipulation, a veiled kind of force. Not a few of Aristophanes' contemporaries were arguing just such points. Were laws imposed by one group on another (as, the democratic majority forcing a helpless 'good' minority) through force of numbers? And was justice established in the interest of the ruling party? If so, were laws really valid, and how could progressive democracy be distinguished from tyranny? Deeply meaningful, deeply troubling questions – but again Aristophanes skates over dark waters on the strong ice of laughter. He gives us no time really to think, let alone indulge in feeling anxious; instead we are diverted by Pheidippides' clever wordplay ("Law was framed by the *ancients*, now it's the turn of us *moderns*,") and the sheer impudence with which, his new law settled, he makes what he regards as a generous concession: all blows received prior to ratification will be held exempt from retribution!

Confident in his power of persuasion, Pheidippides proceeds (g) to an argument from *physis*, nature. "Consider the Cock and other creatures of the field. *They* fight off fathers. Yet how do they differ from us, except for – not using voting booths?"

Taken seriously, this argument develops the problematic implication of what went before. According to the naturalistic view generally assumed and taught by the Sophists, laws evolved gradually, like other social habits, from a natural background of human endowments and human needs; these man largely shares with the rest of animal nature, but he has raised himself by his own boot-straps, emphatically *without* divine guidance or help, to his present civilized state. Yet if older theorists, notably Democritus and Protagoras, stressed the happy contin-

---

[13]) Scholarly discussions of *nomos* and *physis* abound, also of the teaching, individually and collectively, of Democritus (properly, a Pre-Socratic) and the Sophists. Relatively painless for the nonspecialist are Eric A. Havelock, *The Liberal Temper in Greek Politics* (New Haven, 1957), and W. C. Guthrie, *A History of Greek Philosophy*, volume III: *The Fifth-Century Enlightenment* (Cambridge, 1969).

uity with which law builds onto nature in an open-ended success story, later and more radical thinkers, like Antiphon, could stress the discontinuities between "law" and "nature", seeing most human institutions as in fact stifling such permanently real and valid human needs as freedom, happiness, and spontaneity. Man is born free but everywhere he is in chains! A related but less responsible antinomianism proclaimed that (as suggested earlier) Might was Right, tempting the young lions of the day – Plato's fictional "Gallicles", the real enough Alcibiades and Critias – to think of themselves as Supermen and, ignoring the "unreal" constrictions of custom-and-law, to impose their will on others by sheer force.

We can gauge the seriousness of these fifth-century problems by recalling the not so distant impact of the theory of evolution, survival of the fittest, "Nature red in tooth and claw." Much humor has played since then on these sensitivities. Here, for example, is Mark Twain:

> ... and then, by and by, the monkey came, and everybody could see at a glance that Man wasn't far off now. And that was true enough. The monkey went on developing for close upon five million years, and then he turned into a man – to all appearances.[14]

We might pause here briefly to compare Twain's monkey with Aristophanes' cock. Twain was after satire. As so often, he was attacking human pretensions generally and religious orthodoxy in particular; his humor enforces, for all its playfulness, both the scientific truth that man is "only a monkey shaved" and the moral truth that the brutality of so-called civilized men is totally unforgivable. In him, the moralist and thinker come very close to the humorous surface. Aristophanes' satire, by contrast, is only part of the total comedy. Like Twain, he plays on a very sensitive issue, man's place in nature and the meaning of all his works, which had immediate social implications. Yet his humor takes a different turn and a more confident one. The cock is less human than the monkey; it is a funny-looking creature, all the funnier here because it has become inextricably involved with

---

[14] *Mark Twain Tonight*, edited by Hal Holbrook (Pyramid edition: New York, 1967), 183.

the linguistic instruction of the Phrontisterion ("masculine, cock; feminine, coquette") provided by Socrates and regurgitated so enthusiastically by the magic-minded Strepsiades. Now it returns, unexpectedly yet somehow inevitably, to the scene of action.[15]) And funnily enough too, the tide turns momentarily in Strepsiades' favor, for the old countryman, however helpless in the realm of abstractions, *does* know something about cocks. "Well, then: since you're modeling your life on these fowl creatures, why don't you eat shit and sleep on a perch?" Pheidippides is dumbfounded by this splendid vulgarity. He can only riposte with a lame appeal to Personal Authority: "It's not the same thing at all. You just ask Socrates." In fact, Strepsiades has struck a shrewd blow for humanity as well as himself; but there is, again, no time to dwell on its more serious implications, for the old man is quickly showered with blows, and he loses the game shortly thereafter.

The way the argument ends, as it began, on a farcical note (h), reminds us not to make it seriously. "I tell you," says Strepsiades, "don't beat me, or you'll be sorry some day." – "How's that?" – "It's all in order: first, for *me* to beat *you*; then, if and when you get a son, for *you* to beat *him*." – "And what if I don't get one?" replies Pheidippides indignantly. "I'll have done all that crying for nothing, and you'll have the last laugh by being dead."

An Irish Bull of sorts, this last joke is especially funny because it permits the discharge of the usual deep anxieties about personal death and family continuity; the failure of the latter, which any Greek would dread, is ironically presented as a *post mortem* victory for Strepsiades! (A humorous columnist recently suggested that the present younger generation were planning to seal their rebellious efforts by refusing to have children; thus no later generation would turn the tables on them!) The end is appropriate in another way. We have

---

[15]) Socrates was pressing for a more scientific differentiation of grammar, taking proper account of gender (Arrowsmith suggests: "duck" for the male, "duchess" for the female) as part of an over-all rationalization of language and life. It must have been very funny when Strepsiades produced a live rooster to impress Pheidippides with his new learning: one thinks of Harpo Marx producing the "great seal" of Freedonia. The plot thickens if the contestants in the First Agon were compared in the earlier production to fighting cocks or brought onstage in that guise.

sensed all along that father-beating was a comic substitute for parricide. Now, at last, Pheidippides produces what sons generally repress, the picture of his father lying dead; but it is all a joke, tension and hostility are discharged in laughter, and we are reassured at the same time by the strong sense of game. (Daddy wasn't killed by our wish, he was just pretending.) Laughter is the sign of life, of vitality, of the continuity of experience we all so deeply want.

This is the truer, I think, because the scene does not end even with the symbolic death of Strepsiades' defeat. Aristophanes is still building! For even after Strepsiades concedes defeat and repents in the comic equivalent of sackcloth and ashes,

> Well, gentlemen, I do declare,
> His case seems absolutely fair;
> the logic's very tight.
> All sinners ought to weep and wail
> So higher justice may prevail.
> It clearly serves us right. –

even after this (and notice how the fallen Strepsiades includes most of the audience in a sweeping, inclusive gesture of "we sinners") the incorrigible Pheidippides cannot resist pressing his advantage to the hilt. "Cheer up," he says; "it's all right; NOW I'LL BEAT MOM!" At this point the fallen father rises again, in irresistible wrath. As before, in the dinner-scene, Strepsiades' patience finally reached a breaking-point and quite exploded, so now he has simply had all the effrontery and argument he can stand. Pheidippides' modest proposal is the last straw. If I am right, Strepsiades responds to this ultimate challenge not only by rejecting rational argument (Pheidippides was of course willing to justify mother-beating too) in a violent outburst,

> If you can sink so *low*,
> and argue it so well,
> you and your Socrates and Co,
> then don't you bother to pass GO,
> just GO DIRECTLY TO HELL!

but on this last note, he knocks his son down. It is high time.[16]) And with Strepsiades rather groggy yet back on his feet (the clown's inevitable resurrection), and Pheidippides in turn rather dazed, collapsed to the side, looking sulky, Aristophanes moves on to the finale: Strepsiades' revenge on "Socrates & Co", the burning of the Phrontisterion.

Reflection on the father-beating scene must begin with art, only then move to psychology. We are impressed by Aristophanes' inventiveness, his wit, the sheer brilliance of his ideas; by the comic timing and build-up from the Proagon to the two climaxes, of the Quarrel and Defense, and even beyond; and by the metaphorical and thematic integration of the Second Agon into the play as a whole. I frequently mentioned the play of reversals: Strepsiades reduced to second childhood, the cheater's trickery recoiling on his own head, comic justice. Less apparent from our analysis, yet equally important, is the sweeping progress of what we might call the liberation movement, from the expulsion of Zeus from his heavenly throne, through the consequent revolution in ethics, culture, and education, to the practical culmination of all this ferment in the explosive father-son quarrel and the father-beating. It all makes sense, all follows the roles of logic and cause-and-effect, in the nonsense-arena over which the teasing Clouds preside: the world of illusion in which we live, which could be, but here is not, viewed tragically.

I argued earlier that Aristophanes was using a Jack-in-the-box or spring mechanism both in the build-up of the Quarrel and in the way Pheidippides' energy, deflected from chariot-racing, bursts out with new manic extravagance in father-beating. Surely (and this is crucial) the same may be said for Strepsiades. The more he is constrained, whether by debtors, intellectual concepts, or the very treachery of nature (as exemplified by the Clouds), the more he too must burst forth

[16]) This cannot be proved; there is no stage direction, no indication in the dialogue. But something of the sort is clearly required. Strepsiades' violent response must somehow bowl Pheidippides over, much as characters are knocked head over heels by strong words in the Peanuts comic strip. Pheidippides remains rather out of things for a while afterwards; the simplest hypothesis is that he has been knocked down. A good parallel, also long-awaited, appears in *Wasps* when Philocleon at length knocks down his insufferable guardian-son (see above, note 11).

into new outrageousness. This point, rather this feeling, is crucial for enjoying the over-all play. But with the immediate scene in mind, we may pause to consider certain psychological implications of the son's revolt.

For we too have eaten of the apple, have learned from Freud certain reasons for the pressures and Discontents under which civilized people live. Whether (speaking for males only) we murdered the father in dim ancestral times and must pay for that crime with present remorse and guilt; or whether our aggressiveness toward the father, fueled by competitiveness for the mother and frustration at being deprived of instinctual gratifications generally, is turned inward and against ourselves; or whether our very ambivalence, loving and hating at once, creates guilt feelings—no matter, indeed, whether the father is strict or permissive: in all events, we labor under an enormous burden of repressed hostility and guilt. So too, of course, did the Greeks.[17] They gave us Oedipus; also Electra, Orestes, and the rest. Indeed, why belabor Oedipus? Modern psychology could still learn much about the Medea Complex, the Hippolytus Complex, the Agamemnon Complex; father-murder is only part of the spectrum of messy human emotions conveyed in myth and legend. But it is clearly there, in all the more or less familiar stories of young heroes warding off the advances of queens and stepmothers, killing, or being killed by, kings and fathers. Still more suggestively, any Greek who knew his entire Hesiod could tell how Mother Earth had stimulated her son Kronos to castrate and dethrone his father Heaven, and how Kronos was in turn "bound" and dethroned by his son, Zeus—a process which, by various indications, might have continued indefinitely.

[17] See E. R. Dodds, *The Greeks and the Irrational* (Beacon Paperback, Boston 1957), esp. pages 42–48 and notes. To Dodds' perceptive account of anxiety in the archaic period and its causes, I would add the question: what happens when certain sexual preoccupations emerge into consciousness in the fifth-century enlightenment? Sophocles' Oedipus, it has been said, had no Oedipus complex; Jocasta in that play makes light of his fears, remarking that "many people dream of sleeping with their mothers." We might ask, what becomes of Oedipal strains when incest becomes *thinkable*? Are the old anxieties intensified, and are they compounded with a new anxiety about chaos and meaninglessness? Perhaps we should speak of a Pheidippides Complex: see below, note 20, on "mother-beating."

The Unjust Argument significantly refers to these bad old days in the First Agon (as a sceptic might refer today to many disedifying matters in the Book of Genesis). If justice exists, then why did Zeus, the father of Justice, "bind" his father? I translate the Greek verb literally, as "bind", not "imprison", because it so well suggests the sense of constraint we all must undergo by Freud's account, including the fear of punishment (*e.g.*, castration) which we fear or expect must follow on sensual gratification. It is appropriately Dionysus, the Releaser, who loosens these bonds of tension, liberating a flood of pent-up feelings. Yet the nature of our release is determined by its contexts, of festival, theatre, and comedy. *Within the play* it is total, anarchic. King Zeus, the watchful and inhibiting sky-father, is dethroned by Dinos;[18] and it follows as the night the day, that Strepsiades is beaten by his son. We are all invited, old and young alike (for even the oldest among us labored under paternal pressures, not to say an introjected superego) to join vicariously in Pheidippides' coming-of-age revel, his liberation dance. And we do so the more joyfully because we are protected from falling into real chaos by the net of artistic order and comic gamesmanship. The war of age and youth *can* be tragic. The generations can and do kill each other, in real life as well as legend; indeed, if Aristophanes' audience looked up to the Southern metopes of the Parthenon, they could see the war of the generations magnificently embodied in the battle of Centaurs and Lapiths—the fierce old creatures, the brave young men, annihilating each other with savagery and pain.[19] All the better, then, if Dionysus and Aristoph-

[18] In scientific terminology, *dinos* means "whirling, eddy, rotation"; in ordinary life, it is a large vessel for wine; by etymological play, Dinos suggests a 'Son of Zeus' who is, in the family tradition, dethroning his father. (It also hints at the god Dionysus, son of Zeus, who presides over the present revels.) Put all these meanings together and you get *Cosmic Revolution*, or possibly *Revelution* (keep that e, editor!). As so often, there is a world of meaning in a quite untranslatable play on words.

[19] In this battle to the death, which began with a drunken, sexual assault, some Centaurs are killing, some being killed; an older sculpture (XXXI) shows a more primitive violence, a later one (XXX) a dreadful pain and sadness, as of father killing son.

If, however, we turn to the Parthenon *frieze*, we are impressed by the harmony of generations represented there. The young riders in their vigor, grace, and pride, the

anes transport us into that familiar and happy playground where parricide becomes father-beating and father-beating, for all its noise and furor, is altogether painless. By the law of comedy, you can break the law with propriety and justification. There will be nothing to pay.

I am constrained, less by inhibitions than from considerations of space, from entering into further psychological speculation on the subject of mother-beating. Philip Slater's book, *The Glory of Hera*, raises more questions of family psychopathology than Freud dreamt of; and the Strepsiades family, in which an oversexed wife drives on her son to satisfy her ambitions and avenge her frustrations on the inadequate father, would seem a perfect case history for Slater's purposes.[20]) So too might the description in Plato's *Republic*, Book VIII, of the "ambitious" youth spurred on by his mother's contempt for the unsuccessful, "philosophical" father. The point still remains, that much of the tension of these so familiar, and in realife so painful situations, is happily discharged in Aristophanic laughter. Our business here is to enjoy the solution, not elaborate on the problem. We might turn briefly, though, to the contribution of ritual to comedy. The subject has been wretchedly neglected in classical circles ever since Francis Cornford overstated his case, arguing for a definite and

older marshals and magistrates in their dignity and self-control, seem fully complementary to, and at ease with, one another. Is this an indication of the reconciling power of festival and religious observance?

[20]) Philip E. Slater, *The Glory of Hera* (Beacon Press: Boston, 1968). His argument is too complex to paraphrase here; it stresses the mother-son (not father-son) relationship and the "oral-narcissistic dilemma." The Strepsiades family support Slater's thesis perfectly. The mother is over-sexed, the father (as he indicates in an obscene joke) cannot meet her sexual demands; she projects dreams of glory onto Pheidippides and forces him into rivalry with his father. The Unjust Argument's comic description of the young hero Peleus, who won Thetis but couldn't satisfy her in bed, recalls Strepsiades' failure but also might suggest the strain on the son of the mother's demands which he both is and is not called to satisfy. Pheidippides' proposal to "beat" his mother suggests the hostility we would expect: she is, after all, the common enemy! But *typtein*, like "bang" in modern American slang, can also mean "to fuck": *that* is (a) the ultimate challenge to the father, (b) a reason for parricide, (c) in keeping with the incest theme developed earlier, and (d) an expression of the ambivalent feeling of desire and hostility which, in Slater's view, such mothers provoke. It is of course a chief glory of comedy that it can make light of such matters. Jocasta becomes a joke.

8

very complex ritual structure underlying each and every Aristophanic comedy—an attempt as unsatisfying at times as Ptolemy's epicycles.[21]) And yet Cornford was largely right. His work gives an insight into the power and meaning that Old Comedy derives from ritual; this is complemented, not outmoded by our more critical realization today of the distance, in terms of time, art, and tradition, between the two. Very likely, our father-beating scene goes back to the ancient ritual combat of Old King and Young King. There was a time when this combat was real. The blood of the Old King, the victory of the Young, ensured fertility of crops and women for the coming year. Yet the play instinct is quite as ancient as the working of magic, and very early on, the combat must variously have been played out this side of murder. Ritual is subordinated to play, elaborated in art. Fictional conventions developed over centuries stand between Aristophanes' comedies and the ancient rituals from which they are derived. We have stressed the reassuring tendency of these conventions: Daddy hasn't really been killed, he was only pretending! At the same time, the ritual conflict of age and youth has found a regular niche in comedy. Hence the latter's power to liberate deep wishes yet exorcize anxieties. There is a time, in comedy, for killing fathers. There is also a time for fathers, like the Old King of ritual, to be rejuvenated or born again—but that is another story. Pheidippides doesn't care.

May I put it differently? At four, quite ignorant of Freud and Frazer, my oldest son used to say, "When you die, Daddy, I'll be king and marry the queen." (The remark was stimulated by his seeing the death of the old king in *Babar the Elephant*, a picture to which he returned again and again with obvious fascination.) Now, at thirteen, he happily "beats" me at ping-pong and tennis, or else we laugh together at the marvellous aggressiveness of Laurel and Hardy, or the Marx Brothers, against all figures of authority, all representatives of law and order. I also laughed with my father at thirteen. The war goes on endlessly, but there are still the few blessed moments, of saturnalian or Dionysian release, when we can play together like little children. Isn't that, in a sense, what Strepsiades and Pheidippides were doing?

---

[21]) Francis M. Cornford, *The Origins of Attic Comedy* (Cambridge, 1934). The (scattered) remarks on *Clouds* are often suggestive but never quite appropriate to the play we have.

Perhaps it is. Yet one of the odd things about the *Clouds* (which is, as Whitman says, a very peculiar play)[22] is that in the end it provides no clear reaffirmation either of family solidarity or of the limits of saturnalian anarchy. Towards the end, Strepsiades appeals to Pheidippides to join him in destroying "vile Chaerophon and Socrates, who gulled the both of us."[23]) But Pheidippides won't stop playing, he refuses to 'harm my dear ... *teachers*', and Strepsiades' appeal to Zeus Patrôos, defender of fathers, is rejected as ridiculously old-fashioned: this *is*, after all, the Age of Revolution. Comic Justice again, more salt in the wounds. Pheidippides is throwing his father's own words back at him. Yet neither Strepsiades' admission of idiocy for having kicked out Zeus, nor his comic repentance, nor the Clouds' comic moralizing, nor the mighty attack launched on the Phrontisterion (more comic justice!) make it at all certain that the reign of Zeus has been secured. On the contrary, the Revolution is still going on; only Socrates is caught up, house and all, in that marvellous cyclone.

Here is a new problem. We are enabled to join whole-heartedly and joyfully in comedy, as in other games, by the framework of order guaranteed by fixed rules and limits. Within such a context (of religious and political, theatrical and fictional order), Aristophanes can liberate us from anxieties; not least, from worries about cultural change, "future shock", the erosion of familiar and trusted rites, symbols, values, styles of living and thinking. It is just possible that the topsy-turvy world will *not* turn right side up again when we leave the theatre precincts. The rules *are* changing, including the rules of play, of the comic theatre. This earth, which seemed so solid, is floating on air. Our lives are shot through with illusion; nothing holds, neither Law nor Nature. We have clearly come—as in all times of personal or cultural transition—to the dizzy brink of the abyss of meaninglessness and absurdity.

[22]) See above, note 5. Though generally indebted to Whitman's pioneering account of the comic hero and Aristophanic fantasy, I cannot agree with his disparaging treatment of the *Clouds*. Our Agon—essays at eight hundred miles—is just beginning.

[23]) Chaerophon was Socrates' pallid and effete sidekick. In the first version of *Clouds*, he may have represented the Unjust Argument.

8*

In such a world continuity cannot be assured, except for the persist-ence of illusion represented by the "ever-flowing clouds". Olympus itself is, nay, always was, as open to revolutionary change as Athens; one might say that a permanent contest of Old God and Young God,[24] or a permanent self-renewal of divinity, was occurring there. Strep-siades' mistake was to trust a false wizard, to use black magic, to think he could get away with harnessing the forces of cosmic revolution to serve his personal requirements. Inevitably, he was beaten by the greater energy of his son. The first of a long line of permissive, lenient parents in Western comedy,[25] he tries to change with the times, play the opportunist, go back to school, master the new rules (as if they could be mastered!) and win a game of persuasion where the cards are absolutely stacked against him. His failure is very funny, as the energies of youth and change burst out of control — and stay that way. Like every liberal father confronted by a radical son, like everyone who tries to live by reason and persuasion, he is backed to the wall and beaten up. And he cannot be reconciled with his son because the latter cannot, will not, and in a sense should not return to the old world. That would be untruthful: a sentimental, not comic solution. Perhaps, if Strepsiades were dying like Shakespeare's King Henry IV, Pheidippi-des could (like Hal) have been reconciled with him—and taken his place. In Shakespeare's Henry IV plays, written at a time of equally drastic transition from one set of values to another, the succession of the Young King to the throne may also be seen as a renewal or rejuve-

[24] See Cornford (above, note 21). I cannot agree that Zeus' reign is restored by the play's end, and that Strepsiades, as the "repentant minister," of Zeus, avenges his divine cause. But the parallel action of 'Old and Young' in heaven and on earth is very important for understanding the play.

[25] Terence's masterpiece, *Adelphi* ("The Brothers"), plays beautifully on the way a lenient father, apparently so right-minded and successful, is in his turn backed up against the wall. The point is basically ethical and serious, and may go back to Greek New Comedy. You cannot manage by leniency alone; some admix-ture of anxiety and strictness is needed, as even an *adulescens* might come to realize! To jump forward abruptly: Bernard Shaw constantly draws on the humor-ous possibilities of the outmanoeuvered liberal parent; so, in a much starker way, does much modern comedy and farce. Perhaps the enemy must be unmasked before he can become a friend? In any case, the old comic mechanism still works very well.

nation of the Old King.[26]) But Strepsiades, the old scoundrel, has more in common with Falstaff than with King Henry: he has no intention at all of dying; and that, in its own way, is splendidly reassuring.

For it is only partly true that the Clouds is about disappointment and failure—the failure of Strepsiades to escape from troubles, become young again, and rule the world. We must admire him too for his unquenchable energy, his resilience, his (what other word could do?) sheer survivability. Indeed, there is reason to think that we are all called to the clown profession in times of change:[27]) all called, like the clown playing acrobat, to walk our tightrope over the abyss—to stragger, slip, lose control, yet miraculously swing ourselves up again and go on! A ridiculous thing to be sure, the clown profession: but where tragic heroes fail through pride and arrogance, where they fall from their high-soaring winged horses, the clown on his dung-beetle may yet be allowed a sort of triumph.

Comedy offers no serious lesson; how could it? Yet the greater the comedy, the greater the healing it offers, and the deeper the hope. In times of radical transition the very existence of comedy such as Aristophanes' or Shakespeare's is gloriously paradoxical. Born of outward rituals which may yet renew themselves like phoenixes from their own ashes, comedy plays out its game in the cracks in time, the Old-and-New Days, when nothing is clear or certain. It may be that

[26]) Falstaff questions all accepted values, like the Unjust Argument; Hotspur and he, or the Lord Chief Justice and he, represent polarities of Old and New like the two Arguments in the *Clouds*. But although Hal outlives the old world and kills Hotspur, he also ultimately rejects (and symbolically kills) Falstaff; he will take his father's place and rule with justice and (we hope) humanity. Shakespeare thereby offers a pledge of continuity through change, a father-son bond transcending conflict, perhaps a reconciliation of opposed cultural values. The *Clouds* deals with similar themes in an equally profound way, but Aristophanes seems not to arrive at so simple a resolution as Shakespeare. (See, however, C. L. Barber's reservations in *Shakespeare's Festive Comedy* [Princeton, 1959], 213–21, which come very close to our own uncertainties about the ending of *Clouds*.)

[27]) The fool came, as a sort of "ruling figure," to dominate the Renaissance imagination; this odd situation is explained in relation to cultural transition by Walter Kaiser in his *Praisers of Folly* (Cambridge, Mass., 1963). I would predict that in later retrospect the clown will be seen to have dominated the twentieth-century imagination in art and literature. (This includes the sad clown, the juggling clown, and the clown as acrobat.)

as we watch the play, as we surrender ourselves to comic release, the embattled generations may enjoy momentarily a solidarity which has quite disappeared or is yet to be—rather like those Northern and Southern soldiers who used to swim, talk, and exchange presents in mid-river and mid-war. In some such way, war between the generations subsides even as we acknowledge its permanence; and in the very eye of the cyclone, of the revolution, we are somehow kept safe and even afforded a precious glimpse into the continuity of life and its beauty and joy. The truth remains, that life is unmanageable. The ford of reason has been quite washed out. We shall have to swim the straits; and comedy suggests, we might just, somehow, manage.[28])

[28]) Let a youth of thirteen have the last word. Last night he told me that he just wasn't interested in religion. "I know you and Mom are, but we're different." Flat on my back, anxious about our joint predicament (his, ours, and God's), I am perhaps justly punished for drawing morals from comedy. Still, there is comfort in human solidarity; and perhaps, like Strepsiades and Charlie Brown, I shall rise again! Also, I am cheered by recalling the following actual dialogue, of some years back:

> Boy (on the subject of spanking): "It's against the Law of Children."
> Father: "What's the Law of Children?"
> Boy: "Children should have equal rights with grown-ups. If a grown-up spanks a child, he should spank him right back."

And so the game continues.

Chapter 5

THE CONFLICT OF GENERATIONS IN THUCYDIDES

Felix Wassermann

Marquette University

It is obvious that the conflict of generations was Thucydides' concern not for its human aspects as such but, as with all phenomena of *physis anthropeia* (human nature), for its impact on political decision and action. The difference in mood and temper between the two generations contemporaneously engaged in political activities—a difference reflected in Greek epic and dramatic poetry and analyzed especially in Aristotle's *Ethics* and *Rhetoric*—plays a major part in Thucydides' presentation of the decision, and the ensuing responsibility, between war and peace.

It is significant that in the prehistory of the Peloponnesian War when the Athenians have to make up their minds whether or not to interfere in the conflict between Corcyra and Corinth—an issue whose key importance is underscored by Thucydides' use, for the first time, of coupled speeches—the Corinthian envoys, apparently elder statesmen, when advising the dynamic "hawks" in the Athenian *ekklesia* to stay out of trouble,[1] point to the experience of their own mature age (even as warners had already done in Herodotus[2]). It is also significant, as Thucydides stresses, that in line with the *polypragmosynê* (unrestrained zest for action) of Athenian national character this warning voice is lost.

The same motive occurs when the historian has to deal with the most fateful decision in the course of the war: whether the Athenians, against the advice of their otherwise dynamic late statesman, Pericles, ought to accept the alluring opportunity of the Sicilian expedition. This time the fight between cautious and dynamic politics coincides with the natural tension between the rashness of the younger and the

[1] I 42, 1.
[2] R. Lattimore, "The Wise Adviser in Herodotus", *Classical Philology* 34 (1939), 31; H. R. Immerwahr, *Form and Thought in Herodotus* (1966), 73ff.

restraint of the older generation. In one of the most powerful oratorical contests of the *History* each side is embodied in a representative politician, in Alcibiades and Nicias[3]) (both, as we can be sure, pictured from Thucydides' personal recollections). Nicias, with the violence of one who feels he is fighting for a losing cause, attacks his younger opponent's character, integrity, and ability, emphasizing the fact that Alcibiades is not yet old enough for a responsible position. Nicias is aware that the appeal of his arguments is limited to the "doves" of his own age group whom he warns not to be impressed when called *malakoi* (cowards) by the aggressive super-patriots among the youthfully "hawkish" backers of Alcibiades. As behooves their maturity, they are to be convinced that what counts in politics is not *epithymia* (daydreams of easy conquest) but *pronoia* (forethought and calculation of the risks).

Alcibiades, on the other hand, speaks with the ironic self-assurance of one who expresses the thoughts and wishes of his generation as well as the traditional temper of a nation which, as Thucydides has the envious Corinthian competitors say,[4]) is in its ruthless dynamism neither ready ever to rest nor to allow others to rest. Alcibiades even pretends to agree with the objection of *anoia* (lack of judgment) made by the angry and apparently outdated elders against the claims of youth, while at the same time he advances the suggestion of a compromise. The country is to make use of both the drive and energy of his generation and Nicias' *apragmosynê* (shunning of political action and responsibility), as he calls the cautious attitude of his opponent. He sees the foundations of Athenian power and greatness in the cooperation of the *presbyteroi* (the older generation) and the *neôteroi* (the younger generation). Indeed, as Thucydides does not fail to stress, ideal statesmanship, embodied in his picture of Pericles, reveals a balance of *andreia* and *sophrosynê*, of daring and caution. Referring to this as consistent with the *eiôthôs kosmos* (traditional order), the representative of the active and restless younger generation tries to

[3]) VI, 9–18. A. W. Gomme, A. Andrews, K. J. Dover, *A Historical Commentary on Thucydides*, Vol. IV (1970), 230–255; J. de Romilly, *Thucydide et l'Impérialism Athénien* (1951), 177–183; J. H. Finley, Jr., "Euripides and Thucydides," *Harvard Studies in Classical Philology* 49 (1938) 59f.; H. D. Westlake, *Individuals in Thucydides* (1968), 171ff., 219ff.

[4]) I 70.

beat the older conservatives with a catchword expressing their own roots in tradition.

As a parallel to this fight between the two Athenian politicians, Thucydides presents the conflict between Athenagoras and Hermocrates in Syracuse, again through the effective use of coupled speeches.[5] Here it is the younger man, Hermocrates, who offers the more realistic approach to the political situation by suggesting measures against the approaching Athenian navy. His (as we know) justified warnings are rejected by the older democratic demagogue, Athenagoras, to whom these warnings are only the devices of an ambitious *neôteros* and others of his age group to disturb the citizenry and make the situation safe for oligarchic revolt. We know from contemporary sources, including Plato, about the growing dissatisfaction with the usual democratic institutions among quite a few members of the younger set.[6]

Indeed, even the greatest opponent of the Athenian system, Sparta, was not free from generational conflict in the approach to political decision. This appears in the contrast, also illustrated by speeches,[7] between the cautious way the dangerously increasing power of Athens is dealt with by King Archidamus, whom Thucydides makes point to his age and experience, and the tough call for immediate action by the younger Ephor, Sthenelaidas.

As a representative of an age and society which for the first time tried to understand and analyze all the aspects of the *condition humaine*, Thucydides could not fail to observe the clash between the generations, especially when the political and moral crisis of the later decades of the Fifth Century increased the bitterness of this strife. However, in line with his emphatic concentration on the political sphere, he disregarded the general human issue (as it appears, for example, in contemporary drama) and presented instead in striking fashion its impact on political attitudes and decisions.[8]

---

[5] VI 33–40.

[6] V. Ehrenberg, *The People of Aristophanes*[2] (1951), 110, 207ff. (with many references to significant passages in Aristophanes and Euripides).

[7] I 80–86.

[8] Our own times offer enough examples of the role of different age-groups in politics; during the 1972 presidential election-year there was quite a lively discussion about the appeal made by the individual candidates to an electorate of different ages.

Chapter 6

GENERATIONAL STRUGGLE
IN PLATO AND ARISTOTLE*

Lewis S. Feuer

University of Toronto

The generational struggle in politics, as a universal theme in human history, was naturally recorded by the earliest masters of political science, Plato and Aristotle, both of whom recognized its primacy as an independent factor in political change. They thus enunciated a theme which is reiterated in history through changing modes of production and social systems. To Plato, generational struggle constituted virtually the basic mechanism in political change, the always disequilibrating factor in systems of government, the prime agent in the alternation of political forms. If aristocracy gave way to timocracy, the rule of property holders, it was because the aristocrats' sons became alienated from their fathers. As Plato described it, "The character of the son begins to develop when he hears his mother complaining that her husband has no place in the government... that his father is only half a man...." The servants tell him he must "be more of a man than his father...." But then the timocrats become de-authoritized in the sons' eyes: "A time arrives when the representative of timocracy has a son: at first he begins by emulating his father and walking in his footsteps, but presently he sees him of a sudden foundering against the State as upon a sunken reef...." The son, humbled by poverty, takes to "money-making," and the oligarchical form of government is the creature of the money-makers. But oligarchy gives rise to a rebellious generation which institutes a democracy. For the young son in the oligarchy is brought up "in a vulgar and miserly way"; the sons rebel against the money-making virtues; they call temperance "unmanliness," modesty "silliness," "insolence they term breeding, and anarchy

* Reprinted with permission from *The Conflict of Generations; The Character and Significance of Student Movements* by Lewis S. Feuer (New York: Basic Books 1969) 27-30.

liberty." "The lotus-eaters" appeal to the sons; "there is a battle and they gain the day." But democracy itself feels in turn the discord of generational strife. "The father grows accustomed to descend to the level of his sons, and to fear them, and the son is on a level with his father, he having no respect or reverence for either of his parents...." In such a society, Plato continues, "the master fears and flatters his scholars, and the scholars despise their masters and tutors; young and old are all alike, and the young man is on a level with the old, and is ready to compete with him in word and deed; the old men condescend...." Thus democracy founders as the sons are drawn into "a perfectly lawless life"; the son, says Plato, then dares do in reality what hitherto he has done in dream only, "he will commit the first murder." He throws aside the judgments of good and evil which he learned as a child. Democracy breaks down to be replaced by tyranny, the rule of a dictator.

Such is Plato's "model" for generational strife as the causal mechanism in political change. It underlines one fact—that to the ancients the primacy of generational struggle in history was entirely familiar and obvious.[1] Every form of government seemed to breed its own distinctive form of generational contradiction. Generational conflict seemed to them an everlasting threat to political stability. If this truth was so obvious to the ancients, why was it almost wholly lost sight of in modern times? The answer is that the Industrial Revolution brought a relative generational equilibrium to Britain and America; probably it was the first such equilibrium in world history, and it may well be that the tremendous energies unleashed in industrial development and the opening up of a new continent were energies which otherwise would have been spent in generational strife but now found more constructive channels. When discontented, rebellious sons could cross the ocean to build a new world, or become entrepreneurs in new industries, when young university men could take ship for New England, and clerks could fashion empires, the conflict of generations subsided. Thus at the same time that the revolutionary role of technology became obvious to the social scientist, the role of generational struggle receded

[1] Also see *Plato's Epistles*, tr. Glenn R. Morrow (Indianapolis, 1962), p. 220; *Plato's Laws*, XI, 929c.

into the background. The ancients, however, saw it in all its harsh reality, with its bitterness unrelieved by any safety valve such as a developing technology or new world.

To Aristotle, the psychological sources of generational conflict made for its universality. Generational conflict, in Aristotle's view, basically stemmed from the character of the generations. The young, he wrote, love honor and victory, "more than they love money, which indeed they love very little, not having yet learnt what it means to be without it...." Thus Aristotle, in effect, was affirming that an economic interpretation does not apply to the actions of youth. Their idealism was founded on generational comradeship, on their fraternity. "They are fonder of their friends, intimates, and companions than older men are, because they like spending their days in the company of others...." "They trust others readily, because they have not yet often been cheated. They are sanguine ...and besides that, they have met as yet with few disappointments." They think of themselves as an elite which can accomplish what others have not. "They have exalted notions, because they have not yet been humbled by life or learnt its necessary limitations; moreover, their hopeful disposition makes them think themselves equal to great things—and that means having exalted notions." They think in terms of moral idealism rather than social realism, "their lives are regulated more by moral feeling than by reasoning...." They overestimate their knowledge and abilities; they are dogmatists. "They think they know everything, and are always quite sure about it; this, in fact, is why they overdo everything." They are easily and naïvely moved to commiseration and social consciousness. "They are ready to pity others, because they think every one an honest man, or anyhow better than he is....")[2]

By contrast the elderly men, according to Aristotle, were disillusioned, disaffected, materialistic. "They have lived for many years; they have often been taken in, and often made mistakes; and life on the whole is a bad business." They are skeptics. "They 'think,' but they never 'know'; and because of their hesitation they always add a 'possibly' or a 'perhaps.' ...They are cynical; that is, they tend to put the worse construction on everything." Small-minded, ungenerous,

²) Aristotle, *Rhetoric*, tr. W. Rhys Roberts (New York, 1954), pp. 123–124.

money-minded, their passions slackened, they are moved not by feeling but by love of gain. Sexual desire, Aristotle noted, was the one which swayed youth most, but the old men were self-controlled because their sexual desire was gone. Aristotle, of course, placed his trust in men in their prime, who "neither trust everybody nor distrust everybody, but judge people correctly." Without excesses or defects, they combine the valuable qualities of youth and old age. The mind at the age of forty-five was Aristotle's happiest mean. It was then, as we would say today, most free from ideology, of either the juvenocratic or gerontocratic kind.

Generational conflict, furthermore, noted Aristotle, could take an overt political form. At Cridius, for instance, the oligarchy fell apart because the generations fought each other. At cities such as Massilia, Ister, and Heraclea, wrote Aristotle, elder brothers, younger brothers, fathers, and sons, fought each other for the high places of government. Thus an oligarchy, through generational conflict, could be transformed virtually into a democracy. Such was the immense political significance of generational struggle in the Greek towns; it altered the ruling group in Heraclea from a few persons to six hundred.[3]) Political revolutions, according to Aristotle, were caused not only by the conflict of rich and poor but by the struggle between fathers and sons. He documented the embittered strain between the generations as revealed in their proverbs and maxims: "Nothing is more foolish than to be the parent of children." "Never show an old man kindness."[4])

Indeed, the concept of wisdom as it was first formulated in antiquity by the Egyptian and Hebrew sages was precisely cross-generational in purpose. Wisdom was a warning against generational pride and rebellion; the son was to be his father's good pupil. Thus, history's first document on the principles of right conduct, the Maxims of Ptahhotep, was already concerned with the conflict of generations. Ptahhotep, a man of the Establishment, evidently Grand Vizier to the Pharaoh Isesi of the Fifth Dynasty in the twenty-seventh century B.C., as he set down the wisdom of a lifetime, bade youth hearken to their fathers. "A hearkener is one whom the god loves, one whom the god hates is

---

[3]) Aristotle, *A Treatise on Government*, tr. William Ellis (New York, 1928), p. 154.
[4]) Aristotle, *Rhetoric*, pp. 85, 139.

one who hearkens not.... How worthy it is when a son hearkens to
his father! If the son of a man receives what his father says, none of his
projects will miscarry.... As for the fool who hearkens not there is
none who has done anything for him. He regards wisdom as ignorance,
and what is profitable as useless. A son who hearkens ... reaches old
age, he attains reverence. He speaks likewise to his own children,
receiving the instruction of his father.... He speaks with his children,
they speak to their children."[5] The Hebrew Proverbs echoed Ptahhotep's wisdom, yet wisdom proved feeble against the forces of generational uprising. If the fathers were forbidden to send their children into
the fires of Moloch, the children sometimes seemed to seek the flames
themselves in obedience to a demon within.

[5] James Henry Breasted, *The Dawn of Conscience* (New York, 1933),
pp. 129–130.

Chapter 7

THE FILIAL COMPLAINT*

Miriam S. Balmuth

Tufts University

It's all my mother's fault and only hers. She has never put in a good word for me, never, even though she sees me shriveling daily. I am going to tell her how much my head throbs... and my feet too, both of them... and then she will suffer as much as I am suffering.

With these words, Theocritus has the lovesick Cyclops complain about his unsuccessful courting of Galatea in the eleventh *Idyll*.[1] The fault, of course, is entirely his mother's. The words and their tone, although written in the third century B.C., are not unfamiliar today, either to teachers or parents, even mortal parents. It does come as a surprise to some, however, that they are found so widely in Greek literature and in the recounting of Greek myths by Roman authors as well. The examples cited below are meant to be representative rather than exhaustive.[2]

* I wish to thank the Tufts University Faculty Research Fund for making possible the publication of this essay.

[1] The idyll is a "pastoral", but it is of the kind that was composed in the court at Alexandria rather than on a Sicilian mountainside. The account of Polyphemus as a buffoon is in the tradition partly introduced by Euripides in his satyr-play *Cyclops* rather than Homer's man-eating brute, and the Hellenistic sophistication of the poet emerges clearly in his tongue-in-cheek treatment.

[2] I wish to thank students who have taken Classics 175 at Tufts University for several years for their inspiration to make studies and conclusions of this kind. The translation of Theocritus above is my own. For other ancient authors quoted, the translators and editions are as follows:

Homer, *The Iliad*, trans. Richmond Lattimore (Chicago 1951);

Bacchylides in *Greek Lyrics*, 2nd ed., trans. Richmond Lattimore (Chicago 1960);

Vergil, *The Eclogues and the Georgics of Virgil*, trans. C. Day Lewis (Oxford 1947);

Ovid, *The Metamorphoses*, trans. Rolfe Humphries (Bloomington 1963).

As far back as Homer, and as early as the first book of the *Iliad*, Achilles claims that Thetis could be doing a lot more for him.

> Many times stretching forth his hands he called on his mother:
> 'Since, my mother, you bore me to be a man with a short life,
> therefore Zeus of the loud thunder on Olympos should grant
> me honour at least. But now he has given me not even a little.
> Now the son of Atreus, powerful Agamemnon, has dishonoured
> me, since he has taken away my prize and keeps it.' (*Iliad* I,
> 351–356)

> You then, if you have power to protect your own son, going to
> Olympos and supplicating Zeus; if ever before now either by
> word you comforted Zeus' heart or by action. Since it is many
> times in my father's halls I have heard you making claims, when
> you said you only among the immortals beat aside shameful de-
> struction from Kronos' son the dark-misted, that time when all
> the other Olympians sought to bind him, Hera and Poseidon
> and Pallas Athene. (*Iliad* I, 394–400)

Thetis in turn, appeals to godfather Zeus for assistance. With the knee/chin approach, she supplicates: "If ever before in word or action I did you favor among the immortals... now grant what I ask for [honour for Achilles], and explains that if he refuses, she will be "most dishonoured of all gods..."

In Bacchylides' sixteenth *Ode* written in the first half of the fifth century, Zeus is once more appealed to—this time by Minos, and he immediately flashes lightning, "wishing to make his son's place of honor clear in all eyes." Minos has now set the pattern of invoking divine paternity and goes on to challenge Theseus to do the same by throwing into the sea a gold ring. For this, Theseus leaps overboard "to the house of his horseman father [Poseidon]" where Amphitrite, "the stately true wife of his father" robes and wreathes him so that he can return, gifted with proof of his own divine paternity.

The examples from Roman authors are of myths that are still Greek, in styles that are also Greek. Vergil's *Georgics*, written after the middle of the first century B. C., drew on both the Hellenistic and earlier epic traditions as well, but the Orpheus episode, nestled in the fourth book, has received a great deal of attention for its extraordinary position within didactic pastoral. An episode which frames the story has Aristaeus addressing his mother Cyrene, *multa querens:*

> A shepherd called Aristaeus was leaving Thessalian tempe,
> His bees—so the story goes—destroyed by disease and famine;
> And glum he stood by the hallowed river-head, invoking,
> Upbraiding the one who bore him.
> 'O mother, my mother Cyrene, who dwell in the deep below
> This pool, why did you you bear me from the glorious seed of
>   godhead
>
> (If indeed, as you tell me, the god Apollo of Troas begat me)
> To be fate's target? Where, where has your love for me flown?
> Why tell me to hope for heaven?
> Look, even this mere grace of mortal life, which I won
> So hardly by craft and much resourcefulness from the care of
> Harvest and herd—though you are my mother—I must
>   abandon.
>
> Go on, then, with your own hand grub up my happy orchards,
> Be my enemy, set fire to my sheep-folds, murder the harvests,
> Blast the sown fields, hack down the vines with a brutal axe,
> If you find my praise so irksome.

Although translated as "upbraiding" above by Lewis, "multa querens" is probably rendered more accurately as "complaining" by Mackenzie.[3]) Emphasizing "multa" even more strongly is Williams' translation:[4]) "making loud complaint and bitter cry." I would like to suggest "whining" as the most satisfactory in this context.

Late in the first century B.C., Ovid compiled his *Metamorphoses* and continued in the Hellenistic tradition of Callimachus a cataloguing of themes, and in that of Theocritus an attitude less than respectful towards the gods. In the beginning of the *Metamorphoses'* second book, Phaethon complains to Apollo:

---

[3]) K. R. MacKenzie, *The Georgics* (London 1969).
[4]) Theodore Chickering Williams, *The Georgics and Eclogues of Vergil* (Cambridge, Mass. 1915).

9*

> Phoebus, my father, if I have the right
> To use that name, and my mother is not lying
> To hide some guild with false pretense, my father,
> Give me a proof, so people will believe me,
> Know me for what I am, and let my mind
> Be free from doubting!

It was the right to drive the chariot of the sun—the equivalent of the keys to the car—that Phaethon demanded and got. He didn't survive the ride.

Having isolated some of the complaints and complainers, we can now make some observations on the nature of the complainers and some speculations on the interpretation of the complaints.

When we examine the lineage of the complainers, we find that they are all of the blurred kind of quasi-divine status that corresponds to some definition of the word 'hero'.[5]) Polyphemos, Achilles, Minos, Theseus, Aristaeus, and Phaethon: all were born of divine stock. Their stories share the common theme of a sulky child berating his parent for not exerting enough divine energy on his behalf. With the exception of Polyphemos, in what is essentially a humorous treatment anyway, their requests are granted.

The first interpretation we can make is that we are dealing with a stock mythological motif. Surveying mythology, Geoffrey Kirk has identified twenty-four such motifs and eight unusual or bizarre ones ranging from tricks, transformations, changes of sex, and unusual births to eating children (which he calls commendably remote from real life). Kirk reminds us further that "the emphasis on family tensions in ancient Greece should be seen as a broad response to a continuing human characteristic rather than as a specific reaction to extreme social conditions."[6])

[5]) A hero to Homer is simply a free man; in Hesiod, one of the Fourth Age of Men; in Pindar, a member of a race between gods and men: demigods born of mixed divine and mortal parents, or having done great deeds for mankind; later definitions include minor local deities or founders, larger-than-life stature, or accomplishment, or expectations.

[6]) G. S. Kirk, *Myth: Its Meaning and Function in Ancient and Other Cultures* (Cambridge 1970) 194. The commonest themes in Greek (mainly heroic) myths are listed on 187 and the special, unusual or bizarre themes on 194.

Still another interpretation can be made using a different kind of analysis. Work done by Freud and his erstwhile disciple Otto Rank on the "Myth Of the Birth Of the Hero" traces a common pattern of conception, birth, exposure/enclosure, ..., recognition and reconciliation and suggests that this may reflect a common adolescent fantasy, wherein the child's two putative parents turn out to be surrogates for a royal or divine couple that actually produced him.[7]) In this sense, the filial complaint can be interpreted as an extension of Rank's pattern: here, the request for confirmation of divine paternity.

As Classicists, many of us have had to listen to complaints of students (and even colleagues) insisting on relevance and timeliness from our discipline. In our pathetic anxiety to prove this "relevance" we often invoke Plato or Juvenal to show how universal, permanent, and timeless is the schism between parent and child, or between *senex* and *adulescens* in Roman comedy. In these examples, parents complain about their children and about the younger generation in general, a generation which exhibits disobedience and all the other qualities that seem to have characterized younger generations forever. Yet mythology offers us examples of a different kind, not of the parent who complains about his child, but of the child who complians about his parent. Perhaps it is these latter examples that are more relevant today; relevant...timely...timeless, and therefore Classic.

[7]) See Philip Freund, *The Myth of the Birth of the Hero and Other Writings by Otto Rank* (New York 1964). The original essay by Rank, translated from the German by F. Robbins and Smith Ely Jelliffe was first published in 1914 in the *Journal of Nervous and Mental Disease*.

Chapter 8

"O TEMPORA,
O MOS MAIORUM!"*

Erich Segal

Princeton University

The most common dilemma presented in Plautine comedy is that of a young man *amans et egens*, "in love and insolvent," turning to his clever slave for salvation. The desperate youth is usually assured of deliverance, especially if his bondsman happens to be the wily Pseudolus (lines 117–120):

> CALIDORUS: Dabisne argenti mi hodie viginti minas?
> PSEUDOLUS: Dabo. molestus nunciam ne sis mihi.
> atque hoc, ne dictum tibi neges, dico prius:
> si neminem alium potero, tuom tangam patrem.

> CALIDORUS: Will you get me twenty *minae* – cash –
> today?
> PSEUDOLUS: Of course. Now don't annoy me any more.
> But so you won't deny I said it, let me say:
> If I can't swindle someone else – I'll fleece your father.

The young man's reaction to Pseudolus' plan is vehement indeed (line 122):

> Pietatis causa – vel etiam matrem quoque!
> Remember love and loyalty – fleece mother too!

This particular comic twist has more significance than the usual Plautine παρὰ προσδοκίαν, for Calidorus' words have a special Roman moral connotation.[1]) The expression *pietatis causa* appears

---

* Reprinted with permission from *Roman Laughter; The Comedy of Plautus* by Erich Segal (Cambridge, Mass.: Harvard University Press 1968) 15–20.

[1]) In supporting Jachmann's claim that these lines are Plautine additions, Gordon Williams remarks that the young man's "tasteless joke about his mother is out of place" ("Some Problems...," p. 426; see my Introduction n. 13).

on monuments that Roman sons raised to their fathers out of genuine devotion (in contrast to *ex testamento*, which meant that the father's will had ordered it). Plautus has invoked a pious formula only to reverse it: swindle mother as well as father.[2])

This irreverent outburst typifies the attitude of Plautine sons toward their parents. We find another ready example in the *Bacchides*, where young Mnesilochus vows to revenge himself on the mistress he believes has been unfaithful to him. But since he still loves her, this will be a very special retaliation (lines 505–508):

> Ego faxo hau dicet nactam quem derideat.
> nam iam domum ibo atque – aliquid surrupiam patri.
> id isti dabo. ego istanc multis ulciscar modis.
> adeo ego illam cogam usque ut mendicet – meus pater.

> She'll never say she played me for an utter fool.
> I'll go right home and then – I'll steal something from
> father
> To give to her. I'll punish her in countless ways.
> I'll drive her to the point of poverty – for father.[3])

There is surely no need to emphasize that the young man's plan involves a breach of *pietas*, the very cornerstone of Roman morality. This quality alone led Aeneas (*insignis pietate*) to the founding of Rome. The entire *Aeneid* is in fact epitomized by the exclamation of the patriarch Anchises when he greets his son in the Elysian Fields (6.687–688):

> Venisti tandem, tuaque expectata parenti
> vicit iter durum pietas.

[2]) Calidorus repeats this sentiment, ironically, in a later exchange with Ballio the pimp. To the *leno*'s suggestion that he go "filch from father," *surrupere patri* (line 288), a suggestion, by the way, which parallels Mnesilochus' plan (*aliquid surrupiam patri*, *Bacchides* 507), Calidorus indignantly retorts, *atque adeo, si facere possim, pietas prohibet* (line 291), "Even if I could, my *pietas* prevents me." This very plan has, of course, already been set in motion by the pious son and his man Pseudolus.

[3]) Later in the play, Chrysalus, the clever slave, echoes his young master's words in the rhetorical style which Frankel (p. 57) described as uniquely Plautine (line 947):

> Mnesilochust Alexander, qui erit exitio rei patriae suae.

> He will, like Paris, ruin his father's real estate.

For the very Roman association of father and fatherland, see my argument p. 19.

> You've come at last. The *pietas* your father hoped for
> Conquered every hardship on your way.

But, whereas love and loyalty inspire Virgil's hero to brave the dangers of an underworld journey merely to talk to his father, the sons in Plautus have quite different aspirations. Far from desiring parental communion, they would prefer their sires to embark for Elysium as soon as possible, that is, to drop dead. Philolaches in the *Mostellaria*, for example, sees his mistress and cries out (lines 233–234):

> Utinam nunc meus emortuos pater ad me nuntietur,
> ut ego exheredem meis bonis me faciam atque haec
> > sit heres.

> I wish someone would bring me news right now that
> > father's dead
> So I could disinherit myself and give her all my
> > goods!

In addition to longing for his father's swift demise, he is eager to act the prodigal, to give away all his property, an action which would have been almost as shocking to the Roman audience. Nor is Philolaches alone among Plautine *adulescentes* in dreaming of parricide and bankruptcy. In fact young Strabax in the *Truculentus*, like Calidorus, the *pietatis causa* fellow in the *Pseudolus*, is careful to include his mother as well in his aggressive agenda (lines 660–662):

> Eradicarest certum cumprimis patrem
> post id locorum matrem. nunc hoc deferam
> argentum ad hanc, quam mage amo quam matrem
> > meam.

> My plan is this: I'll first completely wipe out father.
> And then I'll wipe out mother. Now I'll take this cash
> And bring it to the girl I love much more than mother.

Freud considered the hostile impulse against the father to be the very origin of all totemism and taboo.[4]) Since the breaking of re-

---

[4]) Freud, XIII, p. 159, in "Totem and Taboo"; XXI, p. 183, in "Dostoyevsky and Parricide."

strictions is at the heart of all comedy, it is not surprising that this primal taboo should be assaulted here. But the frequent parricidal utterances in Plautus gain special significance when we recall that Roman fathers had absolute power over their children and could have *them* killed if they deemed fit.[5]) Typically Roman is the story of Manlius Torquatus, who in 340 B.C. during the Great Latin War had his son executed for disobeying orders, even though the son's courageous but unauthorized attack resulted in a great military victory.[6]) The history of Rome is replete with examples of fathers killing disobedient sons. Lucius Junius Brutus, founder of the Roman republic, had his rebellious sons put to death in the year of his consulship.[7]) Whether the latter story be fact or legend,[8]) its very existence testifies to the Roman preoccupation with filial deference. Of course father-son conflict is a universal psychological configuration, Freud's Oedipus complex being its most famous formulation. But it is of significance that in the Roman version, unlike such legends as the sons of Noah and the son of Kronos (not to mention the son of Laius), it is the father who prevails.[9])

Fears of parricide typify what certain anthropologists call a "patrist" society (as opposed to a "matrist" one, in which the fear of incest dominates).[10]) In Rome, where the patriarchal organization maintained its pristine vigor far longer than elsewhere in Europe, veneration for old age was no less intense than at Sparta. Moreover,

---

[5]) Georgia Williams Leffingwell, *Social and Private Life at Rome in the Time of Plautus and Terence* (New York 1918) [= Columbia University Studies in Politics, Economics and Public Law 81, 1] 58–59.

[6]) Livy 8.7. See also Valerius Maximus 2.7.5 *(de disciplina militari)*. Quite understandably he also cites this incident under *de severitate patrum in liberos*, 5.8.

[7]) Livy 2.3–5 (509 B.C.).

[8]) Cf. Freud, XXI, pp. 124 and 132, in "Civilization and Its Discontents."

[9]) In Plutarch *Cato Maior* 20.5 there is a statement which evokes thoughts of the impious deed of the sons of Noah. The historian says that in Cato's day, relations between the generations were so strict that elders would not undress in the company of younger men. On the psychological significance, see Grotjahn, p. 28.

[10]) The main features of "matrist" and "patrist" systems are outlined and discussed by G. Ratray Taylor, *Sex in History* (London 1954) 83ff. Taylor's concise tabulation of the attitudes prevalent in "patristic" societies (p. 83) bears quoting in full, since so many of these attitudes are prominent in the Rome we are discussing:

patriarch and patriotism were associated in the most literal sense. Take, for example, the speech which Livy places in the mouth of Scipio Africanus, a man renowned for his filial devotion.[11]) Scipio cites the actions of Coriolanus, another (potential) Roman parricide. Coriolanus, he says, was driven by injustices to assault his fatherland (*ad oppugnandam patriam*) but his Roman loyalty prevailed (Livy 28.29.1):

> Revocavit tamen a publico parricidio privata pietas.
> Nevertheless, personal *pietas* prevented him from public
> parricide.

Rome is truly the fatherland. When Cicero brands a man a traitor, he calls him *parricida*. And of course in daily life *pietas* would prevent a Roman from wishing his father dead, just as it prevented Coriolanus from acting out the parricidal urge.

There is a reason why Plautine characters so often mock Rome's most solemn and fearful institution. As Dr. Grotjahn writes, "Jokes grow best on the fresh graves of old anxieties."[12]) Freud himself observed that wit attacks those institutions or religious precepts

> "1. Restrictive attitude towards sex
> 2. Limitation of freedom for women
> 3. Women seen as inferior, sinful
> 4. Chastity more valued than welfare
> 5. Politically authoritarian
> 6. Conservative: against innovation
> 7. Distrust of research, enquiry
> 8. Inhibition, fear of spontaneity
> 9. Deep fear of homosexuality
> 10. Sex differences maximizcd (dress)
> 11. Asceticism, fear of pleasure
> 12. Father-religion"

[11]) Scipio Africanus won renown at age 18 for saving his father's life at the battle of Ticinus; Livy *Periocha* 21, Polybius 10.3. Cf. also Aurelius Victor *De Viris Illustribus* 3.49.

[12]) Grotjahn, p. 115.

which are so respected that they can be opposed in no other way.[13])
It is worth noting that there are no outrages to *pietas* in Terence.[14])
One may compare the Plautine "drop dead" scenes we have discussed
with a similar one in the *Adelphoe*, when the young man is informed
of his father's inopportune arrival in town (lines 519–520):

> Quod cum salute eius fiat, ita se defetigarit velim
> ut triduo hoc perpetuo prorsum e lecto nequeat surgere.

> I wish – as long as he stayed healthy – he would tire out
> And lie in bed for three whole days, unable to get up.

It sounds very much like a parody of Plautus. It may in fact be a
reaction to the general irreverence which characterized all Roman

---

[13]) Freud, VIII, pp. 108–109, in "Jokes and Their Relation to the Unconscious":
"the object of a joke's attack may equally well be institutions, people in their
capacity as vehicles of institutions, dogmas of morality or religion, views of life
which enjoy so much respect that objections to them can only be made under the
mask of a joke and indeed of a joke concealed by its facade."

[14]) We may compare, for example, the instances cited at the beginning of this
chapter, in which Plautus' young men set out to swindle and bankrupt their fathers,
with Terrence *Eunuchus* 380ff, where young Chaerea explains to his slave Parmeno
that he will disguise himself as a eunuch so that he will *not* have to deceive his parent
(lines 386–387):

> An potius haec patri aequomst fieri, ut a me ludatur dolis
> quod qui rescierint, culpent.
> Would it be better if I went and tricked my father?
> Whoever learned of *that* would criticize me...

It is even more revealing to contrast the sentiments of the Plautine lovers who wish
their parents dead because they adore their mistresses so much with Terence
Adelphoe 696ff, when young Aeschinus speaks to his father of his beloved Pamphila
(lines 701–703):

AESCHINUS: Di me pater
omnes oderint ni magis te quam oculos nunc amo meos.
MICIO: Quid? Quam illam?
AESCHINUS: *Aeque.*
AESCHINUS: O father!

> May the gods all hate me if I don't love you above all else.

MICIO *(pointing to the girl)*: Even more than *her?*
AESCHINUS *(a pause for reflection)*:   As much.

popular comedy. When Donatus comments on this Terentian "anti-father" passage, he contrasts to its mild sentiments the harsh ("Plautine") outburst of a young man from a play by Naevius: *deos quaeso ut adimant et patrem et matrem meos*, "I pray the gods to snatch away my father and my mother."[15]) Clearly, such an assault on parental *pietas* had a special appeal for the Roman audience.

Teachers, in Quintilian's words, are "parents of the mind," and since Plautus' characters openly flaunt the Roman dictates of respect for elders, it is not surprising that Lydus, the tutor in the *Bacchides*, does not command the traditional veneration (lines 447–448):

> ... hocine hic pacto potest
> inhibere imperium magister, si ipsus primus vapulet?

> Just how can a teacher
> Show authority – if he himself's the first one to be
> punched?

Where we should expect deference, we find defiance. In a comic reversal, the teacher feels the hickory stick. Homer shows how even Achilles at the height of his wrath was courteous to his tutor Phoenix, but in Plautus the dignity of pedagogue as well as parent is ignored or, as in the case of Lydus, literally assaulted.

We have already seen that many Plautine sons wish their absent fathers dead. But here in the *Bacchides* young Pistoclerus threatens to kill his tutor face to face (lines 154–155):

> LYDUS: Magistron quemquam discipulum minitarier?
> PISTOCLERUS: Fiam, ut ego opinor, Hercules, tu autem
> Linus.

> LYDUS: Does a pupil dare to menace his own teacher?
> PISTOCLERUS: I think I'll act like Hercules. You'll be my
> Linus.

As educator, Lydus might take some ironic consolation in the fact that the murderous threat is couched in a clever mythological refer-

---

[15]) Donatus *ad Ter. Adelph.* 4.1.5.

ence to Hercules brutally murdering his own tutor,[16]) but this hardly
mitigates the shocking breach of *pietas*. Real-life Rome would not
countenance such disregard for an elder's authority, not the people
who spoke admiringly of the *Manliana imperia*, in praise of the general who put his respectful, loving, victorious, yet "nobly" disobedient son to death.[17])

[16]) The tutor replies with an equally clever (and equally hostile) allusion (*Bacchides* 156–157):

> Pol metuo magis, ne Phoenix tuis factis fuam
> teque ad patrem esse mortuom renuntiem.
> By Pollux, I'm afraid you'll turn me into Phoenix,
> That is, the man who tells your father that you're dead.

[17]) See above, n. 6.

Chapter 9

PATRIA POTESTAS AND THE ROMAN REVOLUTION

Joseph Plescia

Florida State University

There seems to be general consensus that there is a universal, innate force which drives sons away from their fathers' power and that there is a counterforce which drives fathers to hold their children under their authority. But there is disagreement about the nature of these opposite forces. According to Freud, the opposition stems from the libido, from sexual rivalry; for him this opposition is one of hostility. According to Fromm,[1]) it stems from the instinct of the growing son to be free from external pressure in order to fulfil himself and assert his identity; therefore, for him the opposition is one of freedom versus authority; it is a struggle for the son to achieve emancipation from his father. Evidently, both explanations of this innate conflict between fathers and sons presuppose an authoritarian, patriarchal society.

Such a society was that of Rome. Indeed, the Roman jurist Gaius claimed, with some exaggeration, that no other nation had an absolute *patria potestas* such as that of the Roman citizens.[2])

I propose that this generational conflict, a private matter between individual parents and sons in normal times, becomes a national[3]) generational one in times of economic crisis and cultural revolution. This essay, therefore, deals first with the notion of the Roman *patria potestas* strictly from the legal standpoint, and then with the economic crisis and cultural revolution that took place in the late Republic (the so-called Roman Revolution period) and resulted in a national

---

[1]) E. Fromm, "The Oedipus Myth," *Scientific American* 180 (January 1949) 22ff.

[2]) Gaius 1, 55: *quod ius proprium civium Romanorum est.*

[3]) By "national" I refer to the fact that the conflict transcends the family level; it does not imply that all the young rise against their elders; on the contrary, only a small percentage emerges as reformer-activists. See below.

generational conflict which, in turn, brought about the downfall of the Republic.

I. The Roman *Patria Potestas.*

Patria potestas[4]) referred to the power exercised by the head of the family, namely the paterfamilias, over the household (*familia*) in accordance with the *ius privatum* (Private Law).

The family was organized as a miniature monarchy, i. e., under the rule of one person with one purse and one worship. In the archaic period the family legal bonds were essentially agnatic,[5]) i. e., based solely on the paterfamilias; they included: (a) the blood relations traced through the male line, excluding all those males and females who had left the family; and (b) those who had come into the family by adoption or marriage *cum manu* (under the husband's power). In the classical period the family legal bonds gradually became cognatic.[6]) In the post-classical period they were totally cognatic.[7])

The paterfamilias was he who had no direct ascending agnates: he was *sui iuris* (of independent status). He exercised the *patria potestas* over the household and such a power was lifelong; the descendants ceased to be under it only by death or by an act of the paterfamilias.[8])

---

[4]) Gaius 1, 156. Cf. F. de Zulueta, *The Institutes of Gaius* (2 vols.; Oxford, 1953.)

[5]) H. F. Jolowicz, *Historical Introduction to the Study of Roman Law* (2nd ed.; Cambridge Univ. Press, 1952; rpt. with corrections in 1954.) Alan Watson, *Roman Private Law around 200 BC* (Edinburgh Univ. Press, 1971) Gaius 3, 10.

[6]) *Digest* (henceforth "D" 38, 17: the *senatus consultum Tertullianum*, issued under Hadrian, enacted that a mother was a legitimate heir to a son who had died intestate, provided she possessed the *ius liberorum* (privileges granted to parents with three or more children). Similarly (D. 38, 17), the *senatus consultum Orphitianum*, issued under Marcus Aurelius, enacted that children were entitled to inherit from their mother in preference to their deceased mother's brothers and sisters and other agnates. Cf. F. Schulz, *Classical Roman Law* (Oxford Univ. Press, 1951) p. 226. *Inst.* 3 and 4.

[7]) *Inst.* 3, 5; 3, 6; Cf. Nov. 118 of 543 and Nov. 127 of 548. P. Voci, *Istituzioni di Diritto Romano* (3rd ed.; Milano: Giuffre 1954) p. 574.

[8]) Ulpian, D. 50, 16, 195, 2.

The paterfamilias had a dual personality, that is, the individual one as a particular person, and the familial one as the embodiment of the family. Due to this dualism of personality, the extent of the *patria potestas* varied in the course of the evolution of Roman law.

In the archaic period the paterfamilias exercised almost sovereign power over the members of his household.[9]) It included: (a) *ius vitae et necis*, that is, the paterfamilias had the power to punish by death a son who had committed a serious offence against the family or the state;[10]) (b) *ius exponendi*, that is, the paterfamilias had the power to expose deformed newly born children;[11]) (c) *ius vendendi*, that is, the paterfamilias, when pressed by economic hardships, could sell his children;[12]) when he sold them outside the territory of Rome, they became slaves; when he sold them within the territory of Rome, they passed *in mancipio quoad ius privatum*, but remained free persons *quoad ius publicum*, i. e., *de iure* they could, for instance, enlist in the army against the orders of the person who held them in bondage (*in mancipio*);[13]) (d) *ius noxae dandi*, that is, the paterfamilias had the option either to surrender his son to the power of the person wronged by the son or to pay for the wrong;[14]) (e) right of marriage and divorce, that is, the paterfamilias had the power to contract or dissolve his children's marriage;[15]) (f) right to give his children in adoption;[16]) (g) right of emancipation, that is, the paterfamilias had the power to release his children from the *patria potestas*.[17])

---

[9]) Cf. C. W. Westrup, *Introduction to Early Roman Law. Comparative Sociological Studies* (Copenhagen, 1934–44); G. De Sanctis, *Storia dei Romani*. Vol. IV, Part II, Tomo II (Firenze: La Nuova Italia, 1957); P. Voci, *op. cit.* above (n. 7); H. F. Jolowicz, *op. cit.* above (n. 5.).

[10]) Twelve Tables, tab. 4, 2a; Gellius 5, 19, 9; D. 28, 2, 11. Cf. S. Riccobono, *Fontes Iuris Romani Antejustiniani*, Vol. I (Florence, 1941.).

[11]) Twelve Tables, tab. 4, 1.

[12]) Twelve Tables, tab. 4, 2b.

[13]) Cf. H. F. Jolowicz, *op. cit.* above (n. 5); P. Voci, *op. cit.* above (n. 7).

[14]) Twelve Tables, tab. 12, 2b; Gaius 4, 76; A. Watson, *op. cit.* above (n. 5).

[15]) In case of daughters, the paterfamilias could dissolve her marriage, only if it had been contracted *sine manu*. Cf. A. Watson, *op. cit.* above (n. 5).

[16]) Voci, *op. cit.* above (n. 7) p. 485f.

[17]) P. Voci, *ibid*.

This sovereign power, however, of the paterfamilias over his children was subject to certain restrictions by statute and by custom. First of all, it was subordinated to the *ius publicum* (Public Law): in case of conflict between the enforcement of a command derived from the *patria potestas* (*ius privatum*) and a command derived from the *imperium* (*ius publicum*), the *imperium* prevailed; furthermore, the *filiusfamilias* (son under the *patria potestas*) as a magistrate could sit in judgment over his father's actions and pronounce sentence against him. Second, the Twelve Tables enacted that if the paterfamilias sold his son three times, the son was released from the *patria potestas;*[18]) they also provided against the irrational use of the *patria potestas;* thus, on grounds of insanity the *consilium domesticum* (family council) could petition the magistrate to place the paterfamilias under the *auctoritas* (authority) of a curator;[19]) similarly, on grounds of dissipating the family property (*prodigalitas*) the *consilium domesticum* could place the paterfamilias under the *auctoritas* of a curator by petitioning the magistrate.[20]) Third, the censors could issue a *nota censoria* (censorial reprimand) against the arbitrary use of the *patria potestas*.[21]) Finally, custom required the paterfamilias to consult the *consilium domesticum* before pronouncing a decision on the fate of a son in serious matters.[22])

In the classical period the sovereign power of the paterfamilias over the household underwent gradual but substantial curtailment. Thus, (a) the *ius vitae et necis*, though not abolished,[23]) was greatly discouraged[24]) in favor of the public authority; (b) the *ius exponendi*

---

[18]) Twelve Tables, tab. 4, 2b.

[19]) Twelve Tables, tab. 5, 7; Cicero, *De Officiis* 3, 31, 112; Livy 7, 4.

[20]) Twelve Tables, tab. 4, 2b.

[21]) Dionysius Hal. 20, 13; Cf. A. Watson, *op. cit.* above (n. 5) p. 29.

[22]) Cf. A. Berger, *Encyclopedic Dictionary of Roman Law* (Philadelphia, 1953) v. *consilium propinquorum.*

[23]) Sallust, *Catilina* 39.

[24]) D. 37, 12, 5: Trajan forced a father, who had treated his son harshly, to emancipate the young man, and prevented him from sharing in the inheritance of the son after the son's death; cf. also D. 37, 15, 1. Similarly, according to D. 48, 9, 5, Hadrian banished to an island a father who had killed his son on a hunting trip, because the latter had allegedly committed adultery with his second wife; cf. also D. 48, 8, 2; D. 48, 9, 16, 2.

at birth persisted throughout the classical period, expecially for daughters and illegitimate children;[25] (c) the *ius vendendi*, though not abolished, was discouraged;[26] (d) the *ius noxae dandi* was permitted only in cases of poverty; (e) the right of contracting the marriage of the children was now subordinated to their consent;[27] vice versa, the son and daughter could not marry without the consent of their paterfamilias; (f) the right of the paterfamilias to dissolve his children's marriage was abolished by Marcus Aurelius;[28] (g) the right to emancipate his children continued throughout the classical period.

In the post-classical period with the triumph of Christianity the divinization of the paterfamilias as the embodiment of the family[29] was rejected and with it his sovereign power came to an end.[30] Thus, (a) the *ius vitae et necis* was abolished by Valentinian; the paterfamilias who killed his son was liable to *parricidium* (parricide)[31] (b) the *ius exponendi* was also abolished by Valentinian,[32] except perhaps in cases of illegitimate and deformed children; (c) the *ius vendendi* was permitted only under economic hardships; the child had to be newly born and the paterfamilias had the right of redemption;[33] (d) the *ius noxae dandi* was abolished by Justinian;[34] (e) the right to give his son in marriage was subject to the son's consent; vice versa, the son could not marry without paternal consent; the daughter's consent was urged but not required, except when she objected to the lower status or bad character of the bridegroom;

---

[25] Cicero, *De Officiis* 3, 8, 19; Juvenal 6, 602; Seneca, *De Ira* 1, 15, 2.

[26] Gaius 1, 116–17; 1, 138; 1, 141; Codex Justiniani (henceforth "C") 7, 16, 1.

[27] D. 23, 1, 13: *filiofamilias dissentiente sponsalia nomine eius non possunt.* Cf. also D. 23, 2, 21: *non cogitur filiusfamilas uxorem ducere.* For the consent of the daughters see D. 23, 1, 11–12.

[28] Cf. F. Schulz, *op. cit.* above (n. 6) p. 152 (Sect. 258).

[29] Val. Maximus 5, 4, 5; Gellius 10, 23, 5; Suetonius, *Claudius* 16. Cf. C. W. Westrup, *op. cit.* above (n. 9).

[30] C. 9, 15, 1; cf. D. 48, 8, 2.

[31] Codex Theodosii (henceforth "C. Th.") 4, 8, 6; 9, 13, 1; 9, 15, 1; C. J. 8, 46, 10; 9, 17, 1. Cf. Lactantius, *Div. Inst.* 4, 4, 11.

[32] C. Th. 5, 9, 1, 2; 9, 14, 1; C. J. 1, 4, 24; 8, 51, 2–3; 9, 16, 7; D. 25, 3, 4.

[33] C. Th. 4, 8, 6; 5, 10, 1; C. J. 4, 43, 1, 2; 7, 16, 1.

[34] *Inst.* 4, 8.

(f) the right to dissolve his children's marriage had been abolished by Marcus Aurelius.

So far we have surveyed the paterfamilias' power over the person of his children; next we will discuss his power over the property of his children.

Whether or not, in the pre-political stage of Rome's history, the family (or, perhaps, better the *gens* [clan]) operated on the principle of joint-property in the sense that the children were regarded *quodammodo domini* (quasi owners)[35]) is a moot question. Assuming, however, this to have been the case, then the paterfamilias: (a) could not have been able to dispose of the family property (the *res mancipi* [Italian land, slaves and animals of draft and burden] only?) by will, if there were *filiifamilias;* (b) could not have been able to alienate immovable property nor movable property of considerable value by transaction (e.g., the *mancipatio* [solemn procedure for the conveyance of *res mancipi*]) without consulting the *consilium domesticum;* probably, he could have disposed of movable property of limited value, the so-called personal property.[36])

By the time of the Twelve Tables, when the family had been emancipated from the *gens*, the paterfamilias had emerged as the sole legal person who had full control over the household: the Twelve Tables granted him the power to dispose of the property not only *mortis causa* (effective only when or if death occurs), but also *inter vivos* (not subject to the death condition). Whether or not he was required by custom to consult the *consilium domesticum* in major transactions may be argued. However, the Twelve Tables granted the *consilium* the power to petition the magistrate in order to place the paterfamilias under the *auctoritas* of a curator in cases of lunacy and prodigality. The principle was that the paterfamilias had to exercise his *potestas* over the household (persons and property) like a *bonus et diligens* (good and diligent) householder.

Just as the paterfamilias' *potestas* over the persons of his children underwent gradual curtailment during the course of Roman history,

---

[35]) Gaius 2, 157; 3, 154a; D. 28, 2, 11. Cf. F. de Zulueta, *The Institutes of Gaius* (2 vols.; Oxford Univ. Press, 1946–1953), vol. 2, pp. 96 and 175.

[36]) C. W. Westrup, *op. cit.* above (n. 9).

so too his *potestas* over the property of his children underwent gradual restrictions.

In the archaic period the filiusfamilias legally was not capable of owning property: whatever he acquired devolved to his paterfamilias.[37] However, the paterfamilias could grant his filiusfamilias a *de facto* ownership over some property. Such a grant of property was known as *peculium;*[38] the *filiusfamilias* was given the paterfamilias' *auctoritas* to manage it at his own discretion; specifically, he "might buy, sell, hire and so on, but not (unless specially authorized by the paterfamilias) make a gift, manumit a slave, leave anything by will."[39]

In the classical period, at the beginning of the Principate, Augustus authorized the *filiusfamilias* to dispose of his earnings as a soldier at his own discretion *inter vivos* and *mortis causa* without the *auctoritas* of his paterfamilias. Such military earnings were referred to as *peculium castrense.*[40] However, the paterfamilias maintained a *nudum ius* (mere right) over the *peculium castrense* in the sense that if the son died intestate while in the service, the father inherited it by the *ius peculii* (right of property granted to a dependent) and not by right of intestate succession. When the son was discharged from the service, the ownership over the *peculium castrense* devolved to his paterfamilias. Hadrian eventually extended the right of the *peculium castrense* to the veterans.[41]

In the post-classical period Constantine enacted that the earnings of a *filiusfamilias* as a public servant, lawyer or bishop were to be considered as equivalent to the *peculium castrense* and were referred to as *peculium quasi castrense:* the *filiusfamilias* could dispose of it *inter vivos* and *mortis causa* at his own discretion.[42] Constantine also enacted that the *filiusfamilias* was the owner of whatever property he

[37] Gaius 2, 86–7.

[38] This *peculium* (derived from the father) was later called *profecticium* in order to distinguish it from property which the son acquired either from others (i. e. *peculium adventicium*) or through his own exertions (i. e. *peculium castrense* or *quasi castrense*). Cf. D. 49, 17, 9; also, D. 15, 1, 5, 4.

[39] D. Daube, *Roman Law* (Edinburgh 1969) p. 83.

[40] Gaius 2, 106; D. 49, 17; *Inst.* 2, 12.

[41] D. 49, 17; *Inst.* 2, 12.

[42] P. Voci, *op. cit.* above (n. 7), p. 500 ff.

received from his mother or her ascendants *(bona materna)*, but that the paterfamilias enjoyed the usufruct of it; in case the son were emancipated, the father kept the usufruct over half of such a property. The *bona materna* were referred to as *peculium adventicium*. Under Justinian, the *peculium adventicium* came to include not only the *bona materna* but also all the earnings acquired directly through the exertions of the son, except the *peculium profecticium* (*filiusfamilias'* property derived from the father), the *peculium castrense* and the *peculium quasi castrense.*[43])

We shall now discuss the *filiusfamilias'* obligations and their relationship to the *patria potestas*. Let us begin with the contractual obligations.

In the archaic period a *filiusfamilias* could bind neither himself nor another to a contractual obligation: he had no legal capacity, because he was not *sui iuris;* therefore, he could neither sue nor be sued on a contractual obligation.[44])

In the classical period a *filiusfamilias* (not a *filiafamilias* [daughter under *patria potestas*]) became capable of binding himself or another by contract: he could sue or be sued in a civil procedure;[45]) but in case of condemnation the execution of judgment was suspended, unless the *filiusfamilias* had the *peculium castrense*. When the *filiusfamilias* became *sui iuris*, then the execution was permissible.[46])

But, where the paterfamilias had given his *filiusfamilias* a *peculium* with authorization to manage it, then the execution could be enforced against the paterfamilias to the amount of the *peculium*.[47])

Let us now deal with the delictal obligations. In the archaic period the filiusfamilias was not directly liable for delicts committed, unless caught in the act; the paterfamilias was answerable for him, but

---

[43]) *Ibid.*

[44]) Cf. A. Watson, *op. cit.* above (n. 5) p. 29.

[45]) F. de Zulueta, *op. cit.* above (n. 35), vol. 2, p. 158.

[46]) However, the *senatus consultum Macedonianum* (*Inst.* 4, 7, 7), issued under Vespasian, enacted that a loan, made to a *filiusfamilias*, to be paid after the death of the paterfamilias, was not actionable.

[47]) Gaius 4, 69–74. The Glossators called the *actiones de peculis* against the *patresfamilias actiones adiecticiae*. The *actio adiecticia* against a paterfamilias was not affected by the end of the *patria potestas*, provided the *actio de peculio* was initiated within the year. Cf. F. Schulz, *op. cit.* above (n. 6) p. 156 f.

the paterfamilias' liability for his son was noxal: he either paid a composition for the delict or surrendered the culprit to the injured party.[48]

In the classical period the archaic rule continued to be in practice, except that (a) the *peculium castrense* was now subject to distraint for delicts or debts; (b) the *filiusfamilias* became personally liable for wrongs committed upon becoming *sui iuris* through emancipation or paterfamilias' death *(noxa caput sequitur)*.[49]

In the post-classical period Justinian abolished noxal surrender.[50]

Finally, we must mention some mutual obligations that existed between parents and children. Judicially father and son were not required to testify against each other; the son could sue his father only by explicit authorization of the magistrate.[51] Economically, father and son had mutual obligation of support; indeed, such an obligation extended agnatically to all ascendants and descendants.[52]

Between mother and children the obligation of support during the archaic period was only moral. Under Justinian the legal obligation of support became cognatic.[53]

In conclusion, the *ius publicum* made no distinction between citizens *sui iuris* and *alieni iuris* (under another's power); according to it, all citizens were *sui iuris*. The distinction was made by the *ius privatum*,[54] which, however, was subordinate to the *ius publicum*. Therefore, the paterfamilias' *potestas* over his sons was based only on the *ius privatum;* by the *ius publicum* the *filiifamilias* could start a military and political career notwithstanding the *patria potestas;* in practice, the career would have been difficult if opposed by the paterfamilias;[55] but it was possible.

As a general rule, most of the *filiifamilias* of the affluent classes followed the political pattern of the family; some deviated from the

---

[48] Cf. A. Watson, *op. cit.* above (n. 5) p. 159.
[49] Gaius 1, 140; 4, 75 ff; D. 5, 1, 57.
[50] *Inst.* 4, 8, 7.
[51] Gaius 4, 78; cf. P. Voci, *op. cit.* above (n. 7) p. 484.
[52] Cf. P. Voci, *op. cit.* above (n. 7) p. 502.
[53] *Ibid.*
[54] Cf. A. Watson, *op. cit.* above (n. 5) p. 29.
[55] Cf. D. Daube, *Roman Law* (Edinburgh University Press, 1969), p. 75 ff.

traditional political image of the family either to the conservative side or to the liberal side because of personal convictions; others turned opportunist with changing allegiances. Their political success, however, depended greatly on the family support, which was seldom denied. The case of emancipated sons was similar; they might have felt freer in their choice of political allegiance, but they might have had less family financial support.

The young men who had become *sui iuris* because of their paterfamilias' death present a different situation. Obviously, most of them carried on the family political tradition; some of them became political opportunists, and others embraced a course of political action because of strong personal convictions resulting mostly from their education, from their cultural and spiritual development. However, they could freely pursue the dictates of their conscience only because of their status as patresfamilias which gave them full legal capacity and full control over the family patrimony.

In the late Republic, due to the cultural revolution that was taking place in Rome among the members of the affluent classes a new breed of young politicians appeared on the stage: they were more committed to the claims of their interests and their consciences than the previous generations.[56] The young men who are generally considered responsible for transforming the economic crisis of the late Republic into a constitutional crisis and who were strongly influenced by the cultural revolution, were *patresfamilias*, namely the Gracchi; and the *popularis* movement which they founded was essentially a young movement.[57] However, the causes they espoused from time to time gained the support of some of the older generation.

[56] See the thesis of R. E. Smith (*The Failure of the Roman Republic*, Cambridge, 1955) on the pre-Gracchan "integrated society" of Rome and its moral disintegration afterwards.

[57] Cf. Sallust, *Catilina, passim;* in section 20 the conflict of age is clearly brought out: *viget aetas, animus valet; contra illis annis atque divitiis omnia consenuerunt.* The Catilinarian movement must be considered as an offshoot of the *popularis* movement; as such the early involvement of Caesar and Crassus could be better understood.

II. The Roman Revolution (134–27 B.C.).

What, then, was the underlying cause of the Roman Revolution which resulted in the fall of the Republic?[58]

According to some scholars, the Roman Revolution was strictly the result of family politics (the *factiones* [factions]) for *clientela* (clientele) and therefore the result of political power; for others it was the result of a constitutional crisis in the sense that the old city-state constitution of Rome was inadequate to meet the new needs of the Empire-state; others claimed that the collapse of the Republic was the result of moral bankruptcy; others attributed it to the rise of the volunteer, professional armies which tended to become personal armies through collusion of interests between generals and soldiers; finally, others believed that it was the outcome of an economic crisis. I submit that the cultural revolution[59] in the late Republic transformed the economic crisis[60] into a constitutional crisis and that the so-called *iuvenes seditiosi* (seditious young men) or *nefas patricium* (patrician disgrace)[61] played the major role. The economic crisis, therefore, was the material cause; the cultural revolution, which strained the individual conscience and asserted the individual internal imperative, was the formal cause; and the young men of the affluent classes were the major actors.

The urban immigration. According to Livy,[62] migration of people from the country towns to Rome reached critical proportions around the middle of the 2nd century B.C.

The major cause was the economic expansion in Rome at this time.

[58] Cf. R. Seager, ed., *The Crisis of the Roman Republic: Studies in Political and Social History* (Cambridge, 1969.).

[59] Cf. E. Gabba, "Politica e Cultura agli inizi del I secolo av. C." *Athenaeum* 31 (1953) 259f.

[60] Cf. H. C. Boren, "The Urban Side of the Gracchan Economic Crisis." *American Historical Review* 63 (1957–58) 890–902.

[61] Seneca the Elder, *Suasoriae* 6, 26. Cf. Cicero, *ad Atticum* 1, 14: "barbatuli iuvenes, totus ille grex Catilinae, dux filiola Curionis"; *Pro Murena,* 49: "Catilinam... stipatum choro iuventutis."

[62] Livy 39, 3; 41, 8; 42, 10; Cicero, *Pro Balbo* 24, 54 on the *lex Licinia Mucia* of 95 B.C. Cf. R. W. Husband, "On the Expulsion of Foreigners from Rome." *Classical Philology* 11 (1916) 315ff.

In fact, the unusual wealth coming from the wars and provinces in the first half of the 2nd century B.C. (c. 210–145 B.C.)[63]) had promoted the greatest public and private works program in the history of Rome up to that time.[64]) This feverish building mood required labor and supplies, which in turn spurred the growth of factories, shops, apartments *(insulae)*, etc., to supply the needs of the fast growing population and of the building projects.[65]) A contributing factor for this economic expansion was probably the devaluation of the coin *as* from 1/6 of the pound (i. e., 2 ounces) to 1/12 of the pound (i. e., 1 ounce) at the end of the 2nd Punic War.[66])

Other causes for the urban immigration were the facility by which the migrants could be absorbed into the citizen tribes; the attractions of city-life, i. e., the higher style of living ("how can you keep them down on the farm after they've seen Paris"); farm-bankruptcy, caused by competition of provincial imports and local big farms; the hardships and small rewards of small farming;[67]) and finally, unemployment in the country, due to the growing use of slaves in the *latifundia*.

The economic crisis after 138 B.C. After the sack of Corinth and the fall of Carthage (146 B.C.), the subsequent wars, such as the Numentine War (143–133 B.C.) and the Sicilian slave revolts (135–132 B.C. and 104–99 B.C.), were actually a drain on the treasury. As a result of this shortage of money in the treasury, there was, after the construction of the temple to Mars in 138 B.C., no further important public program of building for 13 years, i. e., until 125 B.C. In this year the Tepular aqueduct (less than 1/5 as long as the Marcian aqueduct built in

[63]) Cf. T. Frank, ed., *An Economic Survey of Ancient Rome*, vol. 1, p. 109ff; H. C. Boren, *op. cit.* above (n. 60).

[64]) *Enciclopedia dell' Arte Antica* (Roma: Istituo dell' Enciclopedia Italiana), vol. 6 (1965) v. *Roma*.

[65]) H. C. Boren, *op. cit.* above (n. 60).

[66]) I must note that the dates regarding emissions and retariffing of the silver and bronze coins in the Republic are not yet firmly established; the dates, therefore, are probable. Cf. H. Mattingly, *Roman Coins from the Earliest Times to the Fall of the Western Empire* (2nd ed.; London, 1960; rpt. with corrections, 1962). See also T. Frank, *op. cit.* above (n. 63) vol. 1, pp. 47, 190, 262 ff.

[67]) This is not to be taken in the sense that "most" of the small farmers were fleeing to the urban centers, but in the sense that a "significant" percentage of peasants were doing so.

140's and delivering less than 1/10 the volume of water) seems to have been the major public work since 138 B.C.[68])

The combination of drastic decline in public works and of increase in slave labor made unemployment in Rome very severe; Rome, or better the Commoners in the late 130's were in the throes of a serious economic depression. Furthermore, the Sicilian slave revolt of 135–132 B.C. not only was a drain on the national treasury, but also reduced substantially the export of wheat from that island, which had become the granary of Rome, causing a food crisis in the city and skyrocketing the price of wheat.

One of the consequences of unemployment was the incurring of debts, and Roman law was harsh on insolvency.[69]) Another consequence was the increase of the clientele of the rich families. A third effect was the rise of precinctal bosses, of vice and exploitation which were facilitated by the overcrowding of the tenements. A fourth effect was the decline of military manpower, since many small farmers having abandoned their farm or gone bankrupt became ineligible for the service. In short, the economic depression in the late 130's B.C. brought into the forefront the *proletarii* with all their urban problems, potentially capable of becoming an explosive political force.[70])

The political factions. The ruling class of Rome, on the other hand, became splintered into family factions, and in the 130's B.C. they formed three major divisions, namely, the traditionalist-conservative senators, the intellectual-liberal magnates, and the reformer-activists.

The main characteristics of the traditionalist- conservative senators were: (i) strict adherence to the *mos maiorum* (ancestral customs); (ii) a suspicious attitude toward anything foreign, un-Roman; and by foreign and un-Roman they meant anything that was new, different or critical of the *mos*; thus, Cato the Elder condemned the works of the Greeks as subversive of the Roman *mos*, because they undermined the Roman character (*virtus* [courage], *pietas* [duty], *disciplina*

[68]) H. C. Boren, *op. cit.* above (n. 60).

[69]) H. F. Jolowicz, *op. cit.* above (n. 5); P. Voci, *op. cit.* above (n. 7).

[70]) A. W. Lintott, *Violence in Republican Rome* (Oxford, 1968); P. A. Brunt, "The Roman Mob," *Past and Present* 35 (1966) 3 f.

[discipline]);[71]) (iii) non-interventionism in foreign affairs; in this respect the Roman conservatives were similar to the oligarchs of the Greek city-states; however, when they were forced to intervene, they tended like the Spartans to treat the vanquished harshly (remember Cato's slogan attached to his speeches in the senate: *delenda Carthago* [Carthage must be destroyed]); for them to incorporate the conquered people into the Roman state was to corrupt the Roman element; (iv) a certain degree of *inhumanitas*; Cato advised the Roman farmers how to obtain the most with the least expense from a slave; in effect, Cato said: when the slave becomes an invalid, it is cheaper to cast him away than to nurse him.

The main characteristics of the intellectual-liberal magnates were: (i) an open attitude toward gradual evolution of the *mos*; (ii) an open attitude toward education; for them culture was spiritually regenerative; it added a new dimension to their lives, a new consciousness of themselves and of their country;[72]) (iii) interventionism in foreign affairs; but their interventionism was not imperialistic in the sense of subjugation and exploitation, but in the sense of incorporation, motivated perhaps by a consciousness of Manifest Destiny for a Roman *cosmos*;[73]) so they were sympathetic to the demands of the Italians for the Roman franchise; (iv) a certain fair-mindedness; whether it was the result of a sense of equity, statesmanship or political opportunism might be disputed.[74])

---

[71]) Plutarch, *Cato Maior* 22. Cf. R. E. Smith, *op. cit.* above (n. 56) p. 23f. According to Sallust (*Cat.* 10), until 146 B.C. the *metus Punicus* kept the Romans in a state of *virtus* (courage), in which domestic politics were marked by *concordia* (concord); according to him, the *certamen gloriae* (struggle for glory) was displayed in the field: the citizens strove to win *gloria* for themselves and *imperium* for the Republic. After 146 B.C. the disappearance of the *metus Punicus* turned the *certamen gloriae* into *ambitio imperii* (desire for power) and *cupido pecuniae* (love of money) for themselves. Cf. D. C. Earl, *The Political Thought of Sallust* (Cambridge, 1961) above (n. 56).

[72]) Cf. R. E. Smith, *op. cit.* above (n. 56) p. 14.

[73]) R. E. Smith, *op. cit.* above (n. 56) p. 13, where he characterizes the Roman literature of the 2nd century B.C. as essentially "social literature; its epic expressed the faith in Rome's destiny." See also pages 31ff.

[74]) For the gradual incorporation of *aequitas* and *bona fides* in the Roman legal system see P. Voci, *op. cit.* above (n. 7). For attempts at agrarian reforms see Laelius' bill in the 140's (Plutarch, *Tiberius Gracchus* 8).

The reformer-activists were actually a phenomenon of four elements that were present in the 130's B.C., namely: the new affluence,[75]) the cultural revolution, the urban economic crisis,[76]) the reaction against conservative intransigence.[77])

I have already referred to the new affluence that began at the turn of the 2nd century B.C., to the economic crisis that brought into the foreground the *proletarii* and, eventually, the proletarian armies, to the greater concentration of wealth and power that later permitted the rise of military potentates. I shall now deal with the cultural revolution which brought a new consciousness, a new sensibility that deepened and enlarged the issues, molded the strong personalities, exacerbated the feuds among the family factions, in short, precipitated a moral crisis,[78]) and with the activist reform movement among the educated young, led to the constitutional crisis of the Republic.

The cultural revolution in the late Republic. Rome from its very beginnings had been exposed to Greek culture through its contacts with Cumae, Naples, Tarentum, Syracuse and the rest of the Greek communities in southern Italy. Indeed, the origins of Roman literature were rooted in Greek literature.[79]) However, this influence had been an Italian Hellenism, i. e., of *Magna Graecia* (Southern Italy), slowly and selectively absorbed into the mainstream of Roman culture. But after the *metus Punicus* (fear of Carthage) had been removed and the Hellenistic cultural centers came under the sway of or in direct contact with Rome in the late Republic, then the Romans entered on a Renaissance period, underwent a cultural revolution which affected art, literature, jurisprudence, politics, marriage..., in short, every aspect of life.

[75]) Sallust, *Cat.* 10.

[76]) H. C. Boren, *op. cit.* above (n. 60).

[77]) The intellectual, liberal Magnates prevailed in the political life of Rome from c. 200 to 175 B.C.; the conservatives prevailed from c. 175 to 133 B.C.; the reformer-activists appeared on the political stage of Rome in 134 B.C. with Tiberius Gracchus.

[78]) Sallust, *Cat.* 10; see above (n. 70). Cf. E. S. Gruen, *Roman Politics and the Criminal Courts* (149–78 B.C.) (Harvard, 1968); F. de Martino, *Storia della Costituzione Romana* (Napoli: Casa Editrice Jovene, 1961) vol. 3, pp. 1–9; R. E. Smith, *op. cit.* above (n. 56).

[79]) Cf. J. W. Duff, *A Literary History of Rome* (3rd ed., New York, Barnes and Noble, 1953, ed. A. M. Duff, rprt. 1960.).

Some of the famous Greek teachers who had a great impact on the Roman society were the stoic Crates of Mallos, Carneades, who shocked the Romans with his moral relativism,[80] the stoic philosopher Diogenes of Babylon, the peripatetic Critolaus, the encyclopedist Panaetius of Rhodes, the stoic Posidonius of Apamea and many others.

The most influential philosophers, however, on the Roman elite were Panaetius of Rhodes[81] who lectured in Rome for 15 years (145–130 B.C.) and, a generation later, his disciple Posidonius of Apamea (135–50 B.C.). Panaetius, by emphasizing the positive characteristics of justice, i. e., friendship and liberality,[82] became the theoretician of the Scipionic circle, of the intellectual, liberal magnates.[83] At the death of Panaetius this role, as a theoretician of the Roman ruling class, was inherited by Posidonius. In his *World History*, which was a sequel of Polybius' *World History*,[84] Rome was at the center. According to Posidonius, the Roman Empire was actually the realization of the stoic cosmopolis; it had an ideal form of government in which all men could live a just life under the leadership of an aristocracy, enlightened by the divine *Logos*. Panaetius and Posidonius not only justified Roman imperialism, but urged the nations to welcome it for their own sake, because it was the fulfilment of the divine cos-

[80] Cicero, *De Republica* 3.

[81] His book, *On Duties*, not only was widely read in Rome but also served as a source to Cicero's *De Officiis*.

[82] Cf. Aristotle, *Nicom. Ethics*, books 5 and 8: justice must be tempered legally by equity (to which the Romans always added *bona fides*) and socially by friendship.

[83] R. E. Smith, *op. cit.*, p. 25, where he states that Panaetius was able to fuse the Roman *ethos* with his stoicism. For the *popularis* and anti-*popularis* cultural circles see E. Gabba, *op. cit.* above (n. 59).

[84] In his *History* Polybius first extolled the Roman constitution as the realization of the Ideal Government, namely, the mixed Constitution; later, however, as this ideal, mixed constitution began to degenerate under the stress of the conflict between the oligarchic intransigence and the Gracchan radicalism, he seems to have reverted to the peripatetic doctrine of the cyclic constitutional development from monarchy to tyranny to aristocracy to oligarchy to democracy to ochlocracy. Cf. F. W. Walbank, *A Historical Commentary on Polybius* (Oxford: The Clarendon Press, Vol. I 1957, vol. II 1967.).

mos.[85]) Yet, in spite of Panaetius' high tribute to the Roman aristocracy his disciple, the historian Polybius, after 146 B.C., began to notice that the Roman ruling class was showing signs of a moral crisis.[86])

The reform movement. The moral crisis of the ruling class coupled with the economic crisis of the Commons led to the reform movement, i. e., the *populares*. Had there not been a cultural revolution that affected a significant percentage of the young people of the affluent classes, there would have been only specific legislation for particular demands; such had been the case in Roman history so far. But in the late Republic there was a cultural revolution that mobilized the young men of the better classes; this combination of cultural revolution, developing new social, political and religious viewpoints, i. e., new life attitudes, and the young men with their instinct of freedom from their elders, did not only call for specific and limited reforms, but created a general, pantelic movement, embracing all life and mobilizing everything, government, economy, education, marriage...; in short, it aimed at a new society *(nova aetas).*[87]) Such movements tend to be totalitarian, and the result of the Roman Revolution was totalitarian.

The main feature, therefore, of the political life in the late Republic was the shift of emphasis from foreign affairs to internal affairs and

---

[85]) Cf. Cicero, *De Republica, passim.* Evidently, the Panaetian-Posidonian stoicism favored an aristocratic (later, under the Empire, a monarchic) government. Panaetius and Posidonius, therefore, were not sympathetic to the Gracchi and the *popularis* movement.

[86]) Polybius 6. However, for the deterioration of the Roman character after 146 B.C. see, for instance, bk 18, 35. It would appear that bks 1–6 were published around 155 B.C., and the rest were published after 140 B.C. Cf. F. W. Walbank, *op. cit.* above (n. 84). See also R. E. Smith, *op. cit.* above (n. 56); Sallust, *Cat.* 10, and above (nn. 71 and 84).

[87]) Virgil, *Eclogue IV; Georgics; Aeneid.* Cf. S. Mazzarino, *Trattato di Storia Romana. Vol. II: L'Impero Romano* (2nd ed.; Roma: Tumminelli 1962.) See also L. S. Feuer, *The Conflict of Generations: The Character and Significance of Student Movements* (New York: Basic Books, 1969) Chapter One. For the Etrusco-Roman concept of crisis and renewal on the Individual, National and Cosmic levels see M. Sordi, "L'idea di crisi e rinnovamento nella concezione romano-etrusca della storia" in *Aufstieg und Niedergang der römischen Welt*, Bd. I, T. 2, ed. H. Temporini (Berlin 1972) p. 781ff.

the tribunates of Tiberius Gracchus (134–133 B.C.) and Gaius Gracchus (124–122 B.C.) were the turning point.

According to Plutarch,[88] the prelude to the reform movement was the agrarian bill of Gaius Laelius, a prominent member of the Scipionic circle, in 140 B.C. when he was consul. Confronted by an uncompromising opposition in the senate, Laelius withdrew the bill and received the dubious name of "wise" *(sophos)*.

In the summer of 134 B.C. Tiberius Gracchus was elected tribune. As soon as he entered on his office, he introduced an agrarian bill; its purpose was to relieve urban unemployment and strengthen the classes of small and middle farmers.[89]

But opposition to the bill was again uncompromising. It stemmed from a number of reasons, namely: (a) the fact that, since the *tributum* (property tax) had been abolished in 168 B.C., the rents from the public land were extremely important to the treasury;[90] (b) the reclaiming of public land, which had become the possession of families for generations through custom, might cause a serious conflict between custom and law *(mos* vs. *lex)*; (c) the eviction of Italian farmers from public land which they had received from the government would undermine their loyalty.[91]

---

[88] Plutarch, *Tiberius Gracchus* 8. Until 177 B.C. the ruling class had removed some of the excess population of Rome by colonization. From 177 B.C. there were no colonies established. It appears that until 140 B.C. the economic expansion absorbed most of the labor force and there was no need for the establishment of colonies. But after the decline of public and private works the unemployment situation in Rome became acute. Unfortunately, the ruling class failed to respond to the economic crisis.

[89] If 10–15 *jugera* of land were just adequate to support a family, and holdings of more than 100 *jugera* were considered *latifundia*, then Tiberius' proposal to distribute the reclaimed public land into farms of about 30 *jugera* aimed to establish quite adequate family farms.

[90] I. e., 10% of the produce on plough land; 20% of the produce on orchards; a poll tax on grazing land (perhaps, 1% of the value of the animal).

[91] The revolt of Fregellae in 125 B.C. and the Social War in 90–88 B.C. were caused not only by the grievances that they received less booty, smaller and less fertile plots of land than the Roman citizens, and that in the service they were treated more harshly than the Romans, but also by the fear of losing their farmlands and by the fact that they were denied the franchise, which would have given them the legal protection they needed.

The conflict between Tiberius and Senate was then widened and deepened by the subsequent actions of Tiberius; namely the presentation of the bill to the plebeian assembly over the *auctoritas* of the senate, the recall of the tribune Octavius, the allocation of the treasury of Pergamon to finance the law.

The passage of the bill by the plebeian assembly over the *auctoritas* of the senate represented a challenge to the customary hegemonic authority of the senate in the state. The recall of the tribune Octavius redefined the relationship of the tribunate to the people: previously the people delegated their sovereign power to the tribunes unconditionally;[92]) now the recall made the delegation conditional, which entailed the absolute control of the electors over the elected at all times, thus practically nullifying the *ius intercessionis* (veto-power). Finally, the passage of the resolution to finance the agrarian law with the treasury of Pergamon, just bequeathed to the Roman people, not only thwarted the senate's attempt to hamstring the implementation of the law by allocating inadequate funds, but also further undermined the power of the senators who had so far monopolized the finances and foreign affairs more or less unchallenged.

But the political warfare between Tiberius and Senate reached its breaking point in the summer of 133 B.C. when Tiberius ran for re-election. The fear that, if Tiberius were elected a second time, no one would be able to stop him from being elected a third term and so on, i. e., the fear that Tiberius might establish an ochlocracy, mobilized the senatorial opposition, and in the ensuing riots Tiberius was killed. The senate followed its success by establishing a *cognitio extra ordinem* (ad hoc judicial investigation) in order to try and execute Tiberius' associates without the benefit of appeal to the *iudicium populi* (assembly of the people sitting as a court) in an attempt to destroy Tiberius' *factio*. But in an atmosphere of political freedom and cultural revolution the high-handed judicial procedure of the senatorial commission instead of deterring Tiberius' followers actually provoked and coalesced them into a national, though amorphous, movement, i. e., the *popularis* movement.

---

[92]) The normal safeguards were the veto power of the colleagues and the one-year term of office.

162

In the summer of 124 B.C. Gaius Gracchus was elected to the tribunate as a *popularis*. In the following year he was returned to the office. During these two terms various laws were passed either by himself or by his associates; among them the following ought to be mentioned for their economic and constitutional importance: (a) the *lex frumentaria*[93]) which provided for the building of granaries and for the government sale of wheat at below market price, i. e., at $6^1/_3$ *asses per modius;* this law, of course, along with the secret ballot laws,[94]) undermined the dependence of the urban *proletarii* on the *nobiles* (nobles) (b) the *lex viaria*[95]) which provided for employment and facilitated commerce; (c) the devaluation of the bronze coinage, i. e., the *as*, by 50%, namely from 1 ounce to 1/2 ounce (from 1/12 of the pound to 1/24 of the pound);[96]) evidently, the public work program and the devaluation of the coinage were meant to increase the circulation of money and to expand the economy; (d) the *lex de colonis deducendis*[97]) which established colonies in southern Italy; (e) the *lex Rubria*[98]) which, passed in 122 B.C. but repealed in 121 B.C., aimed to establish a large colony on the site of Carthage with allotments of about 200 *jugera* per citizen;[99]) (f) the *lex Acilia*[100]) which gave the knights an independent constitutional function in the imperial politics of Rome and, consequently, coalesced the knights into a political order, namely, the *equester ordo*.[101])

[93]) H. C. Boren, *The Gracchi* (New York: Twayne Publishers, Inc., 1968) pp. 91 and 101.

[94]) Cf. the *leges Tabellariae*, namely the *lex Gabinia* of 139 B.C., *lex Cassia* of 137 B.C , *lex Papira* of 131 B.C. and *lex Maria* of 119 B.C.

[95]) B. C. Boren, *op. cit.* above (n. 93) p. 101.

[96]) Cf. H. Mattingly, *Roman Coins from The Earliest Times to the Fall of the Western Empire* (2nd ed., London, 1960; rpt. with corrections, 1962.).

[97]) B. C. Boren, *op. cit.* above (n. 93) p. 102.

[98]) *Ibid.*

[99]) The colony was to be named *Junonia*. Evidently, it aimed to revive the Carthaginian plantations once so prosperous. Caesar eventually established a colony on the site and called it Carthage. Augustus later expanded it. It soon became the capital of the proconsular province of Africa and grew into one of the most flourishing cities of the Empire.

[100]) H. C. Boren, *op. cit.* above (n. 93), p. 95f.

[101]) Eventually, one of the requirements for membership in the order was property worth 400,000 sesterces, whereas that of the senatorial was fixed at

The struggle between the *populares* and the oligarchs came again to a bloody confrontation in 121 B.C. when the senate sponsored a resolution to repeal the Rubrian law for the founding of *Junonia;* a riot ensued and the senate made constitutional history by decreeing *(senatus consultum ultimum)* a state of emergency, which claimed to authorize the consul to employ every means against the *populares* and to suspend the *ius provocationis* (right of appeal to the people) and the *ius intercessionis* (veto-power).[102]) Once again the oligarchs aimed at the annihilation of the *populares*, but once again the results were the opposite, because the material causes were not removed and, consequently, the formal cause (i. e., the cultural revolution) kept moulding new *populares iuvenes audaces* (audacious young men of the *popularis* movement).

Whether Tiberius' measures were in contravention of the Roman *mos*, i. e., unconstitutional, is debatable. According to the oligarchs, they were against the *mos;* according to the Moderates, they were not unconstitutional; the consul of 133 B.C., P. Mucius Scaevola, an established jurist, refused to employ force against Tiberius on the motion of Scipio Nasica.[103])

Evidently, Tiberius adhered to the principle of interpreting the *mos*, i. e., the constitution, as liberally or democratically as he could. It had been claimed that in this approach he had been influenced by his Greek mentors, Blossius of Cumae and Diophanes of Mitylene. Blossius has been described as the theoretician of a stoic socialism, advocating the subordination of individual interests to those of the commonwealth;

1,000,000 sesterces. The equestrian order seemed to have represented the big business of Rome; the smaller business men, known as *tribuni aerari* with property worth about 100,000 sesterces, seemed to have formed a class of their own, having varying success in the political, judicial arena of Rome. Cf. P. A. Brunt, "The Equites in the Late Republic," *Second International Conference of Economic History*, 1962, *Vol. I, Trade and Politics in the Ancient World*, pp. 117–49. See also, M. I. Henderson, "The Establishment of the Equester Ordo," *Journal of Roman Studies* 53 (1963) 61–72.

[102]) Cf. Cicero, *De Oratore* 2, 30, 132. See H. Last, *Cambridge Ancient History* IX, 84. The constitutionality of the *senatus consultum ultimum* was challenged by Julius Caesar in the case against C. Rabirius in 63 B.C. and by the *lex de capite civis Romani* of Clodius in 58 B.C..

[103]) Plutarch, *Tiberius Gracchus* 19.

Diophanes has been described as the practical politician who translated the ideals of stoic socialism into practical policies. Blossius proclaimed the principle of the supremacy of the common good: everything for the people; Diophanes added that the interests of the people were best served by the people: everything by the people.[104]

The gulf between the Oligarchs and the Populares had become deep and unbridgeable; their differences, irreconcilable. The struggle, therefore, had become one for complete supremacy and for the annihilation of the opponents, such as it had been in Greece between the Oligarchs and the Democrats. The Roman Oligarchs generally relied on the *senatus consulta* (senate's decrees) and the consular *imperium;* the Populares wielded the *plebiscita* (laws passed by the plebeian assembly) and the tribunician *potestas.*

In this total struggle powerful new forces were injected, namely the Italian question of citizenship, the question of the permanent courts, the proletarian levy which militarized the conflict in one form or another, and the monetary chaos. Though the Italian question of citizenship was gradually resolved, the economic crises continued to keep Roman society under strain and stress. The unemployment situation with its extreme and frequent fluctuations was irritating not only because of its hardships but also because of the fact that the empire was being exploited by a very few families.[105] The monetary chaos and the widespread debts further aggravated the crisis. In 91 B.C. Livius Drusus[106] issued silver coins *(denarii)* with 1/8 bronze, apparently in order to overcome a shortage of silver money. This debased silver coinage was probably accompanied by a promise to redeem it as soon as possible. But in 85 B.C. the praetor Marius Gratidianus was compelled to place certain marks on the new issues of debased *denarii* in order to distinguish them from the good money (i. e. the pure silver *denarii*). In 82/1 B.C. Sulla decreed that the debased *denarii* should be

---

[104] Plutarch, *Tiberius Gracchus* 20. Cf. D. R. Dudley, "Blossius of Cumae," *Journal of Roman Studies* 31 (1941) 94 f; T. S. Brown, "Greek Influences onTiberius Gracchus," *Classical Journal I* 42 (1946–47) 471f.; G. Bloch and J. Carcopino, *Histoire Romaine: La République Romaine de 133 à 44 a. J. C.* (3rd ed.; Paris: Presses Univ. de France, 1952) pp. 196–98.

[105] Sallust, *Cat.* passim. Plutarch, *Tiberius Gracchus* 9.

[106] T. Frank, *op. cit.* above (n. 63) vol. 1, pp. 266–71.

accepted at their face value; in other words, the government refused to redeem them. In 89 B.C. the bronze coin *as* was devalued from 1/2 ounce to 1/3 ounce (i.e., from 1/24 of the pound to 1/36 of the pound). Both devaluations seem to have been attempts to increase the circulation of money in order to overcome a severe contraction of the money supply. But the result seems to have been a monetary chaos: "at that time the value of the coins fluctuated so much that no one could tell what he was worth."[107])

Coupled with the monetary crisis was a severe and widespread debt. During the Social War (90–88 B.C.) and the Civil War (88–82 B.C.) many families of the landed nobility ran short of cash, because they were cut off from their estates, some of which suffered much damage, and borrowed heavily. According to Appian,[108]) riots exploded in 89 B.C. between creditors and debtors. The debtors not only were putting off payments on their loans on the plea of money shortage, of the Social War and of the civil commotion, but also accused the creditors of charging interest in contravention of an old law that forbade it, and threatened to exact legal penalties. The creditors, on the other hand, claimed that time had sanctioned the charging of interest and demanded it according to custom. The praetor A. Sempronius Asellio permitted both parties to proceed against each other in court, thus to bring before the judges the deadlock between law *(nomos)* and custom *(ethos)*. But the exasperated creditors killed the praetor. In 86 B.C., according to Sallust,[109]) the consul Valerius Flaccus, on account of the magnitude of the debts, passed a law *(lex Valeria)* which enacted that bronze coins could replace silver coins at par value (on a one to one basis) in satisfaction of the debt. Since one silver sesterce was equivalent to four *asses*, the law has been interpreted to mean a remittance of 3/4 of all debts, i. e., 75% of the debt was cancelled.[110])

Up to the time of Catiline's conspiracy the debt legislation seems to have been concerned mostly with the financially distressed nobility whose assets were largely in land. Periodically, these big landowners

---

[107]) Cicero, *De Officiis* 3, 80.
[108]) Appian, *Civil War* 1, 54.
[109]) Sallust, *Cat.* 33; Velleius Paterculus 2, 23.
[110]) T. Frank, *op. cit.* above (n. 63) vol. 1, p. 270.

ran short of cash and preferred to resort to debts rather than liquidate some of their assets.[111]) But then they proceeded to obtain relief from the debts through legislation. One of the main goals of the reform program of the Catilinarian movement[112]) was to extend the legislative relief from debts[113]) to the Commons. In fact, the unemployment situation during the late Republic was highly fluctuating, due to the intermittent programs of private and public works, and, as a result, many Commoners incurred debts. Similarly, the small and middle farmers had been hit by the social, civil and slave wars even more than the landed aristocracy; their lands too suffered great damage; they too preferred to resort to debts rather than sell their small plots; they too were burdened with debts.

According to Dio,[114]) the Catilinarian movement also championed a land reform bill for the poor people, since the oligarchs had just defeated the Rullan agrarian bill. Indeed, the defeat of the Rullan bill probably strenghtened the Catilinarian group, representing the extreme left of the *popularis* movement. Their advocacy, however, to seize the consular imperium from the Oligarchs if need be by force precipitated a serious crisis in the *popularis* movement. Then the exposure of Catiline's violent threats and the subsequent execution of the leaders damaged it irretrievably.[115])

III. Conclusion

In Republican Rome both religion (specifically, the cult of the ancestors) and family structure *(patria potestas)* were such as to sanction the supremacy of the Elder in the community. Entrenched in the senate, the deliberative and executive council of the state, they essen-

---

[111]) Sallust, *Cat.* 35.

[112]) For the various groups of Catiline's supporters see Cicero, *In Cat. II*, 4; 17–23; Sallust, *Cat.* 17–18; 33; 36–37. For a discussion of Catiline's *tabulae novae* see Z. Yaretz, "The Failure of Catiline's Conspiracy," *Historia* 12 (1963) 485 f.

[113]) Cicero, *De Officiis* 2, 84.

[114]) Dio Cassius 37, 30, 2.

[115]) According to Cicero (*Pro Flacco* 95), the people used to decorate the tomb of Catiline with flowers. The tombs of the Gracchi and many other *populares*, who died for the cause of the common people, we are told, were also strewn with flowers by the people.

tially controlled public life; as heads of their powerful families, they controlled private life.

A gerontocratic society will not generate a juvenocratic movement, unless the Elders are causing an economic and political crisis, which in turn is a result of a moral crisis, and unless there is a free expanding culture which tends to emancipate the young men from their Elders, to replace ancestral authority *(mos maiorum)* with that of reason, i. e., an external criterion *(auctoritas* and *disciplina)* with an internal criterion (conscience).[116]

In Rome until the 2nd century B.C. the senate's authority was paramount in the state; its leadership was mostly unchallenged, because it had been moderately progressive.[117] Furthermore, the younger elements of the community had been engaged in persistent warfare; many of them had been emancipated as settlers of new colonies; and the cultural expansion had been gradual and limited to very few people. But from the 2nd century B.C., after the victorious conclusion of the 2nd Punic War, Roman society began to undergo an economic and cultural revolution, which with the Gracchi developed into a constitutional crisis that led to the fall of the Republic. During this time the Roman youth lived in a social reality which, on the one hand, in principle was domestically despotic, politically oligarchic and economically exploitative;[118] on the other hand, culturally, it underwent a spiritual revolution through its wide-open exposure to the Greek philosophical and political theories and practices.

The situation from 134 B.C. to the fall of the Republic revealed an enormous gulf, both economically and culturally, between the ruling class and the Commons: on the one hand, the few controlled the wealth and the government, on the other hand, the many were experiencing a severe economic depression; on the one hand, the new philosophical and political influence from Greece was developing a new social consciousness among the educated youth of the well to do families, on the other hand, the tragedy of real society persisted.

[116] Cf. L. S. Feuer, *op. cit.* above (n. 87).

[117] Cf. H. S. Maine, *Ancient Law* (10th ed; London, 1884; rpt. Beacon Press, 1963) pp. 20 ff.

[118] Cf. E. S. Gruen, *op. cit.* (above) n. 78, on the institution of the *quaestiones perpetuae.*

The movement of the *populares*, established by the Gracchi, was essentially a movement of the educated youth of the affluent classes of Rome, of the *iuvenes audaces*. It sprang from idealism and psychological fervor; it was motivated by the back-to-the-people spirit.[119] The movement of the *populares*, therefore, was not a creation of the Commons, but for the Commons. It took momentum and caused a constitutional crisis only because, on the one hand, the oligarchy failed to respond adequately to the economic crisis and to the new social consciousness; on the other hand, the idealism and psychological fervor of the intellectual youth, when confronted by frustrating opposition, unleashed its revolutionary instinct and thus transformed an economic crisis into a constitutional crisis by advocating radical reforms,[120] indeed the replacement of the oligarchy by a democracy in the Greek fashion of political struggle.[121]

In brief, were the *populares* political opportunists or reformers turned activists?

The *populares* were a phenomenon of the cultural revolution and economic crisis. Some of them, the core of the *popularis* movement, were sincere reformers, turned activist, when confronted by frustrating opposition; others might have been political opportunists, and perhaps many of them were of doubtful temper with changing allegiances. However, had there not been a nucleus of genuine reformers, the movement would have lost momentum and would have disintegrated when confronted by judicial and physical repression. The fact that they resorted to violence does not impugn their integrity; it only reveals their zeal and dedication; true believers in a just cause are prone to turn activist or, one might say, fanatic. But can force, in the pursuit of a just "social" cause, be justified in order to overcome force and political establishment? In foreign affairs the Roman answer would have been yes; in internal affairs the history of Rome would also give a positive answer. The Roman historical tradition records that the Republic (the *libertas*) was established by revolution; the political

---

[119] Plutarch, *Tiberius Gracchus*.

[120] Cf. L. S. Feuer, *op. cit.* above (n. 87).

[121] Cf. A. W. Lintott, *Violence in Republican Rome* (Oxford: The Clarendon Press, 1968), p. 177.

equalization of the patricians and plebeians (in practice, only the wealthy plebeians) was a result of brinkmanship, military mutinies and civil riots; and finally the enfranchisement of the Italians was the result of open revolt.

In short, an economic crisis, during a cultural revolution, tends to mobilize the young under a national issue against the rule of the Elders, and – due to their emotional idealism – to turn a significant percentage of them into activism and martyrdom: in the pursuit of justice they will oppose power with power, violence with violence; in these conditions the boundaries of the law are blurred and extremism is justified. This seems to have been the case of the Roman Revolution (134–27 B.C.).

Chapter 10

THE GENERATION GAP IN CATULLUS
AND THE LYRIC POETRY OF HORACE

Valerie Broege

Vanier College — Snowdon Campus

I. Catullus

Important keys to understanding the background of the various facets
of Catullus' thinking on the "generation gap" are his life style and his
youth. As Daniel Harmon points out,[1]) Catullus was alienated from
the traditional pursuits and goals of the typical Roman citizen of his
time. With the exception of his sojourn in Bithynia on the staff of
C. Memmius (Cat., poems 10 and 28), he does not seem to have adopt-
ed the political and military career appropriate for a young man of
his prominent patrician family. Instead, in further deviation from *mos
maiorum* (Roman custom), he seems to have focused his attention on
his mistress Lesbia and the writing of poetry in the company of other
poets of the so-called neoteric school. An average Roman would have
thought his preoccupation with an extra-marital liaison ridiculous.
In poems 5 and 72 Catullus seems well aware of the fact that his love
for Lesbia far transcends the casual affair deemed acceptable for a
young Roman. Even in his poetry Catullus was at sharp variance with
the conservative epic-tragic tradition of impersonal poetry with its
Stoic overtones and national relevance. Catullus chose to write personal poetry in a sensual, even hedonistic vein, with only occasional
references, usually negative, to political figures of his time. In his
poetry Catullus' overwhelming interest was, of course, his beloved
Lesbia. One of his early poems, 51, in imitation of a Sapphic ode,
describes Catullus' sensations on beholding Lesbia. From this tribute
to the Greek poetess, Harmon concludes that Catullus wished to be

---

[1]) Daniel Patrick Harmon, *The Concept of Alienation in Catullus' Poetry*,
Northwestern University Dissertation Microfilm, Ann Arbor, Michigan, 1969.

[2]) Harmon, *op. cit.* above (n. 1), 8, 95.

the "Roman Sappho".[2]) Whether or not this was actually Catullus' intention does not alter the fact that even in his poetry Catullus did not conform to the usual standards of his day.

Catullus' rebellious life style was probably due equally to his temperament and his youth. It was a *topos*, or commonplace, in both Greek and Latin literature to think of a man's life in terms of various ages, with a different demeanor and characteristics assigned to each.[3]) Probably the two best known ancient accounts of the ages of man are Aristotle (*Rhetoric* II. 12–14) and Horace (*Ars Poetica* 153–178). Leaving aside Horace for the moment, let us see what Aristotle says on the subject of youth:

> "The young, as to character, are ready to desire and to carry out what they desire. Of the bodily desires they chiefly obey those of sensual pleasure and these they are unable to control. Changeable in their desires and soon tiring of them, they desire with extreme ardor, but soon cool; for their will, like the hunger and thirst of the sick, is keen rather than strong. They are passionate, hot-tempered, and carried away by impulse, and unable to control their passion; for owing to their ambition they cannot endure to be slighted, and become indignant when they think they are being wronged. They are ambitious of honor, but more so of victory; for youth desires superiority, and victory is a kind of superiority. And their desire for both these is greater than their desire for money, to which they attach only the slightest value, because they have never yet experienced want, as Pittacus said in his pithy remark on Amphiaraus. They are not ill-natured but simple-natured, because they have never yet witnessed much depravity; confiding, because they have as yet not been often deceived; full of hope, for they are naturally as hot-blooded as those who are drunken with wine, and besides they have not yet experienced many failures. For the most part they live in hope, for hope is concerned with the future as memory

[3]) For a survey of the appearance of the theme of the ages of man in ancient literature, with some modern parallels, see Cornelia G. Harcum, "The Ages of Man: A Study Suggested by Horace, *Ars Poetica*, Lines 153–178," *Classical World* 7 (1914), 114–118.

is with the past. For the young the future is long, the past short; for in the morning of life it is not possible for them to remember anything, but they have everything to hope; which makes them easy to deceive, for they readily hope. And they are more courageous, for they are full of passion and hope, and the former of these prevents them fearing, while the latter inspires them with confidence, for no one fears when angry, and hope of some advantage inspires confidence. And they are bashful, for as yet they fail to conceive of other things that are noble, but have been educated solely by convention. They are high-minded, for they have not yet been humbled by life nor have they experienced the force of necessity; further, there is high-mindedness in thinking oneself worthy of great things, a feeling which belongs to one who is full of hope.

In their actions, they prefer the noble to the useful; their life is guided by their character rather than by calculation, for the latter aims at the useful, virtue at the noble. At this age more than any other they are fond of their friends and companions, because they take pleasure in living in company and as yet judge nothing by expediency, not even their friends. All their errors are due to excess and vehemence and their neglect of the maxim of Chilon, for they do everything to excess, love, hate, and everything else. And they think they know everything, and confidently affirm it, and this is the cause of their excess in everything. If they do wrong, it is due to insolence, not to wickedness. And they are inclined to pity, because they think all men are virtuous and better than they really are; for they measure their neighbors by their own inoffensiveness, so that they think that they suffer undeservedly. And they are fond of laughter, and therefore witty; for wit is cultured insolence. Such then is the character of the young.[4])

When one reads this description of youth, one realizes how many aspects of it are mirrored in Catullus' poetry. Catullus certainly represents himself as a passionate, sensual person in the Lesbia poems,

---

[4]) Translation by John Henry Freese in the Loeb Classical Library edition of Aristotle, *The Art of Rhetoric*, London, 1926.

particularly 5, 7, and 51, and in 48, one of the Juventius poems. That he has difficulty in controlling his emotions appears clearly in 8, 50, 76, 85, and 104. The length of time it took for Catullus to become aware of Lesbia's true character illustrates the naive trust typical of the young. Even when he had some glimmer of what she was really like, he still hoped for the best (107 and 109) at least for a time. As a lover Catullus, conveniently forgetting the fact that he was an adulterer, always regarded himself as the epitome of nobility and loyalty (37, 72, 75, 76, 87). It is because of Lesbia's faithlessness that he suffers undeservedly (72, 75, 76). Again Catullus seems to conform to the typical youthful characteristic of enjoying the camaraderie of friends (9, 10, 12, 13, 14, 44, 50). It is probably not altogether amiss to attribute Catullus' early death in part to excessive emotional grief over the death of his brother and the loss of Lesbia's love (65, 68, 76). Catullus' tendency to excess runs all through his poetry: the extravagant language with which he praises Lesbia and affirms his love (5, 7, 51, 86) and his equally extravagant denunciation of her promiscuity (11 and 58); the hyperbolic expressions of his joy when in the company of his friends (9, 13, 50); and the vitriolic invective with which he assails his enemies, poetic (14, 36, 95), political (10, 28, 29, 47, 52, 57), and personal (23, 24, 37, 39, 42, 97); the extreme happiness he felt upon leaving Bithynia (31, 46) and the extreme grief he experienced when his brother died (65, 68, 101). He even prefers his wine totally undiluted (27). Also in illustration of Aristotle's remarks on the character of youth, Catullus felt himself suffering undeservedly at the hands of friends who either betrayed him (15, 21, 30, 40, 58, 73, 77, 82, 91, 100) or failed to give him sympathy in his hour of need (38). The final characteristic of youth mentioned by Aristotle is the love of laughter and wit. Again there is considerable evidence to show that Catullus greatly appreciated both, especially in the company of his friends or Lesbia (12, 13, 22, 50, 51, 53, 56, 68, 86).

Having now described Catullus' life style and the biases of his youthful perspective, let us examine how he handles the theme of the "generation gap" in his poetry. For my purposes, I define "generation gap" as any indication of tension between the generations or acknowledgment of significant differences in conduct and/or point of view in the older and younger generations.

In two of his poems, 61 and 62, Catullus offers obvious instances of his adherence to the theory of the ages of man. In 61 Catullus clearly has this idea in mind when he speaks of Manlius and his young male lover. It is time for the boy to put childish things aside, as symbolized by his giving up of the nuts; he must now enter upon manly estate (61.122–136). For Manlius as well such a love is no longer appropriate when a man is married (61.137–144). Women too have duties and activities appropriate to their age and status. As unmarried girls they are virgins looking forward to marriage (61.36–38), upon marriage they are to participate with enthusiasm in conjugal relations (61.147–149), as matrons they will assist in the marriage ceremony of the young bride (61.182–184), and will remain happily living with their husbands into old age (61.152–159). As a couple the husband and wife have the privilege of enjoying themselves together, but also the duty of producing offspring for the continuation of the family line (61.207–211).

Poem 62, another wedding hymn, also has a coming-of-age aspect, particularly in reference to the bride. The chorus of maidens complains that in marriage the girl is cruelly torn from the embrace of her mother (62.20–24) and that she is dear to her own as long as she remains a virgin (62.44–46). The chorus of youths, on the other hand, retorts that the complaints of the maiden about her impending marriage are feigned (62.36–37; cf. 66.15–18), and that it is not fitting for a maiden to grow old unwed. On the contrary, when wed to a suitable husband at the right time, she is more dear to her husband and less distasteful to her father (62.55–57). She should not resist her parents and her husband-to-be (62.59–65), but, by implication, she should cease being a child and enter upon womanly estate.

In 108 Catullus may be hinting at the ages of man concept in his view of Cominius. In antiquity old men, such as Nestor, were frequently granted great respect owing to the store of wisdom and experience they had acquired through the years. Yet it appears in 108 that Cominius has acquired nothing but base morals to disgrace his old age, for which he deserves the gruesome punishment Catullus describes and hopes the people will decree for him.

Catullus alludes in comic fashion to the Roman tradition of *mos maiorum* in describing the generational continuity in speech habits. In 84 Arrius is presented as a parvenu attempting to affect educated speech but making mistakes in the use of his aspirates. Catullus says that his maternal grandparents, mother, and freedman uncle all spoke in the same fashion (84.5–6). In a considerably more solemn context Catullus again refers to the custom of one's forefathers which he is following in the case of the funeral rites for his dead brother (101.7–9).

In two of his poems we find Catullus subscribing to the philosophy of "like breeds like," be it for better or worse. The positive illustration of this concept appears in 61.212–226, in which Catullus is musing on the future birth of a little Torquatus who will be similar in physical appearance and virtue to his parents, just as Telemachus embodies his mother Penelope's high reputation. As a negative example of the same principle, Catullus in 33 vilifies the thief Vibennius and his profligate son, balancing the crimes of the one against the other.

Probably the most maligned symbol in antiquity of inter-generational strife, the step-mother, appears once in Catullus' poetry.[5] In 23 Catullus sarcastically enumerates the various "blessings" the impoverished Furius enjoys. Among them is a step-mother. She is described as

---

[5] In Latin literature step-mothers have a generally bad press. Some of the adjectives applied to them include *saeva* ("cruel;" Vergil, *Geor.* II. 128; Quint. II. 10. 5), *iniusta* ("unjust;" Vergil, *Ecl.* 3.33), and *scelerata* ("wicked;" Ovid *Fasti* III. 853). A proverb indicating the implacability of step-mothers was *apud novercam queri* ("to complain before a step-mother," i. e., "to complain in vain;" Plautus, *Pseud.* 1. 3. 80). Tacitus (*Ann.* XII. 2) mentions the *novercalia odia* ("enmities of step-mothers"), and the "novercales Liviae in Agrippinam stimuli" ("stepmotherly incitements of Livia against Agrippina;" *Ann.* I. 33). Step-mothers were notorious for mixing poisonous brews for their step-children (Ovid, *Meta.* I. 147; cf. Vergil, *Geor.* II. 128–130).

Various mythological tales about the cruelty of step-mothers to their step-children underscore their bad reputation. For example, we have the unedifying stories of Phaedra and Hippolytus, and Phylonome and Tenes. In both cases the step-mother tried to seduce her step-son, was spurned, and then falsely accused the young man of attempted rape, for which there were unpleasant consequences. Medea almost succeeded in poisoning her step-son, Theseus.

Hera was particularly notorious for the malice she bore as a step-mother, not only against Dionysus, but also Heracles. In addition, Hera also had Epaphus, her step-son by Io, kidnapped, and she persecuted her step-son Arcas along with his mother Callisto.

The story of Ino provides us with a plethora of crimes committed or attempted by step-mothers. First Ino plotted to kill her step-children, Phrixus and Helle, but was thwarted by their real mother, Nephele. Later Hera drove Athamas and Ino

being *lignea* ("like dry wood"; 23.6), with teeth capable of chewing even a flint stone (23.3–4).

Many of Catullus' comments on the generation gap stem either directly or indirectly from his unconventional relationship with Lesbia. There seem to be hints in Catullus' poetry that his father and perhaps his other relatives disapproved of his liaison with Lesbia.[6] It is obvious that they could scarcely be happy about Catullus' dead-end love affair with a married woman, who could not bear him any legitimate children to carry on his family name. Thus, when Catullus' brother died prematurely, he could truly lament the fact that his family would have no hope of an heir (68.19–26; 90–100).

Cicero (*De Officiis* I. 160) expresses the common Roman sentiment about a man's hierarchy of duties—his first duty is to the gods, the second to his state, the third to his parents. Thus, it is significant that Catullus breaks from this tradition to affirm that Lesbia comes first; he loves her more than himself and all his own (58.1–3; 68.159–160). He has even had to do battle because of his relationship with her (37.11–14). The mutterings of the stern old men in 5.1–3 may indeed be those of Catullus' father and other relatives who find themselves unable to share Catullus' celebration of life and love with a promiscuous, married woman.

Perhaps owing in part to the probable altercations he had with his father about Lesbia, Catullus in several instances seems to view an old parent as a burden. He emphasizes the weakness of the aged parent, particularly with his repeated use of the word *tremulus* (17.11–12; 61.51–52, 157–159; 68.142).[7]

mad, since he had colluded with his wife Ino in harboring the infant Dionysus, Hera's step-son. Some time afterward, believing that Ino had been killed by wild beasts while hunting, Athamas married for a third time, siring twin sons by Themisto.When Ino returned to the palace alive, Themisto tried to have Ino's sons killed, but Ino, perceiving her intentions, by a ruse had Themisto's twins killed instead.

[6] See Phyllis R. Young, "Catullus on Parenthood," *Classical Journal* 63 (1968), 267–268.

[7] See also Catullus 64. 305–307 and 316 for his characterization of the Three Fates as old women. The adjective *tremulus* ("trembling;" 307) makes yet another appearance in the context of old age. T. E. Kinsey, "Irony and Structure in Catullus 64," *Latomus* 24 (1965), 924, believes that Catullus is poking fun at the gods in this section of the poem.

In spite of these rather negative comments about old parents, Catullus elsewhere seems to have strong feelings about what a child and his parents owe each other. A parent should have children on whom to depend (61.66–68); Catullus draws a very poignant picture of an aged grandfather, belatedly presented with a grandson and heir by his only daughter (68.119–124). Up to the time of marriage mothers and daughters are very close (cf. 3. 3–10), as symbolized by the taking of the bride by force from her mother's arms (61.56–58; 62.20–25). Yet the suitable marriage of a child, particularly a daughter, is regarded by the parents as a blessing (cf. 64.379–380); the daughter is then less distasteful to her father (62.56–57). A daughter should not resist the choice of spouse made by her parents; it is her duty to obey her mother and father (62.26–30, 59–65). The old matrons have the duty of settling the young bride in the marriage chamber (61.182–184). An old distinguished family has the duty of continuing its line with the birth of offspring (61.207–226) who resemble both their parents in looks and virtue. The young couple should employ their vigorous youth in conjugal love with a view to producing children (61.228–231).

From these remarks of Catullus it seems that he had a traditionalist view, at least in theory, of the respective duties of children and parents. However, because of the probable conflicts with his father over his relationship with Lesbia, he was unable to fulfill the ideal role of son. Instead he has lavished on Lesbia the kind of love that a father has for his sons and sons-in-law (72.3–4). Although he has advised the young bride of 62 not to fight against her parents' choice of a prospective marital partner, Catullus seems to have scorned parental advice about Lesbia (cf. 37.11–14). Instead of pleasing his family with the sanctified marriage of a Manlius and Junia, Catullus has had to settle for clandestine meetings at a friend's house when Lesbia could spare the time from her husband and other lovers (68.67–69, 131–137, 143–158).

Probably Catullus felt a good deal of tension and anguish in having to defy his father because of his love for Lesbia. I believe that traces of this anguish can be found in the way that Catullus has handled some of the mythological material in his poetry. In this connection I find his treatment of the Ariadne and Theseus episode in 64 especially relevant. I agree to a certain extent with the autobiographical approach of

Putnam[8]) that would see Catullus' plight mirrored in part in Ariadne's fate. In succumbing to her overwhelming love for Theseus, Ariadne has forsaken her father, sister, brother, and mother in preference for Theseus (64.117–120, 132–133, 149–151, 180–181), just as Catullus has given Lesbia the highest place in his affections. Theseus has proven to be forgetful of his promises of marriage to Ariadne; his words are written in the wind (64.58–59, 139–142). Catullus uses similar imagery to describe Lesbia's faithlessness (70). Because Ariadne has deserted her native land and relatives only to be abandoned by her perfidious lover, she prays that a similar misfortune might befall Theseus (64.200–201).

I believe that it is no accident that Catullus describes carefully just how beloved Theseus was by his father. Aegeus says that his son is dearer to him than a long life of his own (64.215), just as Catullus calls Lesbia "his life" (104.1; 109.1), dearer to him than his own life (68.159–160). Catullus makes it clear that the old man Aegeus lives only for his son (64.215–245), just as Theseus was the focal point of Ariadne's existence and Lesbia was that of Catullus'. So it is a *quid pro quo* when Theseus causes the death of his father through negligence just as by the same fault in character he had destroyed Ariadne emotionally (64.246–250). Although Catullus does not invoke a curse on Lesbia for her infidelity, it is clear that he experienced a crushing sense of desolation with nothing but an emotional and physical breakdown to show for it (76). He hasn't even followed the well-intentioned advice of his father, which Theseus had at least honored (64.158–163) in regard to any relationship with Ariadne. Catullus' plight was even worse than that of Ariadne. Although she estranged herself from her family for the sake of Theseus, only to be rejected in turn by him, at least she had the consolation of marriage with a god. By contrast, Catullus had grieved his father for nothing, and I believe his anguish in having done so led him to choose the death of Aegeus as a blow for Theseus of sufficient magnitude to match the sufferings of Ariadne. It must be remembered that Catullus was unique in linking Ariadne's

---

[8]) M. C. J. Putnam, "The Art of Catullus 64," *Harvard Studies in Classical Philology* 65 (1961), 165–205; see also Douglas F. S. Thomson, "Aspects of Unity in Catullus 64," *Classical Journal* 57 (1961), 49–57.

curse with Aegeus' death. He must have had a reason for doing so. Presumably Catullus could have structured 64 in such a way as to have used, for example, the episodes of Theseus' disillusioned departure from Athens and subsequent death by treachery as appropriate fulfillments of Ariadne's curse, since these events parallel to a certain extent what happened to Ariadne.

Continuing our discussion of 64, we can make some interesting points regarding Catullus' views of the "good old" generations of the past. It is a well-known propensity of the ancient Greeks and Romans to look upon the past, or at least certain parts of it, with rose-colored glasses.[9]) Important for our purposes here is Hesiod's version of the five ages of man's history. The first age of gold is the best, with a steady decline until we reach the fourth age of the heroes, which marks an improvement. It is this age of the heroes with which Catullus deals in 64. As Curran points out,[10]) at first glance one might be tempted to say that Catullus views the age of the heroes as a kind of ideal, especially when he addresses the heroes as having been born in the happiest time of the ages (64.22–25; cf. 68.153–154).

But dark shadows haunt even the marriage of Peleus and Thetis, which was regarded as particularly blessed. Although Catullus makes Thetis a willing bride, one must remember that most of the versions of the story indicated that Thetis was strongly opposed to marriage with Peleus and had to be tricked and wrestled into it. Also of significance is Catullus' brief mention that Zeus himself has set aside his love for Thetis and given her to Peleus (64.26–27). We know that he did this perforce, since he did not wish to fulfill a prophecy that should he marry Thetis, he would sire a son stronger than himself. The unpleasant aspects of this episode are alluded to when Prometheus appears at the wedding, bearing the traces of an old punishment (64.294–297) which he suffered at the hands of Zeus partly because he would not reveal the secret prophecy to Zeus immediately.

---

[9]) See Arthur O. Lovejoy and George Boas, *Primitivism and Related Ideas in Antiquity*, Baltimore, 1935, especially 23–102 on chronological primitivism in Greek and Roman mythology and historiography.

[10]) Leo C. Curran, "Catullus 64 and the Heroic Age," *Yale Classical Studies* 21 (1969), 171–192; see also Kinsey, *op. cit.*, 911–931.

Even more disturbing is Catullus' description of the glorious future offspring of Peleus and Thetis. His most bloodthirsty aspects are emphasized. The Phrygian streams will flow with Trojan blood, mothers will mourn their sons killed by Achilles mowing the fields with slaughter, the Scamander's channels will be choked by the corpses of Achilles' victims (64.343–360). To cap this gory recital of the future hero's deeds, Catullus describes the pathetic sacrifice of an innocent maiden, Polyxena, over Achilles' grave (64.362–370). Catullus seems to be indicting the values of the heroic code, as is also implied in his reference to the third heir of perjured Pelops (64.346). Such a reference reminds us that from Tantalus to Electra and Orestes the family was a veritable hotbed of crime and intrigue.

Having seen the many dark aspects of what was thought to be a nearly ideal marital union, Catullus' rather pessimistic view of the heroic age is further intensified by the murder and betrayal involved in the story of Ariadne and Theseus. Even though Ariadne is saved by Bacchus, who claims her as his bride, the main emphasis in the account is on Ariadne's abandonment by Theseus and the curse she invokes on him.

At first glance the conclusion of poem 64 seems to contrast the piety of the age of heroes with the present state of degeneration in morals, but on closer inspection certain ambiguities appear, echoing Catullus' treatment of the myths in the earlier part of the poem. Catullus makes the point that in the days of yore when people were pious, the gods deigned to show themselves in mortal company. But, as Curran points out,[11] Catullus expressly states that even for the occasion of the wedding of Peleus and Thetis, the mortal guests withdrew before the gods arrived with their gifts (64.276–279). Furthermore, Apollo and Diana refused to attend the wedding celebration (64.299–302)—an ominous sign when one remembers the enmity that Apollo will bear against Achilles, contributing to his death.

It is also interesting to note that examples can be cited from the heroic age in illustration of some of the various crimes that Catullus imputes to his contemporary, degenerate age. Catullus mentions fratricide (64.399); Thyestes with the help of his son Aegisthus killed

[11] Curran, *op. cit.* above (n. 10), 185–186.

his brother Atreus. Eteocles and Polynices killed each other in the siege of Thebes. Catullus also alludes to two types of irregular sexual relationships—a father sleeping with his son's wife and a mother sleeping with her son (64.401–404). The latter sin obviously reminds one of Oedipus and Jocasta, although Catullus seems to attribute unconsciousness of the deed only to the son, whereas both Oedipus and his mother were married unwittingly. However, even within the scope of poem 64 in the Ariadne episode, one might be reminded of her mother Pasiphae's unnatural lust for Poseidon's bull, and Catullus' reference to Pelops and his line might make one think of Thyestes marrying his own daughter, Pelopia. Examples might be multiplied of other incestuous relationships in the heroic age—e.g., Cinyras' unconscious seduction by his daughter Smyrna—but it suffices to point out that such relationships were by no means to be found only in the degenerate present.

Thus, it can be seen that Catullus' reaction to the past is complex. On the one hand, he can look to the heroic age with a certain degree of nostalgia, but at the same time he seems to see the seeds of the present moral degradation in the past. Past and present are not all that dissimilar. Particularly in his treatment of Achilles, to quote Curran, "there is tension between simple heroism and a more civilized sensibility, between admiration for the hero and awareness that he was just a very efficient killer."[12]) Perhaps Catullus believed that all utopian views are ultimately illusory, and, to return to the autobiographical approach to 64, he may be projecting his disillusionment with his "ideal love affair" with Lesbia.

Catullus seems to be obsessed by the theme of improper family relationships as expressed in perverse sexual unions. To supplement his generalized catalogue in 64, in a number of his other poems he names some contemporary individuals who indulged in incest of various types. Noteworthy in this respect is Gellius, usually identified as L. Gellius Poplicola, the variety of whose sexual irregularities is duly recorded by Catullus. He seduced his aunt (74, 88, 89), his mother (88, 89, 90), and his sister (88, 89),. in addition to numerous other girls of his acquaintance (89), including Lesbia (91; cf. 116). In 91

---

[12]) Curran, *op. cit.* above (n. 10), 191.

Catullus comments with a certain amount of irony that he would have thought that Lesbia was safe from his clutches since she was neither his mother nor his sister.

It is tempting to see the Aufilena of 111, accused of having children by her uncle, as a female counterpart to Gellius. In 78 Catullus claims that all the generations will know of Gallus' infamy in tutoring a nephew in the arts of seducing his uncle's wife. Perhaps Gallus is the brother of Gellius' uncle.

A complicated story of nefarious sexual activities appears in 67. The lady in the poem when married for the first time gave her virginity not to her impotent husband but to his father (67.19–30). Not stopping there, she enjoyed adulterous relationships with Postumius and Cornelius (67.35–36), and a third tall, red-haired gentleman not named (67.41–48).

We might speculate on what has prompted Catullus to pillory incestuous relationships as being so reprehensible. Perhaps his shock and disillusionment upon hearing about Lesbia sleeping with her brother (79) has something to do with his condemnation of such activities. Apparently Catullus does not regard sexual intercourse as an approved method of closing the generation gap!

The final topic I would like to consider is the part the generation gap may have played in Catullus' criticism of Caesar and Pompey and their associates. Caesar, born in 100 or 102, and Pompey in 106 were clearly old enough to be Catullus' father. However, none of the invective directed against them appears to focus on any age differences. Instead, as Harmon points out,[13]) it seems to be a question of Catullus being outraged that they do not live up to the traditional ideals associated with Roman statesmen. Perhaps this is unfair of Catullus to play the armchair critic, particularly when he seems to have deliberately eschewed any political career for himself. But one is reminded of some modern-day hippies who decry the political situation in the U.S.A. but do nothing but drop out of the mainstream of life, living idly on welfare.

Catullus seems to demonstrate in his poetry a curious schizophrenia. There is a vast chasm between the ideals he seems to profess and the

[13]) Harmon, *op. cit.* above (n. 1), 7, 72 ff.

conduct of his own life, especially in regard to love and marriage, but also politics. On the one hand, he can lament in 10 and 28 that he has not been able to make any profit during his stay in Bithynia on Memmius' staff. He criticizes Memmius harshly for not passing the loot around sufficiently. Clearly Catullus is not troubled by the effect on the provincials of the often iniquitous system of Roman administration. He seems only to be concerned about the fact that Bithynia was a poor country and that he personally did not get his fair share of what proceeds there were, in order that he might impress his friends with his ill-gotten wealth. In 28 he expresses his sympathy for his friends, Veranius and Fabullus, who seem to have suffered the same fate under Piso. One feels quite certain that Catullus would have had no complaints whatever had he and his friends enriched themselves sufficiently in their respective provinces.

Therefore, Catullus cannot altogether escape the charge of hypocrisy when he inveighs against Caesar, Pompey, and Mamurra in 29, when he accuses them of allowing Mamurra to bleed Gaul and Britain dry. In spendthrift fashion, Mamurra has already run through his ancestral property, the booty brought back by Pompey and his troops after Mithridates was defeated, and what wealth he was able to gain during his Spanish service. One wonders to what degree jealousy plays a role in Catullus' denunciation of Mamurra. Caesar and Mamurra are attacked again as birds of a feather in 57. Again one must smile when Catullus rails against their adulteries—another case of the pot calling the kettle black (cf. 94 on Mamurra). Mamurra is attacked further, via his mistress, in 41 and 43. Catullus exclaims in 43 that his age is indeed tasteless and ill-bred if its values have sunk so low that Ameana can be compared to Lesbia. Vivid accounts of Mamurra as spendthrift in the handling of his estate at Firmum are found in 114 and 115. One is reminded of Catullus' social-climbing claim to having a Tiburtine country estate, to which he retired after suffering a cold in the course of his attempting to mooch a good dinner from Sestius (44).

Another interesting political poem is 52, in which Catullus reviles Vatinius, the upstart supporter of Caesar and Pompey, who is already arrogantly anticipating a consulship, which he was to hold only for a few days as *suffectus* (vice-consul) in 47. Although the identity of Nonius is not certain, he too would appear to be a supporter of

Caesar or Pompey.[14]) So again Catullus is enraged at the success of worthless minions of the triumvirs. But Catullus was not above boasting in order to impress Varus' girlfriend (10) about the non-existent benefits he had reaped in Bithynia. Even though one might argue that the poem was written in such a way as to tell a joke on himself, Catullus seems rather petulant that the girl catches him out. As Quinn points out,[15]) Catullus begins by saying that she is a "scortillum ... non sane illepidum neque invenustum" ("a little harlot not indeed unmannerly nor unattractive;" 10.3-4). Halfway through the poem she becomes *cinaedior* ("rather wanton"; 10.24) and then finally she is "insulsa male et molesta... per quam non licet esse neglegentem" ("wickedly tasteless and troublesome, not allowing Catullus to be careless;" 10.33-34).

We learn from Suetonius (*Jul.* 73) that Caesar felt that Catullus had inflicted everlasting marks of disgrace on him as a result of his scurrilous verses about Mamurra, but that a reconciliation between Caesar and Catullus took place, Caesar inviting him to dinner on the same day. Caesar also continued his customary friendly relations with Catullus' father. One might be tempted to see the reconciliation as a confrontation between the generations, with Catullus' father acting as the mediator in bringing his arrant son to reason. But it must be remembered that the *Lex Cornelia* prevented Caesar from entering Italy, so if he were to have a personal interview with Catullus, one logical place for doing so would be at the home of Catullus' father in Verona.

Caesar would be particularly interested in having Catullus on his side, since Catullus' poetry was potentially a vehicle for propaganda, favorable or unfavorable, and there is evidence that Caesar liked young people in general and looked for their support in his political and military campaigns.[16]) Caesar's army tended to consist of younger men at all ranks, including his *contubernales* (tent-mates), scions of the illustrious families of Rome. Instructive in this regard was the rapid elevation of responsibilities entrusted to P. Crassus, the younger son of

[14]) See C. J. Fordyce, ed., *Catullus*, Oxford, 1961, 222.

[15]) Kenneth Quinn, ed., *Catullus the Poems*, London, 1970, 121.

[16]) See Jean Granarolo, "La Jeunesse au Siècle de César d'après Catulle et Cicéron," *Assoc. G. Budé, Congrés de Lyon, Actes*, Paris, 1960, 483-519, especially 488-489.

the triumvir. Caesar allowed his young recruits of Cisalpine Gaul, who were excellent soldiers, to adorn and perfume themselves after the fighting was over. Caesar treated all the young men in his army with marked preference, relying on them to carry out dangerous enterprises.

Politically some of Caesar's moves seem geared to obtain the support of the younger men of good family – the abolition of debts and the destruction of the *tabulae novae* (old account books). Such measures could not but fail to appeal to dissolute young men who had spent money too freely. Caesar also seemed fond of having younger men, such as Curio, active on his behalf in Rome. In short, Caesar seemed to be well aware of the value of young men as a political tool and was eager to have Catullus join his camp.

Catullus' initial hostility to him seems rather strange when one realizes that, in spite of the more idealized sentiments he expresses, Catullus' actual life style was very similar to that of the type of young man for whom Caesar had great appeal – an individual of good family used to a rather idle, hedonistic existence who wanted to make money (Cat. 10, 28), but did not seem to have much of it (10, 13, 26, 28, 44). That Catullus considered financial status as an important criterion in judging a person's worth appears in his criticism of Furius, a rival for Juventius' affections, as a pauper (23, 24, 26).

Even stranger to account for, in my opinion, is Catullus' sneer at Caesar's literary efforts (57); Mamurra is similarly ridiculed in 57 and 105. From what we know about Caesar's writing (cf. Cic. *Brutus* 251–262), he is of the Atticist tradition as was Calvus (cf. Cic. *Brutus* 280, 283–284), whose poetry Catullus greatly admired (50). It is difficult to say, then, why Catullus found Caesar's writing objectionable other than perhaps he viewed it as pretentious for a politician and soldier to try to be a writer, and was ready to criticize Caesar for whatever he did. The use of the adjective *eruditulus* ("dilettantish;" 57.7) might apply in particular to Caesar's work of scholarship, the *De Analogia*, a treatise on grammar.

In closing this section of the paper, we may recapitulate the most important factors shaping Catullus' views on the generation gap: the dichotomy between the ideal and the real in Catullus' interaction with Lesbia, his parents, and the social and political life of the Rome of his day.

II. Horace

We have already noted the concept of the ages of man in Catullus' poetry. In the case of Horace the ages of man are of prime importance in interpreting his views on the generation gap. Horace has his own description of the ages in the *Ars Poetica* (153–178). To a much greater extent than Catullus, Horace has a changing perspective on age in his writing since his career dates from about 35 B.C., when the first book of his *Satires* was published, to 13 B.C., the publication of the fourth book of *Odes*.

When Horace was a young man he exhibited the fiery spirit (*Ode* III. 14.25–28), if not the courage, of youth by participating in the battle of Philippi in 42 B.C. in command of a Roman legion (*Sat.* I. 6.48). Although we should not take literally his description of himself as being spirited away from the battle in epic fashion by Mercury, the patron of poets, and his abandoning of his shield (*Ode* II. 7.9–14), it can safely be said that he did not exactly distinguish himself as a soldier (*Epist.* II. 2.46–48; cf. *Epode* 1). Again, as is typical of the young man, *amata relinquere pernix* ("swift to abandon things loved;" *Ars Poetica* 165), we find Horace's ardor for military service and the restoration of the republic cooling, when instead of following his friends back into the seething straits of war (*Ode* II. 7.9–16), he chose to return to Italy under an amnesty offered by the victors. Unfortunately he found himself with his wings clipped and destitute of house and farm (*Epist.* II. 2.49–51), probably as the result of confiscation of his property to be given to the victorious army.

As Horace ages, he continues to apply the concept of the ages of man to himself in consideration of what activities are appropriate for him. In *Epistles* I. 1.1–32 and II. 2.51–144 he seems to regard himself as too old for the folly of writing lyric poetry; instead in his middle years he deems it appropriate to turn to philosophy (cf. *Epist.* I. 2.).

In the realm of love Horace seems to be of the opinion that in his middle years the role of appreciative spectator is more suitable than that of active participant. In *Ode* II. 4 Horace praises the beauty of Phyllis, the beloved handmaiden of Xanthias. In lines 21–24 he assures Xanthias that he should not take amiss Horace's praise of Phyllis' arms, face, and shapely ankles since he is already forty years old.

Ode III. 14 was written on the occasion of Augustus' return from his Spanish campaign in 25 B.C. In the poem Horace again refers to his own reduced vigor in love campaigns when he tells a servant boy to go to Neaera's house and bid her to join the celebration. But if the doorkeeper offers any delay, the boy is to hurry away, since Horace's white hair softens a spirit prone to strife and wanton brawling (*Ode* III. 14.21–28). In *Ode* I. 16 Horace begs a girl to forgive his abusive verses – the product of the erstwhile passion and madness of his youth.

Horace in *Ode* IV. 1 begs cruel Venus to cease trying to bend him to her commands, since he is nearly fifty years old. He is not the same man he was under the sway of good Cinara (*Ode* IV. 1.3–4). Instead Venus should go the house of the young nobleman, Paulus Maximus (*Ode* IV. 1.7–16). Horace claims that neither a girl nor a boy can delight him any more in love (*Ode* IV. 1.29–32). But in the last two stanzas (33–40) Horace indicates that he still has the power to love after all, since he can produce at least an occasional tear over his unrequited love for Ligurinus. Since this poem forms the introduction to book four of Horace's *Odes*, which he wrote after some ten years of inactivity, there is the strong possibility that Horace can simultaneously be referring to his reluctance to write more lyric poetry but that he still has the ability to do so (cf. *Ode* III. 26; Suet. *Vita Hor.*). *Ode* IV. 11 continues the theme of Horace's more advanced age and waning powers of love. He tells Phyllis that she will be his last love (31–34).

Horace again pleads his age as an excuse in *Epode* 17, in which he begs Canidia to cease her magic spells against him. He thinks that he has paid sufficient penalties in that his youth has fled away along with his rosy bloom, his bones are covered with yellow skin, his hair is white, and he is tormented day and night with no possibility for easing his straining chest by taking breath (*Epode* 17.19–26). Both his age and keenness in sense of smell are adduced by Horace as reasons for his relative lack of passion when he sleeps with the anonymous, but odoriferous, woman of *Epode* 12.

Horace does not stop at applying the theory of the ages of man to himself. In a number of his poems he deals with the theme of individuals not exhibiting the kind of conduct generally deemed suitable to their years. His thinking along these lines may be somewhat rigid, as indicated in the *Ars Poetica* (153–157; 176–178) in which he does not seem to make allowances for individual differences in temperament, but instead seeks to explain all characteristics of people from the point of view of their age. This tendency is further revealed in *Satire* II. 3.247–249 in which Horace states that if such childish activities as building toy-houses, harnessing mice to a small cart, playing odd and even, and riding a long stick delighted a bearded man, he would be insane. Many modern-day adult builders of sand castles on the beach and collectors of toy-trains might vociferously argue the point!

Horace continues his critical view of the old acting young in a series of poems – *Epode* 8, *Ode* III. 15, and *Ode* IV. 13. In *Epode* 8 Horace gives a repulsive description of an ugly old woman who has the nerve to upbraid the poet for his lack of virility. Although Horace does not state the implication definitely as he does in *Odes* III. 15 and IV. 13, we get the impression that the old woman is behaving in a manner that in no way befits her age and appearance.

In *Ode* III. 15 Horace censures the old woman Chloris, who instead of tending to the spinning and weaving of wool appropriate for a decorous old Roman matron, is sporting about like a maiden in quest of love. Horace feels so strongly about her unsuitable conduct that he even characterizes it as wanton and infamous (*Ode* III. 15.2–3). One is reminded of the similar attitude Catullus had about the old man Cominius of 108.

The situation in *Ode* IV. 13 is somewhat more complicated. Horace has prayed in spiteful fashion to the gods that a former girlfriend of his, Lyce, should become old. His prayer has been answered, and he seems to delight in describing in graphic detail the degeneration in her appearance. She, like Chloris, is still behaving as a young maiden, and with little success. A further element is added in *Ode* IV. 13 that we did not encounter in *Ode* III. 15: Lyce is an object of ridicule among the passionate youths who see the torch now fallen to ashes (26–28). So in *Ode* IV. 13 improper behavior for one's age has become not only disreputable but ridiculous.

Horace's view of old age in the *Ars Poetica* (166–176) is quite negative. In spite of his statement that advancing years bring many blessings with them (175), he fails to enumerate them, having concentrated on the disadvantages associated with old age instead. Elsewhere in his poetry there are only a few hints of any of the advantages to be enjoyed by the aged, such as more indulgence in eating (*Sat.* II. 2.82–88). Even virtuous old Cato was often accustomed to warm himself with wine (*Ode* III. 21.11–12).

Horace's obviously pessimistic view of old age in the *Ars Poetica* is certainly reflected in a number of his lyric poems. For example, *Ode* III. 19.22–24 has a brief reference to the old man Lycus who is jealous of Horace's mad drinking bout and who is not a fitting suitor for the maiden living next door. One is reminded of Horace's characterization of the old man as *difficilis, querulus*, and a *castigator censorque minorum* ("troublesome, querulous, and a chastiser and critic of younger people;" *Ars Poetica* 173–174).

That Horace regards old age as burdensome and sorrowful clearly appears from the large number of his poems that pit the pleasures of youth against crabbed old age. Noteworthy in this regard is the famous Soracte ode (I. 9). Shields[17] discusses the artistic use of whiteness and immobility in the description of the snow-capped Mt. Soracte which is used to point up the moral of the poem, to enjoy one's youth while one may. In this connection the juxtaposition of antithetical qualities in "virenti canities abest morosa" (*Ode* I. 9.17–18) should be mentioned. As Shields puts it,[18] "the underlying motif of the ode, the tension between youth and old age, *virenti canities*, green-white, *stet-dissolve*, is magnified by the contrasted word portraits, the winter scene at the beginning and the summer scene at the end." The contrasts are continued in the fact that the winter scene is rural, involving no people, whereas the summer scene is urban and full of life. By implication Horace seems to be saying that old age is lonely, immobile, and rather forbidding, whereas youth is convivial, active, and merry.

Lockyer[19] also has some interesting interpretations of this ode. He sees Horace as approving sports and love as the proper activities of youth, which he recommends to Thaliarchus. As Lockyer sees it, there is nothing better that Thaliarchus would like to do but sneak off

[17] M. G. Shields, "*Odes* 1.9: A Study In Imaginative Unity," *Phoenix* 12 (1958), 166–173.

[18] Shields, *op. cit.* above (n. 17), 171.

[19] Charles W. Lockyer, Jr., "Horace *Odes* 1.9," *Classical Journal* 63 (1968), 304–308.

to his girlfriend. Instead it looks as if he will have to spend the day with Horace quietly drinking. Although Horace at the time this ode was written was probably in his late thirties or early forties, he seems to us, and no doubt to Thaliarchus, a garrulous old man reminiscing about the pleasures of youth, as the typical aged "laudator temporis acti se puero" ("man praising the bygone days of his past;" *Ars Poetica* 173–174). In short, the poem is an excellent illustration of the generation gap.

A number of Horace's other poems are similar in tone to *Ode* I. 9 with its *carpe diem* theme in regard to the enjoyment of youth's pleasures. In *Ode* II. 3.13–16 Horace bids the servant boy to bring wines, perfumes, and the too brief blossoms of the lovely rose, while Fortune, youth, and the Three Fates allow it. Horace in *Ode* II. 11.1–12 enjoins his friend Quinctius Hirpinus to cease to be anxious concerning military issues since fresh youth and beauty are speeding away behind them and wizened old age is banishing sportive love and easy sleep. The advice of enjoying youth while they may seems particularly apropos in this case because they seem to have little of it left, as indicated by Horace's reference to their white hair (*Ode* II. 11.13–17). Thus, it seems all the more necessary that the courtesan Lyde come to them quickly (*Ode* II. 11.21–24).

The horrors of growing old for a woman are adumbrated in *Ode* I. 25. The aging Lydia is being sought less frequently by the gay young blades, and Horace says the situation will grow worse yet when she is an old woman, burning with passion but disdained by lovers. Horace shows a certain inconsistency in viewing Lydia when old as still burning with passion. Perhaps, however, old women are different from old men, since Horace states in the *Ars Poetica* (171–172) that the old man lacks fire and courage in all that he does, is dilatory and slow to form hopes, and is sluggish.

Ode IV. 10 is a kind of companion piece to *Ode* I. 25 in that Horace describes for a young boy, Ligurinus, how unpleasant it will be for him when he grows old. There is a malicious tone to the poem, probably because this is the same Ligurinus whom Horace mentions in *Ode* IV. 1 as spurning him. The end of the poem has Ligurinus expressing an age-old, universal regret about the nature of life, why it is that the beauty of youth cannot be combined with the wisdom and expe-

rience of age (*Ode* IV. 10.7–8). I believe that Fraenkel[20]) is right in
pointing out that here, as well as in other similar passages, Horace is
lamenting the passing of his own youth, as indeed does probably
every other individual growing old. But even youth is not exempt
from death, that great leveler of both the young and old alike (*Ode*
I. 28.15–20).

In three poems – *Odes* I. 23, II. 5, and III. 11 – Horace offers his own
suggestions for how the generation gap between the old and the young
can be closed. In *Ode* I. 23 we are presented with Chloë, another
individual who is not manifesting the type of behavior appropriate
for her age. Only instead of being an old woman who pretends she is
still a young girl, Chloë is a nubile young lady still clinging close to her
mother in childish fashion. Horace tries to reassure her that he will
be gentle and that she should not fear his advances. It is high time for
her to have a mate!

In *Ode* II. 5 Lalage appears to be somewhat younger than Chloë and
is not yet ready for a lover. To some anonymous addressee (Horace
himself?) the poet gives the advice to wait awhile, for the years that
are taken from him will be added to her (*Ode* II. 5.13–15). Soon the
tables will be turned and Lalage will aggressively seek him as her lover
(*Ode* II. 5.15–16). Surely the whole poem smacks of wishful thinking
on Horace's part.

The Lyde of *Ode* III. 11 is like Lalage in being yet too young for
wedlock or a lover (7–12). Hence, it seems somewhat extravagant and
even inconsistent with the theory of the ages of man for Horace to
cite the tale of the Danaids to warn Lyde not to spurn him as the
Danaids, with one noble exception, killed their bridegrooms. Horace
seems to be urging Lyde to emulate the merciful conduct of the one
Danaid who allowed her husband to live. For Lyde this would mean
the acceptance of Horace as a lover.

As was the case with Catullus, we find that many of Horace's
remarks on the relationship of parents and children were probably
conditioned by his relationship with his own father. Unlike Catullus,
it appears that Horace got on famously with his father and expressed

---

[20]) Eduard Fraenkel, *Horace*, Oxford, 1957, 414–415; see also Hans Oppermann,
"Späte Liebeslyrik des Horaz," *Beiträge zur Alten Geschichte und deren Nachleben,
Festschrift für Franz Altheim zum 6. 10. 1968*, Berlin, 1, 459–476.

his gratitude to him for seeing to it that he received the best education both in the home and at school (*Sat.* I. 6). Horace gives his father the ultimate tribute when he says that should he live his life over again, he would not choose a different father (*Sat.* I. 6.93–99).

In the light of Horace's own experiences it is not surprising, then, when he stresses in a number of his poems the importance of one's parents setting a good example for their children and offering them love and protection. The consummate musician, Orpheus, learned his art from his mother (*Ode* I. 12.7–12); Proculeius, who divided his property between his brothers who had lost theirs in the civil wars, will have lasting fame for the fatherly spirit he showed towards his brothers (*Ode* II. 2.5–8).

In several of his poems Horace sets up Augustus as a paragon father-figure. Augustus has exhibited a fatherly devotion to the young Neros, Drusus and Tiberius (*Ode* IV. 4.22–28). Both father and step-sons illustrate the maxim that only from the brave and good are brave youths born; both family training and natural talent are necessary to create the brave of heart, and lack of proper training mars even what talents nature has given (*Ode* IV. 4.29–36). As a further illustration and proof of his beliefs, Horace reviews the contributions made to the state by an earlier member of the Claudian house, Claudius Nero (*Ode* IV. 4.37–76).

Augustus is also elevated to the status of father of his country (*Ode* I. 2.50; cf. *Ode* III. 24.25–30). In *Ode* IV. 5.1–2 Augustus is called best guardian of the race of Romulus, but in a kind of reversal of roles he is likened to the long-absent son for whose arrival his mother anxiously watches, just as Rome looks for the return of Augustus (*Ode* IV. 5.9–16). Such an analogy reveals the tendency of the Romans to view their city as feminine, even to the point of deifying it as the goddess Roma. But the rulers of Rome were always masculine, thereby reflecting the strongly patriarchal social system based on the *patria potestas* ("power of the father").

In both *Odes* IV. 5 and IV. 15 Augustus figuratively acquires the role of a culture hero, since it is he who has ushered in a new Golden Age at Rome. Among the characteristics of the Golden Age are harmony and piety in the home. The chaste household is not polluted by adultery; mothers are praised because of children who look like their parents

(*Ode* IV. 5.21–24; cf. Cat. 61.212–226). Men with their wives and children piously pray to the gods, and in the manner of their forefathers hymn the glories of Troy, Anchises, and the Julian line (*Ode* IV. 15.25–32).

In the *Carmen Saeculare* Horace continues to express his concern that family life in Rome be uplifting. The chorus of youths and maidens chosen to sing the hymn in honor of the gods are chaste scions of Rome's most illustrious families (*Ode* IV. 6.31–44; *Carmen Saec.* 1–8). Horace prays to the goddess of childbirth to produce offsrpring and to bless the legislation concerning marriage (*Carmen Saec.* 13–20). Horace shows his concern for the well-being of both the younger and older generations, in his prayer that the youths may be receptive to learning virtuous morals and the aged may enjoy tranquil peace (*Carmen Saec.* 45–48). Horace even goes so far as to assert that Faith, Peace, Honor, and Modesty – the ancient virtues that made Rome great – have now had the courage to return (*Carmen Saec.* 57–60).

It appears from the *Carmen Saeculare*, as elsewhere in his poetry, that Horace agrees with the traditional view of the importance of morals and solid family life in contributing to the general welfare of the state. In *Epode* 2 (cf. also *Odes* I. 12.39–44; III. 6.37–44) we find a further example of the kind of well-ordered family life that Horace idealizes.[21] A modest wife tends the home and her dear children like a Sabine woman or the well-tanned wife of a sturdy Apulian, accomplishing various household and outdoor tasks in preparation of the homecoming of her weary husband (*Epode* 2.39–48).

---

[21]) But see Steele Commager, *The Odes of Horace: A Critical Study*, Indiana, 1962, 106–107, for the view that Horace in *Epode* 2 may be satirizing the exaggerated praises the country often received, since the usurer Alfius, the speaker in the poem (67–70), cannot resist the call of his profession, in spite of his intentions to become a farmer. But see also the non-satiric *Ode* I. 1. 15–18 in which a seagoing merchant, temporarily disaffected from his occupation, tries to become a farmer, only to return to his original calling. Might not *Epode* 2 be in part a reiteration of the idea implicit in *Ode* I. 1 that each person has his own profession which he usually has not the ability, even if the occasional desire, to change? But if one accepts *Epode* 2 as a satire, Horace at least on this occasion is probably making fun of the traditional austerity and virtue asociated with family life of the early republic. Or, as Fraenkel, *op. cit.*, 59–61, sees it, Horace adds a satiric tag to the poem to check his over-enthusiastic idealism.

Horace's view of the protective parent also appears in *Epode* 1, in which Horace expresses his desire to be with Maecenas at the battle of Actium, even though he is unwarlike and might get in the way (1–16). Yet Horace feels that he would rather be present even if he cannot help, just as the mother bird more keenly dreads the attacks of serpents on her unfledged nestlings when she has left them, although she could lend them no more aid were she at hand (*Epode* 1.17–22).

We have been looking at the positive examples Horace offers of parent-children relationships; now it is time to examine his negative illustrations. The uncongenial figure of the step-mother, whom we have previously encountered in Catullus 23, makes an appearance in *Epode* 5 and *Ode* III. 24. *Epode* 5 is a gruesome poem in which a young boy is suffering a lingering death, so that the witch Canidia can use various parts of his body for a love charm. The boy asks Canidia why she gazes upon him as a step-mother (*Epode* 5, 9–10),[22]) thereby betraying her evil intentions.

Horace's other reference to the step-mother occurs in *Ode* III. 24, an interesting poem contrasting the good morals of the Scythians and Getae, regarded as noble savages, with those of present-day, degenerate Romans.[23]) As one index of the moral superiority of the Scythians, Horace mentions that among them children bereft of their mothers need have nothing to fear from their step-mothers (*Ode* III. 24.17–18). Scythian family life has other virtues – the dowered wife does not rule over her husband nor take up with a dazzling paramour (*Ode* III. 24.19–20). The bride's dowry is the great virtue of her parents and her own sense of fidelity to her husband; it is a crime to sin, for which the penalty is death (*Ode* III. 24.21–24).

Horace then contrasts the unsound family life of the Romans (*Ode* III. 24.53–62). The free-born boy untrained in sterner tasks does not know how to ride a horse, and he fears to hunt, more skilled in games involving the Grecian hoop or the dice forbidden by law. Perhaps this is to be expected when his father dishonestly cheats his business partner and friends in order to build up a large inheritance for his unworthy son. Because of the great pessimism Horace expresses about Roman

[22]) Cf. Seneca (*Contr.* IV. 6) *novercalibus oculis intueri.*

[23]) See Lovejoy and Boas, *op. cit.* above (n. 9), 315–344, for a survey of ancient views, some far from eulogistic, on the Scythians and the Getae.

morals in this poem, Williams[24]) dates it to about 28 B.C., when Augustus' first attempts at moral legislation failed (cf. *Ode* III. 24.25–54).

Horace also castigates the education of Roman girls as improper (*Ode* III. 6.21–32). The maiden takes delight in being taught Grecian dances and the arts of coquetry and adultery, to the point that during her husband's drinking parties she indiscriminately takes on younger lovers, not without her husband's knowledge.

There are a few other Horatian allusions to individual instances of troubled parent-child relationships. In *Epode* 3, Horace's mock epic on the devastating effects of garlic, he condemns any man to eat of garlic, deadlier than the hemlock, should he with impious hand strangle an aged parent (1–3). For the Romans even striking one's parent was apparently a crime of such magnitude that offenders were consigned to Tartarus for eternal punishment (Vergil, *Aen.* VI. 608–609). But the tables are turned in the tale briefly alluded to by Horace in *Ode* I. 7.21–32, in which Teucer's father has unreasonably banished Teucer, holding him responsible for the death of his brother Ajax. Here it is a case of a father showing cruelty to his son. Reciprocal enmity is involved in the story of Lycambes and Archilochus referred to in *Epode* 6.13. Lycambes refused to let Archilochus marry his daughter as he had promised, whereupon Archilochus inveighed against him with such effect that he hung himself.

A more extended charge of unfilial behavior is uttered by both Europa and her father in *Ode* III. 27.33–66. Europa, innocently picking flowers in a meadow, was attracted to a beautiful and docile white bull, Jupiter in disguise. Unfortunately when she sat upon the bull he carried her off, and Jupiter made her his mistress. Europa laments that she has forsaken the name of daughter and her duty to her father, overcome by madness. She hopes that what happened was just a dream. For Europa to have left her household gods and to continue to remain alive is shameless. She seeks to wander naked among the lions and to feed the tigers for her sin. But apparently Europa is not prepared to undergo the even more torturous death of being a prey to wild beasts only after a period of famine and exhaustion (*Ode* III. 27.53–56). Europa's preoccupation with her beauty is

[24]) G. Williams, "Poetry in the Moral Climate of Augustan Rome," *Journal of Roman Studies* 52 (1962), 28–46.

at great variance with the obliviousness of physical appearance displayed by the frenzied Ariadne, another sinful woman facing death (Cat.
64.60–75).

Horace pictures Europa's father as urging her to kill her worthless
self, even helpfully offering two alternative methods for effecting her
demise, perhaps since Europa has said that one death is not sufficient
for her sin. The father represents the staunch, uncompromising patriarchal view of female sexual indiscretions, preferring death for his
daughter rather than that she should live in dishonor as a slave card-
ing her mistress' wool or as a concubine given over to a barbarian
queen. The point of view taken by him is similar to that of Lucretia
and Virginia's father—chastity for women was regarded by the Romans, at least in theory, as worthy of the highest accolade of praise.

But I believe that Horace may be mocking the "death before dishonor" point of view to some extent. The speeches of Europa and
her father seem somewhat exaggerated and melodramatic. Then Venus,
laughing treacherously in enjoyment of these proceedings, arrives on
the scene as the *deus ex machina* just in the nick of time to explain
things and to prevent any bloodshed involving either Europa or vengeance against the bull. Europa's reparations for the inconveniences of
the rape will include the naming of a continent after her. Since Horace
often indulges in subtle ridicule of extremist emotions,[25] is it not
possible that he could be providing us here with a spoof of the traditionalist view of chastity and filial piety?

The final theme I wish to discuss in regard to Horace's use of the
generation gap as a literary theme is his view of the generation of the
ages. Horace was keenly sensitive to the vicissitudes of the political
situation in Rome. In his poetic reactions to events affecting the state
he runs the full gamut of emotions from pessimistic escapism to per-
functory celebration of Augustus' rule. A large number of Horace's
political poems employ to a greater or lesser degree the motif of the

---

[25] For example, see Commager, *op. cit.* above (n. 21), 33, 132, 135–139, 144,
150–156, 239–240, who views such poems as *Odes* I. 5, 13, 16, 19, 22, 33; II. 9;
III. 9 as parodies of the elegiac view of love as the most important thing in life. We
have already seen Horace's burlesque of the Homeric hero in having himself rescued
by Mercury in a dense cloud at Philippi (*Ode* II. 7). We have also mentioned the
possibility that *Epode* 2 satirizes the traditional blessings attributed to country life.

ages of man's history. *Odes* IV. 2, IV. 5, and IV. 15, as we have seen, laud Augustus' accomplishments to such an extent that he is represented as ushering in a new Golden Age at Rome. But what we are concerned with here are Horace's more pessimistic poems, written when the outcome of the civil wars was yet uncertain. In these poems Horace regards his contemporary Romans as the detestable result of man's long history of degeneration from the Golden to the Iron age. As we shall see, Horace's individual instances of inimical relationships between parents and children that we have summarized will be writ large in his description of the hardships besetting Rome before Augustus was her unequivocal master.

Epodes 7 and 16 are among the most pessimistic of Horace's political poems. In both poems Horace views the current generation of Romans as of accursed stock. Romulus' murder of his brother Remus is seen by Horace as an archetypal act of civil war which has plagued the Romans ever since (*Epode* 7.17–20). The seeds of Rome's destruction at her own hands is implicit in the circumstances of her founding. From the evidence of this poem one might infer that Horace sees a continuity of evil in the nature of the Romans from the first generation to the present.

An analogous point of view occurs in *Ode* III. 3.17–24 in regard to the circumstances involved in the founding of Troy and the cause of its ultimate destruction. Laomedon employed the gods Apollo and Poseidon to build the walls of the city, but then cheated them of the pay he had promised. Likewise Paris was guilty of treachery in spiriting away Helen from her husband Menelaus, thereby causing the Trojan war. Horace implies that treachery is an integral part of the Trojan character in calling the house of Priam *periura* ("perjured;" *Ode* III. 3.26–27). Although Horace does not allude in detail to the role that the Trojan horse played in Troy's downfall, I am sure that he would consider it as most fitting and ironic for a nation tainted by treachery to succumb as the result of this same trait being directed against it, just as Rome is destroying herself by her "primal sin" of fratricide.[26]

---

[26] Vergil (*Geor.* I. 501–502) traces Rome's sufferings all the way back to Laomedon's crime, linking Troy with Rome's history and implying that there is a

The opening section (1–14) of *Epode* 16 reiterates much of what Horace has said in *Epode* 7. There are the same themes of the current generation being ground to pieces by civil war in Rome, Rome destroying herself, and the Romans being impious and accursed. However, Horace's despair over the situation in Rome carries him to an even greater degree of hopelessness in *Epode* 16. He can only counsel as a solution of Rome's ills the emigration of the better citizens to the Isles of the Blessed where they will enjoy a Golden Age existence. Jupiter has set apart these shores for a righteous people ever since he dimmed the luster of the Golden Age with bronze and then hardened the ages with iron (*Epode* 16.63–65). Even though Horace and his contemporaries are living in the Iron Age, an escape is offered for the pious (*Epode* 16.65–66). Perhaps, if we accept the implications of *Epode* 7, we can conclude that Horace regards the whole history of Rome as falling within the Iron Age, but, as we shall see, certain of his other poems seem to contradict this theory.

In *Ode* I. 2 Horace pictures Jupiter, father of gods and men, as being displeased with the events in Rome and indicating his wrath by sending storms to assail the city (1–5). A mythological analogue is adduced in the description of Deucalion's flood, which the people of Rome fear may return (*Ode* I. 2.5–12). Angered at first by the impiety of Lycaon and his sons, Jupiter later resolved to destroy by a flood the whole race of men, with the exception of a few honorable individuals. Horace apparently regards the Rome of his day as equally deserving of destruction. He continues the flood motif in his description of the Tiber river inundating two of Rome's most venerable landmarks, the Regia and the temple of Vesta (*Ode* I. 2.13–16). The execution of Ilia, mother of Romulus and Remus, is given as the reason for the Tiber's vengeance against Rome. Again the notion is implicit of a primal crime needing expiation by the Romans. But contrary to his views in *Epodes* 7 and 16. Horace appears to consider the youth of his time victimized by the sins of their fathers (*Ode* I. 2.21–24), instead of being equally culpable. Horace ends *Ode* I. 2 on a more optimistic note, praying that Augustus may be a beneficent

continuous line of debased descendants from Laomedon to Vergil's Roman contemporaries.

father for his country (41–52), rather than demonstrating the vengeance of the divine father Jupiter.

The theme of Jupiter as the divine guardian of the human race and Augustus as his human counterpart on earth appears again in *Ode* I. 12. Although Horace still mentions Jupiter's more sinister aspects of striking down polluted groves with his thunderbolts, thereby implying that some men are still impious and deserving of punishment, it appears that Augustus is more firmly ensconced as ruler of the world, which he governs with justice (*Ode* I. 12.57–60).

Jupiter and Augustus are also linked in *Ode* III. 4. In counseling Augustus to temper brute force with wisdom, Horace describes the victorious battle of the Olympians led by Jupiter against the insolent Titans, Giants, and Aloeids. Perhaps one can infer from the intergenerational nature of the conflict of the younger Olympian gods with the older Titans and Giants that Horace is making an analogy to the successions of generations involved in Rome's civil wars, with the moral drawn that only force plus wisdom, as exemplified in the character of both Jupiter and Augustus, is sufficient to put an end to the struggle once and for all.

Returning to *Ode* I. 12, we find an example of Horace's tendency to be a *laudator temporis acti* ("praiser of the past").[27] In the poem Horace catalogues some of the great heroes who lived during the kingship and early republican period in Rome. As opposed to the impression we received in *Epodes* 7 and 16 that the Romans were impious from the first, here it appears that they were once upright and moral, but have since fallen from this high estate. How do we account for this inconsistency in Horace's thinking? Poetic license may be partly responsible, as well as Horace's attitudes to the changing political situation in Rome. When it was at its worst, Horace was all doom and gloom about Rome past and present, but when a ray of hope appeared that Augustus may yet put things right, Horace was reassured and found it congenial to contemplate Rome's virtuous men of old, whose morals were being reincarnated in Augustus (cf. *Ode* I. 12.).

---

[27] See Margaret E. Taylor, "Horace: *Laudator Temporis Acti?*," *American Journal of Philology* 83 (1962), 23–43.

Ode I. 35 contains a striking juxtaposition of optimism and pessimism. In lines 29–32 Horace prays for the success of Augustus' expedition against the Britons and the safety of the newly recruited band of youths who will be campaigning in the East. But it appears that even Horace's hopes for the success of foreign campaigns cannot help but remind him of the kind of warfare Rome has previously been engaging in for so long (*Ode* I. 35.33–47). He laments those fallen in the civil wars, and again asserts that his present age is of iron which has shrunk from no iniquity. The very youth he has prayed for in the above stanza he now characterizes as *contemptores deorum* ("despisers of the gods") but prays that they may reforge their blunted swords and turn them against the Arabs and Massagetae (cf. *Epode* 7.1–10; *Ode* I. 2.21–24). Although the effect of reversal in perspective Horace achieves in the last three stanzas of *Ode* I. 35 may be in illustration of the reversals caused by Fortuna, to whom he dedicates this poem, Horace's contradictory thoughts also undoubtedly reflect his own uncertainty in simultaneously hoping and fearing for the future of Rome (*Ode* I. 35.1–16).

Ode II. 15 is another poem lauding at the expense of Horace's contemporaries the virtuous practices of ancestors living during the times of Romulus and Cato. Horace is railing at the current extravagance shown in enlarging and beautifying private estates. Instead the ancestors expended the best building materials of marble on public works, adorning their towns and the temples of the gods rather than their own houses (*Ode* II. 15. 17–20).

As a kind of antidote to the effeminate practices so often indulged in by the youths of his time (*Ode* III. 24.51–58; *Sat.* II. 2.50–52) Horace prescribes his own program of training. The youth should be hardened by active military service and feared for his ability in horsemanship and with the lance; he should be able to endure hardships and humble circumstances (*Ode* III. 2.1–12). In this poem Horace is describing the typical view the Romans had of warfare as a means of glorifying themselves and the state, and as Horace puts it, the young man just as well should die a hero in battle since death comes to cowards as well (*Ode* III. 2.13–16). Perhaps Horace's emphasis on training the youth to be good soldiers seems incongruous in the light of all of his lamentations about the civil wars oppressing

Rome, but it may indicate just how deeply entrenched the military ideal was in the Roman consciousness. Add to this the fact that Horace does not seem to have been much of a soldier himself and may be prizing all the more an ideal that he wished he could have attained.

Ode III. 5.1–12 castigates the traitorous behavior of the troops of Crassus living in wedlock with Parthian brides – an indication of the overturned morals of Horace's day. Horace then illustrates the Roman penchant for precedents in recounting the Stoic bravery of Regulus. In the face of agonizing death in Carthage he reported the Roman Senate's refusal to ransom some young Roman soldiers who had surrendered to the Carthaginians without a struggle. Regulus was willing to die to prevent a ruinous precedent from polluting the coming ages (*Ode* III. 5.13–18). He felt that there would be no use in ransoming the youth since when once true courage has vanished, it does not care to be restored to the degenerate (*Ode* III. 5.25–30). The young men have failed to live up to the military ideals outlined by Horace in *Ode* III. 2, and therefore they are a disgrace to their country and deserving of death. To what degree such ideals have been tarnished in later years Horace has illustrated in the first part of *Ode* III. 5 and in *Epode* 9.7–20, with his references to the treason of Sextus Pompeius and Antony. For Horace there is indeed a "generation gap" between the conduct of degenerate men of his own time and the virtuous men of Rome's illustrious past.

The last of the so-called "Roman Odes," III. 6, is an amalgam of several of the themes we have been discussing. As we shall see, there is a certain amount of internal inconsistency within the poem itself. The beginning of the ode is reminiscent of *Ode* I. 2.21–24 in that the current generation of the Romans, though guiltless, will expiate the sins of its ancestors until the shrines, temples, and statues of the gods are restored. Just as Jupiter vented his wrath upon Rome in *Ode* I. 2, the neglected gods are depicted as visiting many woes on Italy in the form of defeat and near-defeat by enemy troops while the country has been beset by civil strife (*Ode* III. 6.7–16).

Next, in contradiction of the innocence he attributes to the Romans in line 1, Horace asserts that the generations are teeming with sin, having polluted marriage, their offspring, and their homes. This

disastrous degneration of morals in the family then eventually engulf-
ed the citizenry and state of Rome (*Ode* III. 6.17–20). We have already
alluded to the instruction in depravity, in whose lessons the young
maidens took delight (*Ode* III. 6.21–32). It is clear from Horace's
remarks that he sees the home as being of prime importance in the
inculcation of virtue. Without the proper training of the youth at
home, the state at large can hardly help but feel the unfortunate
effects.

Using the same technique seen in *Ode* III. 5, Horace then contrasts
the sorry behavior of contemporary young women with that manifest-
ed in the "good old days" of the victory of Roman youths over the
Carthaginians, Pyrrhus, and Antiochus (33–36). The young men
of the past were given a strict upbringing at home unlike the maidens
and youths of Horace's time (*Ode* III. 6.37–44; cf. *Ode* III. 24).
Horace's final stanza of III. 6 is his own statement of the classic view of
the degenerating ages of man – time injures everything; the age of
our parents, worse than that of our grandparents' has brought us
forth less worthy, and soon about to give birth to offspring still
more wicked. Notice how the thought here forms yet another contradiction to what Horace expresses in line 1, but at least it does
not altogether contradict Horace's belief in the virtue of the Roman
soldiers of old, since the final stanza implies that depravity has only
affected the most recent generations of Romans.

The pessimism of *Ode* III. 6.45–48, as well as the reference to
Augustus' building of temples, has led Fraenkel[28] to date the ode
to 28 B.C. The poem certainly is a companion piece in tone and theme
to *Ode* III. 24, also dated to 28 B.C., which, as we have seen, was
the year of Augustus' initial abortive attempt to institute moral
legislation.

In summarizing Horace's use of the generation gap as a literary
theme in his lyric poetry, it is clear that the bulk of his remarks
concerning the subject stem wholly or in part from three concepts –
the ages of man, the ages in man's history, and the development
of a child's ethical values as being dependent on his parents' example.

[28]) Frankel, *op. cit.* above (n. 21), 261–263.

Chapter 11

THE GENERATION GAP IN THE FIFTH BOOK
OF VERGIL'S *AENEID**

Stephen Bertman

University of Windsor

Through his poetry, the Roman poet Vergil sought to help his people find their way through a radical crisis in their history. In the Fifth Book of his major work, the *Aeneid*, the polarity of generations – of old and young – is given symbolic and forceful exposition.[1]

The geographic setting of Book Five is Sicily. Sicily was the last land Aeneas and his people touched before they were driven by winds to Carthage, and now, after a year spent with Dido in Carthage, the Trojans are compelled to visit Sicily again. It was exactly a year before that Aeneas' father, Anchises, had died there, and it is to the city where his bones lie that strong winds now blow them. Welcomed by the aged ruler Acestes, Aeneas announces heroic competitions to be held in his father's memory – contests in sailing, running, boxing, and archery open to Sicilians and Trojans alike. While they are being held, Juno has Iris persuade the Trojan women to burn the Trojan ships. This way, Iris tells them, they will compel their men to settle in Sicily and will not have to face further hardships on the mainland of Italy. The fire the women set is extinguished by Jupiter, but not before four of the ships are lost. Now Aeneas must decide whether to stay in Sicily with his people, or somehow go on. Acting upon the advice of aged Nautes, advice later confirmed by his father's ghost, Aeneas decides to leave the women and the weak, and go

* An earlier form of this essay appeared in *Vergilius* 17 (1971) 9–12. It is reprinted here with the permission of the Vergilian Society.

[1] In *Iliad* 23, the Homeric book which *Aeneid* 5 most resembles, the theme of young and old is indeed present (cf. esp. 589–590 and 787–788), but seems to play only a minor role. Vergil may well have given it a greater role in his own work because of the greater significance it seemed to have for his own day. For a sensitive interpretation of the funeral games in *Aeneid* 5 see Sister Johanna Glazewski, "The Function of Vergil's Funeral Games," *Classical World* 66 (1972–73) 85–96.

on to Italy in his remaining ships with men who are young and brave. This in essence is the action of Book Five.

In Book Five as in no other book of the *Aeneid* Vergil emphasizes his characters' ages. The important characters of this book are either markedly young or markedly old and the poet frequently refers to their age. In addition, a number of scenes involve conflict or constructive interaction between a younger and an older character. In so developing his story, Vergil exhibits concern with the strengths and the weaknesses that characterize each time of life and their effects upon civilization.

The positive aspect of old age is symbolized by four characters: Entellus, Acestes, Nautes, and Anchises.

The boxing-match between old Entellus and young Dares reveals with force and clarity the distinction between the two generations they represent. Dares is the Trojan champion – young, self-confident, well-conditioned – who claims victory for himself when no one stands up to challenge him. Entellus is the Sicilian champion: past his prime, slow, reluctant to take up the challenge until prodded by Acestes. Young Dares seems to have the edge, until Entellus swings, misses, and falls on his face. When he gets up, Entellus is a different man for he now remembers the champion he *was*. The sting of pride brings his old strength and experience back to life again in an invincible hammering of blows that pummels Dares senseless. Here age emerges triumphant, not because of strength alone (Dares too was strong), nor only because of experience (Dares was not untried), but because age had within itself resources of spirit that could revive strength and experience to defeat a younger opponent. In short, Entellus was victorious because he possessed a past that added an invincible dimension to his present.

In the last of the four competitions, archery, old Acestes competes with younger men. The target is hit before Acestes' turn, but Acestes' arrow, then released, becomes a flaming prophecy as it shoots across the sky. Aeneas declares him the winner because it was Acestes through whom Jupiter spoke.[2]

---

[2] Henning Mørland ("Zu der Bogenschützenepisode in der Aeneis," *Symbolae Osloenses* 37 [1961] 58–67, esp. 59) observes that the older the contestant is in the archery match, the better his shot is.

Throughout the book Acestes is presented positively as a figure benevolent toward Aeneas and his homeless people. Acestes is willing to share his substance and his lands because of his ancestral kinship with the Trojans. The roots of his kindness thus reach back into the past and his sensitivity to the past engenders acts of friendship.

The third character who is old and who is viewed positively is Nautes. His single function in the book is to provide Aeneas with solid, practical advice. After the burning of the ships, the aged Nautes counsels Aeneas to go on to Italy with the strong, leaving the weak in spirit behind.[3])

The wisdom of Nautes' advice is later confirmed by Anchises, who appears to his son Aeneas as a vision in the night. Anchises, in fact, has a power even when he is not present, for his symbolic function in Book Five chiefly resides in his absence and the response of others to his absence. Through the time-consuming ceremony of remembrance in Book Five, Vergil seems to be saying that the essence of civilization is not speed but tradition, not rapidity but continuity, and that in a very real way the strength of the present and the meaningfulness of the future depend upon a respect for the past.

The first of the heroic competitions – the boat-race – provides the clearest evidence that there are negative aspects as well to greater age. In that competition Menoetes, helmsman of the Chimaera, is thrown off the ship into the sea by its young captain, Gyas. Menoetes receives this treatment because he had been cautiously steering the

---

[3]) Nautes' advice to Aeneas is comparable to Jethro's advice to Moses in *Exodus* 18. In each case an elder offers the wisdom of his counsel to a younger leader who finds himself in an administrative dilemma. More significantly, the effect of Nautes' advice (and of Aeneas' ultimate decision to accept it) can be likened to the journey of the Israelites to *their* promised land, for the forty years of migration through the Sinai desert served to eliminate an enervated older generation and allowed a hardier younger generation to come of age (see esp. *Exodus* 16: 2–4 and *Numbers* 11: 4–6 and 14: 26–35; note also *Numbers* 32.) For further likenesses between Vergilian poetry and Biblical literature see Moses Hadas, *Hellenistic Culture: Fusion and Diffustion* (New York: Columbia University Press 1959) ch. XIX, and Cyrus H. Gordon, "Vergil and the Near East," *Ugaritica* 6 (1969) 267–288. The aging of Aeneas' people during their Mediterranean journey is noted by Ellenor Swallow, "The Strategic Fifth *Aeneid*," *Classical World* 46 (1952–53) 177–179, cf. 177 (bottom) f.

ship out to sea to avoid hidden rocks. Here Menoetes' long years of experience produced a degree of caution incompatible with victory.

Such an unwillingness to take risks in characteristic also of the Trojan women who set fire to the ships to prevent yet an eighth year of painful searching for a home that ever eluded them.[4]) It is not accidental that as spokeswoman for their position Iris assumes the guise of Beroë, described as the 'aged' wife of Doryclus. Nor is it accidental that the Trojan woman who then excites her comrades with the revelation of Iris' identity is specifically described as the oldest woman there, Pyrgo, who once nursed Priam's sons. Nor is it only women who are weary and too weak in spirit to sail on. Tired men too are to be among those who stay in Sicily, a land with ancestral roots that will hold Anchises' tomb, the ultimate symbol in matter and spirit of the Trojan past. To identify the Sicilian settlement even more with the old, Aeneas names it for Troy, the kingdom of the past, and leaves his people in the charge of an aged king.

In Book Five Vergil also shows that youth like old age has positive and negative aspects. Here the prime symbol of youth is Iulus, the son of Aeneas. As a climax to the heroic competitions which had earlier involved their fathers, he and the companions he leads carry out an elaborate series of spear-carrying maneuvers on horseback to their fathers' delight. In their role as soldiers-to-be the boys symbolize the future generation of Trojan – and ultimately Roman – warriors. Indeed, the very maneuvers they perform will, as Vergil tells us, someday be learned by Roman boys. In these youths their admiring fathers see their own fathers' faces. For even as the boys will be the transmitters of tradition into the future, so are they the embodiment of the past. The reverence their fathers feel is a reverence that comes of seeing the present in a deeper dimension, in a wider framework of time, one in which past, present, and future reinforce one another mystically and stand as one.

---

[4]) Swallow (above, n. 3) 178 attributes the attitude of the women to their having suffered without the recompense of glory given their men. In a larger sense, their attitude can be likened to that of other women in the poem (Dido, Amata) who by their emotions impede the course of progress, i.e., the realization of Rome's imperial destiny.

The virtue of the young is the courage to sail on, to take risks, to face the unknown. Perhaps they possess this virtue because unlike the old their physical strength is not past its prime, perhaps because they have seen and suffered less, perhaps because their lives have been broken by fewer disappointments, their idealism dimmed by fewer failures; but whatever the reason they have this spirit of adventure nonetheless. Their face is turned forward – to the future – unencumbered by the past, but also (we must now add) unenlightened by its experience.

At the first sign of fire young Iulus charges off and berates the women, but to no effect; his father knows better and prays to Jupiter as the only possible source of relief. Likewise Hippocoön, the only one of the four archers named as young (and very probably the youngest of all[5]), makes the worst of four shots – perhaps because he has the least experience. In the boat-race the helmsman Menoetes may have been too cautious, but young Gyas – who threw him overboard to the laughter of the crowd – loses anyway because he lacks a helmsman and is none himself. And though Dares, the young braggart boxer, has strength and nimbleness, he lacks the proud reservoir of the past that Entellus can draw upon.

It is, indeed, the god Janus who seems to preside over Book Five with its contrast of age and youth, its two faces looking in opposite directions and set back to back, each with limitations and strengths intrinsic to its pose. Perhaps this is consonant with the symbolism at the book's beginning and end: before the landfall in Sicily Aeneas gazes backward to Carthage, but when he leaves Sicily his eyes are fixed ahead. In both scenes he sails a dark sea with some truth unknown to him.

Sicily is indeed a Carthage-ago and an Italy-yet-to-be, an island with all the power to suspend time that islands can possess, a land poised between Aeneas' rejection of a woman's love and his surrender of self to war.[6] It thus becomes a proper setting for a consideration of past and future through a study in contrast of the generations that are their incarnation. It is in this place that a resolution must

[5]) See Mørland (above, n. 2).
[6]) On Sicily as a "place between" see Swallow (above, n. 3) 177.

be achieved, a resolution achieved through the mediation of Aeneas who is to symbolize in his own person the virtue of each extremity in the continuum of generations.

To Vergil's eyes neither the young nor the old are without fault. The old can be wise but also afraid; the young can be brave but imprudent. Vergil's solution is to draw upon the best from each: to use the wisdom of the past to guide the brave. It is from the old that the answer comes – from Nautes and (dead) Anchises – and the self-effacing answer they give is that the future belongs to the brave, to those who have the courage (in Tennyson's words) "to strive, to seek, to find, and not to yield."[7]) Only through their courage can the dream become reality.

Yet the clearest evidence of Vergil's attitude is the patriotic purpose of his poem, a poem written for a people who had lost their sense of national purpose, who had lost faith in themselves. It was to restore this faith that Vergil told his people a story out of their past, a story of personal and communal commitment. In the same way Augustus rebuilt crumbling temples and renewed ancient rites. For both believed that only through a courageous rededication to the sustaining values of the past could a meaningful future be found.

[7]) Tennyson, "Ulysses".

Chapter 12

GENERATIONAL CONFLICT IN PERSIUS

Phyllis Young Forsyth

University of Waterloo

Paul Merchant has recently stated that "the writers of the early Empire... are more aware of their duty to Rome and the Emperor, rather too eager to compose a celebration ode or panegyric, rather too dependent on patronage to 'rock the boat' too vigorously."[1]) Such an attitude might appear to be ill-conducive in literature to expressions of disgust and dissatisfaction with society, especially during the somewhat repressive reigns of Caligula, Claudius, and Nero. Yet during this period the poet Persius *was* inclined to 'rock the boat' by satirizing a "sick society" badly in need of medication. From his position as an educated young man of means he castigated the Roman Establishment for its folly and ignorance, hoping thereby to point out the way to the virtuous life.

Persius has been referred to as an "angry young man" type of poet[2]) eager to flail the Establishment in the manner of Lucilius; as he himself writes in Satire I:

> ... secuit Lucilius urbem,
> te Lupe, te Muci, et genuinum fregit in illeo; (114–115)

> And yet Lucilius flayed our city: he flayed
> you, Lupus, and you, Mucius, and broke
> his jaw over you.[3])

Such is the license Persius desires, even though it may win him no friends in powerful places (I. 107–109). In this disregard for popular

---

[1]) Paul Merchant, *The Epic* (London, 1971), p. 23.

[2]) Cynthia S. Dessen, *Iunctura Callidus Acri* (Urbana, 1968), p. 38 et passim.

[3]) Text and translation of all passages from the Loeb edition: G. G. Ramsay, *Juvenal and Persius* (London, 1918).

opinion the poet is, of course, very much like modern social critics who speak out without care of the personal consequences of their speech. The modern medium is different, but (*pace* McLuhan) the message is basically the same.

What has this to do, however, with the generation gap? The answer is two-fold: first, we have in Persius a unique opportunity to see how a young poet reacted towards his society—a poet whose premature death in A.D. 62 has left us with six satires and a prologue poem which are the creations of a young mind and which were not revised in the light of later experience. Persius' death from a stomach disorder at the age of 28 (according to the *Vita Persi* attributed to the commentary of Valerius Probus) enables us to examine the poetry of an "under 30" Roman who seems to have disliked much of what he saw in his society—a society characterized by a succession of despotic rulers, the abrogation of personal freedoms, and decadent morality; in short, a society that we today can understand from past and present experience.

Secondly, the extant poetry of Persius frequently makes use of the theme of conflict between youth and older age to put its "message" across. The poet, moreover, is quite consistent in the roles he assigns to each side in these conflicts: generally "youth" is presented in a rather negative light, whereas the representative of the "older generation" is seen in a positive light. Such generational conflict is indeed a major theme in the Satires of Persius.

If we are to examine the role of this generational conflict in the poetry of Persius, we must first deal with the problem of the poetic *persona*.[4] Simply put, is the voice which speaks to us in the Satires of Persius actually that of the poet himself, or is it rather a dramatic creation of the poet's which may have little resemblance to its creator? If the voice is purely the latter, it has been argued, then we are quite wrong to see in Persius' work a reflection of this young poet's actual thoughts and emotions. The poet and the poems become two very separate entities, and the biographical approach to literature crumbles.

Such a dichotomy is, however, most unlikely, for even the act of

---

[4] Cf. Dessen (above, note 2), pp. 7 ff. and Niall Rudd, "The style and the man," *Phoenix* 18 (1964), 216–231.

choosing a *persona* tells us something about the poet, though critics may disagree on what that something is. And realistically, as Niall Rudd so well says, even "admitting that there is no necessary parallel between a man's outward behaviour and his inner life as revealed in his writings, we can... point out that (as everybody knows) such a relation does commonly exist."[5]) One could also note the dictum of of Wordsworth that the collected poems of an author form a kind of autobiography.[6]) To quote the famous (or infamous) statement of Buffon, "style is the man".

We are now in a position to examine the Satires of Persius for themes of generational conflict and to draw from Persius' treatment of these themes some conclusions about the man and his times quite relevant to our own times. Indeed when any classical author has *nothing* to say to us we had best turn in our lexicons. The magnificence of classical literature, however, has always been its modernity in every time.

Like other zealous young men, before and after him, who want to reform a sick society, Persius assumes in his Satires an extreme position. He pictures himself at times in the role of a physician trying to heal a most recalcitrant patient (Satire III. 88–106), and the prescribed medicine is a heavy dose of Stoicism; his satire "not only operates on a sick society but provides a necessary release for the pent-up feelings of the satirist: *facit indignatio versum.*"[7]) Aware of the wide gap between his convictions and those of society as a whole, the satirist bitterly castigates the Establishment in poems often noteworthy for their lack of humour. Thus Persius comes to be termed "a young doctrinaire" by a perceptive critic,[8]) and certainly two of the most noticeable characteristics of other "young doctrinaires" are bitterness and the lack of a sense of humour.

The first satire of Persius illustrates this gap in values quite well. In dialogue form, the poet presents an exponent of the "old" values (let us call him Persius) in argument with an exponent of the "modern" values (usually called, simply enough, the Friend). The values they are

[5]) Rudd (above, note 4), p. 219.
[6]) Cf. Merchant (above, note 1), p. 92.
[7]) Kenneth J. Reckford, "Studies in Persius," *Hermes* 90 (1962), p. 500.
[8]) Charles Witke, *Latin Satire* (Leiden, 1970), p. 79.

discussing are literary: from Persius' point of view, modern literature and literary taste are corrupt (I. 13–23); modern poets in their over-whelming desire for fame and praise compose degenerate verse for a degenerate public: as Nisbet writes, "the pretensions of the literary establishment are intolerable, but the poetry-loving public is just as bad. It thinks only of the smoothness of verses, and supposes that the technique of a modern poet is equal to anything."[9]) It is the old argument with which we are quite familiar: the "new" *must* be better than the "old"—i. e., progress becomes an end in itself.

The anonymous Friend praises modern poetry as smooth and graceful:

> ... quis enim, nisi carmina molli
> *nunc demum*[10]) numero fluere, ut per leve severos
> effundat iunctura ungues? scit tendere versum
> non secus ac si oculo rubricam derigat uno. (63–68)

> Why what else but this—that *now at last*[10] we have
> verses flowing smoothly along, so that the critical
> nail glides unjarred over the joinings. Our poet
> knows how to draw his lines as straight as if
> he were directing a ruddle cord with one eye shut.

He adds at line 92:

> Sed numeris decor est et iunctura addita crudis.

> But you will admit, anyhow, that grace and
> coherence have been added to the uncouth
> measures of our sires.

In reply, Persius wonders whether such "verse" could have been written

> ... si testiculi vena ulla *paterni*[10])
> viveret in nobis? (103–104)

> Would such things be written if one drop
> of our *fathers'*[10]) manhood were still alive
> in our veins?

[9]) R. G. M. Nisbet, "Persius," in *Critical Essays on Roman Literature: Satire* (London, 1963), p. 45.

[10]) Emphasis mine.

In the "good old days" of Rome, the poetic drivel of Persius' day would have been inconceivable; Persius, in his disgust for present-day Rome, looks back in time to a utopian society in which corruption, both social and literary, did not exist. The angry young poet rejects the current poetic establishment, which, one ought to remember, counts as its most illustrious member none other than the Emperor Nero![11])

Persius ends his first satire with a clear statement of his own desires as a poet—*not* for fame and a mass audience (since it is corrupt), but for those readers schooled in the invective of Old Greek Comedy; only such an audience could appreciate the "different" verse of Persius. In this way the poet becomes isolated from the general public and strives only to please himself in his poetry, only to release his own emotions; what the Establishment thinks of him is of no importance. It is, in fact, his disregard for popular acceptance that sets Persius apart from his contemporary fellow-poets, who fawn upon the public.

In the first satire Persius points to "the corruption of literature and literary taste in Rome, as a sign and accompaniment of a similar corruption in morals;"[12]) in his second satire the poet attacks still another symptom of his society's sickness, current religious practices. Here Persius maintains his position as a "scorner of the present day"[13]) and as a glamourizer of the past: according to him, religion has degenerated to the point where people pray for one thing (such as 'a fair name' or 'good credit') in public, but for quite another thing (such as money) in private. This religious hypocrisy of his own day is flailed by Persius in a manner quite comprehensible to today's world, in which the gap between pretense and reality is rapidly becoming a chasm, witness the arms manufacturer who worships the Prince of Peace on Sunday.

Persius also attacks the folly of men who infer from their own love of wealth that the gods also value material possessions. Since men prize gold, he says, they now gild the statues of the gods (52–58); hence

[11]) The evidence indicates that the first satire was one of Persius' last poems, written when Nero ruled.
[12]) Ramsay (above, note 3), p. 312.
[13]) Witke (above, note 8), p. 81.

> aurum vasa Numae Saturniaque impulit aera
> Vestalesque urnas et Tuscum fictile mutat. (59–60)

> Gold has now ousted Numa's crockery, and the
> bronze vessels of Saturn; it has supplanted
> the urns and Tuscan pottery of the Vestals.

Clear is the implication that religious practice was purer in the olden days of Rome. Persius carefully selects details that point to a long-lost Golden Age: Numa, according to the historian Livy, was the Roman king famous for justice and piety; Saturn is, of course, commonly a symbol in Latin poetry of the distant Golden Age; the Vestals are also associated with right reverence.

The second satire concludes with an attack on the sinful desires of the flesh and with a plea for a different mode of worship: offering the gods not treasure, but

> compositum ius fasque animo sanctosque recessus
> mentis et incoctum generoso pectus honesto.
> haec cedo ut admoveam templis, et farre litabo. (73–75)

> a heart rightly attuned towards God and
> man; a mind pure in its inner depths,
> and a soul steeped in nobleness and
> honour. Give me these to offer in the
> temples, and a handful of grits shall
> win my prayer for me!

In short, the young poet advises those who worship god with costly ritual to recognize that deity has no interest in material wealth, but rather in riches of the *spirit*. The message itself may be clichéd and commonplace, but the need to hear it continues.

The generation gap as a theme is even more pronounced in Satire III. As in his first satire, Persius makes use of a dialogue form, here in order to present his Stoic thesis that philosophy illuminates human existence. Speaking in behalf of the study of philosophy is a man (usually called the "mentor") old enough to remember the days of his youth wistfully (44–51); the object of his advice is a young man who is snoring heavily as the poem opens and who is rebuked throughout the satire for his laziness (cf. especially 1–6). However, as Housman pointed out many years ago,[14]) this lazy young man is none other than Persius himself; moreover, the older man too is Persius, so that "the dialogue is conducted between the satirist's higher and lower selves,"[15]) and the object of this dialogue is to bridge the gap which the higher self sees between itself and the lower self.

Through the course of the satire, Persius' higher self (the mentor) expostulates with his lower self (the youth) to cease his folly and pursue the life of virtue as taught by the study of philosophy. His argument is simple: childish actions (exemplified by sleeping off last night's debauch or avoiding one's homework) are appropriate to childhood (15–51) but *not* to adulthood, when the study of philosophy should lead one to the right way of life (52–62). The "higher" Persius continues with a general call for the study of philosophy (66–76), and with the analogy of the sick patient who willfully ignores the sound advice of his physician (88–106). When the "lower" Persius asserts that he is not physically ill, his mentor points out that there *is* such a thing as spiritual illness, which requires the healing brought by philosophy (107–118).

This picture of an older person advising a youth continues in the next satire of Persius. Here, however, Persius presents historical figures rather than two "versions" of himself: the philosopher Socrates and the politician Alcibiades. The poet emphasizes the age differential between the two at the start of his satire: Socrates is called "the bearded sage" (1.1), while Alcibiades is sarcastically criticized by the philosopher for pretending to be wise "before your beard" (1.5). The beard, then, becomes a symbol not only of maturity but also of the wisdom which maturity should bring.

The message of Socrates is a variation on the ancient theme of "know thyself". The philosopher exclaims

> Ut nemo in sese temptat descendere, nemo,
> sed praecedenti spectatur mantica tergo! (23–24)

> Not a soul is there—no, not one—who
> seeks to get down into his own self;

[14]) A. E. Housman, "Notes on Persius," *Classical Quarterly* (1913), 12–32.
[15]) Nisbet (above, note 9), p. 54.

all watch the wallet on the back
that walks before!

After chastizing Alcibiades for his profligate way of life, Socrates
offers some final advice:

respue quod non es, tollat sua munera cerdo;
tecum habita: noris quam sit tibi curta supellex. (51–52)

Cast off everything that is not
yourself; let the mob take back
what they have given you; live
in your own house, and
recognize how poorly it is
furnished.

Once again, the poet portrays an older figure in the role of mentor to
the young.

The fifth satire presents a change of pace: Persius, the young poet,
offers "an enthusiastic acknowledgment...of all that he owes to his
beloved guide, philosopher, and friend, L. Annaeus Cornutus."[16]
We have again two main figures, the young man and the older mentor,
but now the generation theme merely serves as a prelude to a lengthy
discussion of the Stoic thesis that no man is truly free save the philosopher (11.52–191).

This prelude, however, is certainly one of the most personal passages
in the Satires of Persius. Beginning with line 30, Persius tells of how
he came under the influence of Cornutus as a green youth:

me tibi supposui. Teneros tu suscipis annos
Socratico, Cornute, sinu... (36–37)

I placed myself in your hands,
Cornutus; you took up my tender
years in your Socratic bosom.

In this reference to Socrates we hear an echo of the previous satire,
in which Socrates was imagined to be speaking. Thus one could identify
the frequent figure of the "older mentor" in Persius' poems with the

[16] Ramsay (above, note 3), p. 365.

historical Cornutus, who (so it seems) actually played such a role in the poet's life. The recognition of this fact solves one puzzling aspect of Persius' presentation of a generation theme—that is, here is a young poet who nevertheless castigates youth in his poems while venerating older figures, a far cry from present practice in this area! If, however, Persius loved his mentor as much as he professes (esp. 11.26–29) and saw him as the corrector of his potentially wayward adolescence, we have an explanation of Persius' respect for and admiration of elder figures in his Satires.

A logical extension of Persius' respect for his elders appears in the sixth satire, where the poet himself assumes the role of older mentor to his own heir (43–80). When the young man objects to Persius' enjoyment of his resources (which will, of course, leave less for him to squander when Persius dies), the poet, in a very Horatian tone, argues his right to use pleasurably what is his own:

> ungue, puer, caules! mihi festa luce coquatur
> urtica et fissa fumosum sinciput aure,
> ut tuus iste nepos olim satur anseris extis,...(69–70)

> Here, boy, drench the cabbage
> with oil, and damn the expense!
> Am I to have my holiday dinner
> off nettles and a smoked pig's
> cheek with his ear split through,
> in order that some day or other
> your young ne'er-do-well may
> regale himself on a goose's liver?

Persius insists upon his right to enjoy what he possesses; let his heir fend for himself!

Thus, the theme of generational conflict can be found in every satire of Persius, whether in the form of old tastes and practices in conflict with modern tastes and practices, or in the form of an older and wiser figure offering sound advice to a younger man. In either case, Persius venerates the old, which he sees as a vital guide to the young, as a "mentor".

Such a position strikes one today as quite one-dimensional; not every elder is wise, not every young person is imprudent. We rightly see virtues and vices in both, with each side able to contribute to a mutual understanding. For Persius, however, as for many "young doctrinaires" there can be only one "right side". His is the voice of the past, from which he finds hope for the future; hence the frequent wistfulness of his verse, his sense of "temps perdu". That a young poet felt so strong an attachment to the past merits our attention; we need not be myopic on the subject, but we ought to recognize that the values of the past are not without meaning for the present.

Chapter 13

YOUNG AND OLD IN IMPERIAL ROME[1]

Barry Baldwin

University of Calgary

Life did not begin at forty for the Romans; rather it began to run out. This belief, a gloomy contrast to the psalmist's canon of three score years and ten (hopelessly unrealistic for any ancient society—and not a few modern ones), dated all the way back to the earliest period of Rome's history. Servius Tullius, one of the traditional seven kings who reigned from c. 753 to c. 510 B.C., drew up the centuriate register of male citizens as the basis for military census. According to Aulus Gellius,[2] a scholar and antiquarian of the second century A.D., it was devised on the following principles:

> *Puer:* one to sixteen years of age
> *Junior:* seventeen to forty-six
> *Senior:* forty-six and up.

These were calculations for military purposes, and the upper limit is not unreasonable. However, subsequent generations accepted and refined the general principle. A man was normally exempted altogether from military service, regular and emergency, at the age of fifty. At sixty, he was excused jury-service and, if it applied in his case, atten-

---

[1] The topic requires no strict chronological limits. However, in general, this paper concentrates on the period A.D. 14–235, whilst looking back or forward when applicable. The chosen period allows a study of the first two centuries or so of imperial Rome at its apogee. The fifty years of civil war after 235 are too ill-documented and too unnatural to be included, and the world they produced was very different from the one discussed here.

[2] Aulus Gellius wrote twenty books on miscellaneous matters called *Attic Nights* (abbreviated to *NA*). They are translated by J. C. Rolfe in the Loeb Classical Library series (LCL in subsequent notes), published by Heinemann in England and Harvard University Press in North America. The passage in question is *NA* 10.28; Gellius is quoting from the earlier historian, Quintus Tubero.

dance at the senate.[3]) The latter point is a reminder that, although the word "senate" is connected etymologically with the word *senex* ("old man"), this body was not permanently comprised of dotards any more than the House of Lords.

Should the above regulations be thought of as concessions to age or disqualifications? In human terms, the answers would vary. Obviously, not every Roman was decrepit, physically or mentally, at sixty, and the hale will not have wanted to withdraw altogether from public life just because they happened to have reached some talismanic age limit. A glance at Greek history would reveal to them that a Spartan king (Agesilaus) had still been on the battle-field at eighty, and many a Roman felt that anything a Greek (even a tough Spartan) could do, he could do better. By contrast, Seneca's *De brevitate vitae* ("On the brevity of life"), written in the first century A.D., states that men looked forward to retirement at fifty or sixty; those who did will have welcomed the regulations as concessions.

As soon as we start talking about people being too old or too young, the spectre of that horrid invention of the mass (crass?) media, "the generation gap", rears its head. This essay will, I hope, demonstrate that, for various reasons, age versus youth was hardly a real issue in imperial Rome. However, the matter was bound to crop up in personal cases and attitudes, and sometimes at the institutional level as well. The Romans had a tag: *Sexagenarios de ponte* ("Sixty-year olds off the bridge"). The origin of this saying became blurred by time, provoking thereby a colourful explanation and a prosaic one. Legends effloresced about sexagenarians thrown into the Tiber and drowned, with at least one virtuous son hiding his father and so on. The more sober and plausible (for human sacrifice, despite the later horrors of the arena, was very rare in Roman history) explanation is that the bridge was the one crossed by voters in the Assemblies, and so the saying indicated that sixty-year olds were debarred from voting. A more personal and human (or rather, inhuman) illustration of the point, probably inspired by the saying, is provided in the second century A.D. Lucian, the malicious, Greek-speaking satirist (sometimes

[3]) For discussion of these details (and references to the primary sources), see J.P.V.D. Balsdon, *Life and Leisure in Ancient Rome* (published in North America by McGraw-Hill, 1969), pp. 169 ff.

dubbed "the Voltaire of Antiquity"), claims in a pamphlet written against an enemy called Peregrinus that the latter had strangled his sexagenarian father because at that age he had lived long enough.[4]) The ultimate in generational gaps? Maybe so; or perhaps a jesting reversal of the Roman concept of *patria potestas* over a son.

Naturally, although there are no examples of longevity so spectacular as those regularly reported from the Soviet Union,[5]) Greece and Rome produced their share of the impressively long-lived. The same Lucian is credited (or debited, since most scholars find it a bore and wrongly ascribed) with a treatise entitled *The Long-lived*,[6]) which lists Greeks who survived to a ripe old age. It closes with a promise by the author to furnish a similar list of Romans. *The Long-lived* is addressed to a Roman patron, and the author's intent may simply have been to boost his patron's hopes of long life. Though perhaps silly, the treatise is an interesting example of the literature concerning old age which preoccupied the Roman world. In the last century B.C., Cicero had written his *De senectute* ("On old age"). Seneca's *De brevitate vitae*[7]) has already been remarked. Both Cicero and Seneca achieved sexagenarian status. Plutarch addressed himself to the question *An seni res publica gerenda?*[8]) ("Should the old govern?"). And so on.

We are dealing with a society that had upper age limits for civic and social responsibilities but no legal age for retirement from jobs, no life insurance policies (the premiums would have been ruinous, if they had had these), and a low expectancy of life for both sexes and all classes.[9]) Now law has been happily defined as the crystallisation of popular prejudice (Goldfinger in the Bond saga quoted this in the context of drug laws!). The relation between prejudice or superstition and legislation applies to all societies.

[4]) Lucian, *On the Death of Peregrinus* 10 (translated in vol. 5 of the LCL edition).

[5]) And occasionally from the United States; whilst writing up this paper in April, 1972, I read a newspaper account of a former slave celebrating his one hundred and thirtieth birthday.

[6]) Translated in vol. 1 of the LCL edition under the title *Octogenerians*.

[7]) Translated in vol. 2 of the LCL edition of Seneca's *Moral Essays*.

[8]) Translated in vol. 2 of the LCL edition of Plutarch's *Moralia*.

[9]) For statistical tables and comparisons between ancient and modern figures, see A. R. Burn, 'Hic breve Vivitur', *Past & Present* 29 (1953), pp. 1 ff; also Balsdon, p. 355.

Not least to imperial Rome. This increasingly legalistic civilisation exhibits many irrational and inconsistent superstitions concerning age. Lucian, for instance, claims to have abandoned a successful career of public speaking at the age of forty;[10]) this was the time of life (he says elsewhere) at which a man should be turning towards philosophy.[11]) His contemporary, the philosopher-emperor Marcus Aurelius (who reigned in the period A.D. 161–180) also said in his *Meditations*[12]) that wisdom and the age of forty went together. This point in life is a good deal below that fixed by Plato for the full attainment of wisdom, but it made more sense in a world where men were soon living on borrowed time. Aulus Gellius laid it down that sixty-three is the most dangerous year in an older person's life,[13]) an idea echoed unwittingly in the Beatles' beautiful song *When I'm sixty-four*! This same Gellius also heaped scorn on opsimaths,[14]) men who began to study late in life; presumably Gellius would not support the concept of adult education. In his *Lives of the Sophists* (written in the third century AD), Philostratus maintained that fifty-six was still young for a professor, but was the beginning of senility in all other learned professions.[15]) This is encouraging for professors, less so for their students. Has Philostratus unconsciously anticipated the North American academic issues of tenure and competence?

So Romans did not look forward to a ripe old age with modern confidence. This in itself reduced the possibility of a "generation gap" concept. As did the norms at the other end of life's scale. Manhood and womanhood came early. This may have been partly to do with the physiological development of those who live in the Southern Mediterranean. Perhaps more to the point, it took account of the harsh realities of life expectancy.[16])

[10]) *Bis Accusatus* ("Twice Accused") 32 (LCL edition, vol. 3).
[11]) *Hermotimus* 13 (LCL vol. 6).
[12]) *Meditations* 11. 1 (translated in LCL).
[13]) *NA* 15. 7.
[14]) *NA* 11. 7.
[15]) *VS* (the usual abbreviation of his title) 543; translated in the LCL.
[16]) Greek and Latin epitaphs of the Roman period frequently register the deceased's life down to years, months, and days. See the discussion (with examples and inscriptional references) in R. Lattimore, *Themes in Greek and Latin Epitaphs* (University of Illinois Press, 1962), p. 16; there is even a dedication to a dead wife

The cardinal issue of a father's *patria potestas* over his children is very relevant to this section, but detailed discussion falls outside my scope.[17] A boy normally assumed the *toga virilis* (roughly equivalent to getting the key of the door—or, I suppose, the key of the car in North America) round about his fifteenth year.[18] This, however, was not strictly fixed in law; there are cases of its assumption as early as fourteen and as late as nineteen. Such flexibility is perhaps significant of the Romans, and is paralleled in other contexts to the point of vagueness. For example, scholars have believed that the word *iuvenis* had honourable connotations, whereas *adulescens* or *adulescentulus* implied a sneer.[19] Yet Aulus Gellius, in whose writings the alleged distinction has been particularly claimed, can quote the text of a censorial decree in which the rival terms are used as synonyms.[20] Roman terms for collateral family relationships are notoriously ill-defined. Again, it is Gellius who points to the apogee, with his information that in early Latin the plural *liberi* was used to designate a single child.[21]

In the period under discussion, Rome accepted four teenaged emperors (Nero, Commodus, Elagabalus, and Alexander Severus), none of whom had a formal regent (informal domination by elders is another matter). At a lower level, Octavian (the future emperor Augustus) delivered a public funeral oration at the age of twelve.[22] Romans would be amazed at the current debates in Canada and the United States over the advisability of lowering the voting and drinking age (a nicely absurd collocation in one respect, since it is usually impossible to buy a drink legally on voting days!) from twenty-one to eighteen.

Maturity, then, came early to the Romans. One cannot resist adducing the more modern saw that "Youth is too precious to be wasted

which takes the count down to the odd number of hours lived (see Lattimore, p. 280, for text and discussion).

[17] See the paper by J. Plescia elsewhere in this book.

[18] See Balsdon, p. 120.

[19] See the discussion by J. C. Rolfe in vol. 1 of the LCL edition of Gellius, p. xiii.

[20] *NA* 15. 11.

[21] *NA* 2. 13.

[22] Suetonius, *Life of the Deified Augustus* 8 (LCL edition, vol. 1).

on the young." Still, it should not be assumed that the Roman approach is better than ours. Especially in the case of girls. For Roman law permitted a girl to marry (or to be married off, which is often more to the point) at the age of twelve.[23]) This in spite of the fact that Graeco-Roman medical writers recognised that puberty (evinced by the beginning of menstruation, breast development, etc.) did not begin until the fourteenth year. On the basis of inscriptional and literary evidences, it has been calculated that the normal age for a girl to get married was fourteen. This conclusion is also founded partly upon hope, since one does not like to think about the physical and emotional distress likely to be brought on by the consummation of such early marriages. There is one tragic example attested of what could happen. Quintilian, the Spanish-born professor of rhetoric in the first century A.D., tells us in a moving passage that his wife died in her nineteenth year, having borne her husband two sons, one of whom died at the age of five.[24])

I can remember an absurd scandal in England in the late fifties, when the American pop singer Jerry Lee Lewis was driven from the country, his tour aborted, when it was revealed that he was married to a child bride from the Southern States. This nonsense confirmed Oscar Wilde's dictum that the British public is never so ridiculous as when engaged in one of its periodic fits of morality (Wilde, of course, would know about that!). A Roman would have wondered what all the fuss was about.

Marriage should not be confused with betrothal. A girl could be affianced before twelve. The minimum age varied.[25]) Augustus thought ten was an appropriate one; Roman law later reduced this to seven. Augustine, in his thirty-first year, contracted with a girl of ten. The ultimate absurdity was the betrothing of the daughter of the emperor Claudius (A.D. 41–54), the always hapless Octavia, at the age of one.

---

[23]) See Balsdon, pp. 119 ff.; also his *Roman Women* (London, 1962), pp. 173 ff. Articles on the subject in general include those by A. G. Harkness in *Transactions & Proceedings of the American Philological Association* 27 (1898), pp. 35 ff., and K. M. Hopkins in *Population Studies* (1965), pp. 315 ff.

[24]) *Institutes of Oratory* 6. Proem. 1 ff. (LCL edition, vol. 2).

[25]) See the very detailed discussion in L. Friedlaender, *Roman Life & Manners in the Early Empire* (London, 1913), vol. 4, pp. 123 ff.

Later on, when eleven, Octavia was married off to the sixteen years old Nero; in A.D. 62, Nero had her liquidated at the age of twenty.

A girl could marry at twelve, a boy at fourteen. This difference in minimum ages was not designed to give young males two extra years of freedom (for the most precocious youth cannot sow many wild oats at this time of life). The point was that, after the emperor Augustus, a girl was expected to have had at least one child by the time she was twenty. The crucial age for the male was twenty-five; at this age, he could hold the quaestorship (an early rung on the political ladder), and was expected to be a husband and father.

In this paradoxical society of teenaged engagements and arranged marriages, the Romeo and Juliet syndrome seems at once ubiquitous and improbable. Yet it would be absurd to suppose that love matches did not exist—or develop. Legally and socially the dice were loaded against the girl. For example, she could only object to her father's choice of a husband on the grounds of moral turpitude, and what respectable Roman girl could admit to knowing anything about that? Marriages were not made in heaven, but between two families.[26] A good match helped the man's career; Tacitus is frank about this when describing the matrimony of his father-in-law, Agricola.[27] The old Republican ideal for a matron was to be *univira* ("having only one husband"); this comes out forcibly in Virgil's treatment of Dido's anguish over her affair with Aeneas. But in no society has the sexual double standard been more marked than at Rome. The man could have his mistresses and boy-friends as an extramarital bonus; even such archetypal spokesmen of the Republic as Cato the Elder and Cicero sanctioned the sowing of wild oats by young males. It was the "liberated woman" who got short shrift from the satirist Juvenal in the late first century A.D.[28]

Of course, most of the above relates to the upper and middle classes. The lower orders, in fact if not in theory, were not much haunted

[26] See the lively and up-to-date account of J. A. Crook, *Law and Life of Rome* (London, 1967), pp. 99 ff.

[27] *Agricola* 6: "He married the well-born Domitia Decidiana; this match adorned and enhanced his political career."

[28] See, in particular, his *Sixth Satire* (translated in LCL; also in the Penguin Classics series with a good introduction by Peter Green).

by Augustus' legislation concerning celibacy and childlessness.[29]) The distinction between Party and Prole in Orwell's *1984* is crudely comparable. At the top of imperial society, it is very hard to find an emperor who never married. The concept of marriage as the social goal for the man filtered down to the Greek literary romances of the period.[30]) In this, as in other things, Rome anticipated the ethos of North America.

Hence, the young were encumbered with social, financial, and human responsibilities from an early age. This helped to draw young and old closer together; ironically, the older person was often freer than the younger. Difference in years rarely involved a mutual incomprehension of life styles. Not that one can furnish a schematic account of Roman attitudes to youth and age, since the universal considerations of accepted standards and individual point of view obtain as much for Rome as for any other society.

On the highest level, take the attitudes to Roman emperors. In the period A.D. 14–235, four came to the throne as teenagers: Nero was seventeen, Commodus nineteen, Elagabalus fourteen, and Alexander Severus thirteen, The first three of these are depicted as "bad" rulers by the primary sources, but it is more a question of their own characters and the influences of older people upon them than their youth. The nearest approach to "generation gap" chatter is provided by the historian Tacitus. For instance, he says of Domitian (A.D. 81–96), who was twenty-nine at his accession, that "he knew his youth was scorned by the older generation."[31]) But since Domitian is an emperor particularly loathed by Tacitus, this needs to be taken with a pinch of salt. Again, by the same token, Tacitus claims that the septuagenarian ruler Galba (seventy-two at his short-lived accession in A.D. 69) was an object of ridicule to the young, who compared his age and looks unfavourably to those of his predecessor Nero and current rival, the

---

[29]) See any modern account of Augustus for details of these laws; in particular, R. Syme, *The Roman Revolution* (Oxford, 1939), pp. 443 ff.

[30]) See Lattimore, p. 193, n. 156; for amusement (and some instruction), compare Germaine Greer's remarks on romance and male fantasising in *The Female Eunuch* (Paladin paperback edition, 1971), pp. 171 ff.

[31]) *Histories* 4. 86.

thirty-seven year old Otho.[32]) Certainly, there will have been some who felt this way. However, there was a very good reason why such comparisons were standardised in the first century. For by a striking series of coincidences (it would be rash to go further than this), there was a continued alternation between old and young emperors after Augustus. Tiberius was fifty-five, Caligula twenty-five, Claudius fifty, Nero seventeen, Galba seventy-two, and Otho thirty-seven. It should also be noted that the more senior names in the above register get no better a press from Tacitus in most respects than the younger ones.

The above is more in the realm of political attitudes. Let us approach Tacitus from a more human viewpoint. He consistently sprinkles in his *Annals* and *Histories* formulaic phrases about the lusts of the young.[33]) Some might infer sexual jealousy on the part of an older man from this; not every older man agrees with the praise of old age as the liberator from passion expressed in Plato's *Republic*. Possible, but too glib. Round about the age of twenty-four, Tacitus married the thirteen-year old daughter of Agricola, the governor of Britain whose biography he wrote. Of his young bride (whose name he does not bother to register), he merely states that "she was then a girl of excellent promise" (*egregiae tum spei*).[34]) Promising what? Our Lolita generation might dub Tacitus a nympholept, or think only a Humbert Humbert could find anything to praise in a girl of thirteen.

Illumination of the point is provided by Tacitus' friend, the younger Pliny. In one of his *Letters*,[35]) Pliny writes a touching obituary of the daughter of a certain Minicius Fundanus, dead before her thirteenth year: "She blended together the wisdom of age and dignity of woman-hood with the tender modesty of youthful innocence." Appended to this are tributes to her shows of affection towards father, father's friends, and nurse; to her devotion to books and restraint in play; to

[32]) *Histories* 1. 7.

[33]) E. g., *cupiditates adulescentiae* (*Histories* 1. 15); *mobilis adulescentium animos* (*Annals* 4.17). Tacitus also has his clichés about the old as being given to atavism and opposed to change; see, e.g., *Annals* 13. 3 ("Old men like to spend their time comparing past and present"). Notice also a striking phrase (*Annals* 3.8): *cum incallidus alioqui et facilis iuventa senilibus tum artibus uteretur* ("His youthful easy directness then resorted to the wiles of an old man").

[34]) *Agricola* 9.

[35]) *Ep.* 5. 16 (LCL edition, vol. 1).

the courage she displayed in her fatal illness. Quintilian, as was noted earlier, is similarly affecting on his own young wife, so tragically deceased before her twentieth year.

It is pertinent to recall that the Romans had two sets of platitudes, one for each sex (and not completely cynical to bear in mind their proverb *de mortuis nil nisi bonum*—once translated as "Speak only humbug of the dead." Fundanus' daughter is a younger version of all those tediously virtuous matrons of the Republic: dutiful, wool-spinning, polyphiloprogenitive.[36]) Young men's folly might be excused in words that hint at the so-called "Permissive Society". There is a classic passage in Cicero's speech *Pro Caelio*, delivered in 56 B.C., but of timeless relevance. The orator had to defend his rackapelt young client's private life against the prosecution. Hence, the following formula is produced in Cicero's best manner: "Indeed, I have both seen and heard of in Rome many men whose entire youth was given over to pleasure, from their young lips to the tips of their fingers, so to speak, but they eventually got over it and became respectable and distinguished citizens, devoted to virtue. Everyone allows that youth should have its head, for nature herself makes young men blaze with passion. Provided that these passions hurt no one and no household, they are regarded with tolerance."[37]

There is a nice gloss on this urbane philosophy. Nice because it is credited to a man who anathematised the "new morality" which was supposedly coming from Greece and the East to infect young Romans: old Cato. This John Bull figure was said to have praised a young man whom he noticed slipping out of a brothel for preferring fornication with whores to adulteries with married women. Admittedly, some versions continue the anecdote to make Cato rebuke the same youth for living there, when he again saw him around the same bordello. But a Cato sanctioning youthful whore-mongering is as improbable (superficially, at any rate) as a Richard Nixon legalising pornography. For Cato was not the sort to pose as a "swinging oldie."

Imperial Rome exhibits a miscellany of public and private attitudes and phenomena. Augustus paid some special attention to youth by

[36] See Lattimore p. 271, for the archetypal example of these.
[37] *Pro Caelio* 28.

creating a sort of cadet movement called the *Iuventus*.[38]) It is useful to recollect that he himself had only been nineteen when Caesar's will pronounced him heir in 44 B.C.; and that his age had prompted the sexagenarian Cicero into fatally miscalculating that such a young man could be used as a pawn in politics. And it may be significant that Augustus designated his grandsons and putative successors as *Princeps Iuventutis* ("Youth Leader"). But an emperor did not need to worry about politically alienated youth. Opposition to the principate came from mature historians and older Stoic philosophers on an ideological level.[39]) If any element of imperial society was "radicalised", it was not youth.

Young marriages, the continuing importance of family life (in spite of Juvenal's fulminations), and the nature of higher education all meant that young and old spent a lot of time in physical and mental togetherness. Aulus Gellius' accounts of his tertiary education, in Rome and Athens, constantly stress the close contacts between himself and his fellow students and their mentors and teachers. Education indeed, formal and informal, formed a link between the generations that is becoming alien to our own society with its troubled schools and "polarised" campuses. The hardheaded materialism of at least one of the characters in Petronius *Satyricon* softens when he discusses his sons and education.[40]) Even Juvenal shows a fondness for children. Admittedly, this is partly a rhetorical contrast to his Swiftian diatribes on the horrors of old age, but many see sincerity in his line *maxima debetur puero reverentia* ("The greatest respect possible must be paid to a boy").[41]) Reminius Palaemon, a famous teacher of the first century A.D., horrified people by having sexual intrigues with his pupils.[42])

A neat summation of the theme of this paper is neither possible nor desirable. Roman legal sanctions were not always logical or consistent.

[38]) See Balsdon, p. 161; Syme, pp. 445 ff.

[39]) The best modern account is R. MacMullen, *Enemies of the Roman Order* (Harvard Univ. Press, 1966), pp. 1 ff.

[40]) *Sat.* 46 (Echion the scrap dealer on his boys' education).

[41]) *Sat.* 14. 47. See also *Sat.* 10. 188 ff. and *Sat.* 11. 211 ff; for Juvenal in general, see G. Highet, *Juvenal the Satirist* (Oxford, 1954), especially pp. 122, 127 ff., 145 ff., 237.

[42]) Suetonius, *Lives of the Grammarians* 23 (LCL edition, vol. 2).

Much less so were the attitudes of individuals. Philostratus the biographer can be handily cited as evidence of two types of prejudice. On the one hand, he says that Isaeus the sophist turned from a misspent youth to decency and success (echoing Cicero's *Pro Caelio* in sentiment).[43]) By contrast, he depicts the scholarly Hermogenes as a youthful prodigy whose intellectual talents moulted with mature age[44]) (burnt himself out, as we would say). Conventional praises of young girls are balanced by poems in the *Greek Anthology* which award the palm, in the manner of Stephen Vizinczey's *In Praise of Older Women*,[45]) in respect of beauty and sexual expertise to mature women.[46]) Crackling epigrams about the impetuous passions of the young are offset by epitaphs which set out the intellectual and artistic attainments of boys just in their teens.[47])

That there was no American-styled cult of the young in Rome is not surprising news. The absence of any through-going distrust of the young and consequent veneration of the older generation is perhaps more pleasantly unexpected. One good reason for this state of affairs is not that Rome was less endowed with moralisers than we are (quite the reverse!), but the difference in moralising techniques. Men like Juvenal and Tacitus revered old ways, not old people. They had little good to say about their own societies, but did not blame it all on to one age group. Emperors, foreigners, women: these, not youth, were the whipping-boys.

No one piece of evidence can be taken as an accepted general

[43]) *VS* 513.

[44]) *VS* 543.

[45]) Available in paperback (Contemporary Canada Press, 1965); the theme is obviously a commonplace in modern erotic literature.

[46]) See, in vol. 1 of the LCL edition of *The Greek Anthology*, 5. 13; 5. 258. The first of these claims well-preserved hair, breasts, skin, and libido for the sixty-year old woman Charito; the second admits that a certain Philinna is wrinkled and sagging in the bosom, but the poet prefers this to the standard charms of a young girl (he sounds like the man in Richard Needham's jest about the man who claims he only buys *Playboy* for the Interview feature).

[47]) See Lattimore, p. 268, for an epitaph on the talents of a deceased thirteen-year old boy called Cladus, who was better at wrestling but not hopeless in the arts. New Testament tags such as "Let no one despise your youth" (1 *Timothy*, 4. 12) may be adduced.

opinion, at least outside legal contexts (and not always then). However, we have to end somewhere, so consider the following sentiment from Pliny's *Panegyricus* (his tediously important speech in honour of the emperor Trajan): *Cur enim posteris amplior honor quam maioribus haberetur?* ("Why should the younger generation be more honoured than the older one?")[48]) Before modern parents chorus their approval of Pliny's question, I hasten to add that the context is not a debate about the generations but a matter of tax exemptions. And Pliny went on to ask: "And why should justice not apply equally to young and old?"

[48]) *Panegyricus* 38. 7 (LCL edition of Pliny's *Letters*, vol. 2).

Epilogue

VULCAN'S LEGACY

Thera, Aetna, Vesuvius: from the Bronze Age of Greece to the Imperial Age of Rome the Mediterranean was periodically convulsed by volcanic fury, by fiery, subterranean forces that erupted through the rigid crust of earth, bringing blazing destruction to the works of men. In like manner the long stable cultures of ancient Greece and Rome were convulsed by a youthful power that violently broke through the crust of convention and tradition. The volcanic eruptions, like the generational upheavals, were born of mounting pressures within, pressures that demanded ventilation if the earth, like human institutions, was to grow. Indeed, within the destructive fury of volcanoes was the primal energy of creation itself, straining against an aging planet.

When the last lava flow had cooled, when the last grey ash had settled to earth, what men were left returned to reconstruct their lives, broken but wiser for having learned the limits of their own power, for having learned that no generation—however strong—truly owns the earth. No less a lesson was learned by those who faced and survived the conflict of generations in their society.

In their wisdom the Greeks and Romans saw in Hephaestus, or Vulcan, two natures. Caverned within a volcanic home, he was god of the earth's destructive fire. But in that home they envisioned him working his forge as a creator, hammering metal softened by intense heat into constructive works of beauty and use. If we are wise we will see in Vulcan's dual nature a symbol that can help us transcend the violence of generational conflict, for within the potentially destructive fire of youth there is also the very power that can lead us to acts of creation and constructive change.

Stephen Bertman

235